Noble, Wretched, and Redeemable

Noble,
Wretched, &

REDEEMABLE

*Protestant Missionaries to the Indians in Canada
and the United States, 1820–1900*

C. L. HIGHAM

University of New Mexico Press
Albuquerque

University of Calgary Press
Alberta

Cover Background/Frontispiece Illustration: Plate 134—Meech-o-shin-gaw.
From George Catlin's *Letters and Notes on the Manners, Customs, and Conditions
of the North American Indians,* vol. 2 (New York: Wiley and Putnam, 1841).
Courtesy of Cushing Memorial Library, Texas A&M University.

Cover Inset Illustration: Egerton Ryerson Young in Native Attire. From the
frontispiece of Egerton Ryerson Young's *By Canoe and Dog Train: Among the
Cree and Salteaux Indians* (New York: Abingdon Press, 1890).

Library of Congress
Cataloging-in-Publication Data

Higham, C. L.
Noble, wretched, and redeemable : Protestant missionaries to the Indians in
Canada and the United States, 1820–1900 / C. L. Higham. — 1st ed.
p. cm.
Includes bibliographical references and index.
University of New Mexico Press ISBN 0-8263-2165-8 (cloth : alk. paper)
University of Calgary Press ISBN 1-55238-026-2
1. Indians of North America—Missions—History—19th century.
2. Indians of North America—Public opinion. 3. Public opinion—
United States. 4. Public opinion—Canada. 5. Protestant churches—
Missions—United States—History. 6. Protestant churches—Missions—
Canada—History. I. Title.
E98.M6 .H54 2000
266′.0089′97078—dc21
00-008249

CONTENTS

ACKNOWLEDGMENTS

THIS WORK could not have been completed without the help and direction of a vast number of people. First, I must thank Howard Lamar for introducing me to Western American history, and Alec Douglas and John Herd Thompson for introducing me to Canadian history. I heartily thank the Canadian government for their grant, and Judith Costello, Dr. Clark Cahow, and Patrice LeClerc for their help in my completion of the Canadian research. I must also thank the following archivists for their patience and assistance: George Miles and Susan Bach of the Beinecke Rare Book and Manuscript Library at Yale University; Tom Clark of the Duke University Divinity School Library; Patricia Birkett and Timothy Dubé of the National Archives of Canada; Dorothy Keally, Laurel Parsons, and Terry Thompson of the Anglican Church Archives; Ian Mason of the United Church Archives; the staff of the Archives of Ontario; Ann Yandle of Special Collections and University Archives at the University of British Columbia Library; Brian Moore of the British Columbia Archives; Vernon Leighton at Winona State University. Additionally, I would like to thank John Webster Grant, Jean Friesen, and Robin Fisher for answering what I know they considered to be strange questions. They were all more help than they may ever know.

I owe a special debt of gratitude to my advisors, John Herd Thompson and Peter Wood. They never said no to any of my ideas and let me puzzle them out on my own. I greatly appreciate the freedom that they granted me in this endeavor. Additionally, I would like to thank Frederick Hoxie, Jean Barman, and my colleagues at Texas A&M University: Thomas Dunlap; Larry Yarak, who read various sections of the manuscript and provided invaluable insight into the writing process; and Daniel Bornstein, for suggesting the term "redeemable savage." Much of the credit for this completed work goes to Durwood Ball, James Rosenheim, and Julia Kirk Blackwelder. Their comments and insights shaped the final restructuring and conceptualization of what exists here. I also owe special thanks to Al Broussard for his faith and support.

I could not have finished this work without the support of my family: my parents, who provided a place to write for several summers and an understanding of academia; my in-laws, who took pride and interest in the project without asking too many questions; and my sisters, Susan and Martha.

Last but by no means least, I thank Christopher Alexander. No other political scientist on the face of the earth knows more about Protestant missionaries than this man. From riding in a small car across Canada to helping me fight with computers, I owe him for his patience, his willingness to do anything to complete this work, his ability to keep me going, his friendship, his humor, his faith in me, and his love.

INTRODUCTION

Noble, Wretched, and Redeemable compares how nineteenth-century Protestant missionaries viewed the native inhabitants in western Canada and the United States. By tracing the changing images of these indigenous groups, it examines how three kinds of institutions—the missionary societies, national governments, and various secular scholarly institutions—influenced the process of image formation.[1] Within this context, the chapters demonstrate that despite important institutional differences in the two countries, and contrary to the perceptions of both past missionaries and current scholars, Protestant missionary attitudes toward Indians were similar in Canada and the United States during the nineteenth century. To demonstrate the similarity of these attitudes, the book investigates how the missionary societies, the Canadian and U.S. governments, and various secular scholarly institutions placed financial and political pressures on individual Protestant missionaries that shaped how these missionaries portrayed the Indians to these institutions, as well as to the literate, white Christian public.

For purposes of comparison, this book approaches image creation in three ways. First, it outlines general histories of the Canadian and American western frontiers and the government policies that regulated them. These histories reveal how different Canada and the United States were throughout the nineteenth century. Second, it explains how the shift of financial support from the missionary societies, the various governments, and the secular research institutions, created pressures for missionaries and encouraged new alliances between them. Finally, this book examines how Protestant missionaries on the western frontiers discussed and described the Indians in their writings and lectures and how these portrayals changed in relationship to changing institutional pressures and changes on the Canadian and American frontiers. Despite expectations of many scholars to the contrary, Protestant missionary writings display attitudes toward

Indians in Canada and the United States that appear to be similar and interchangeable, suggesting comparable viewpoints in society at large.

Through their copious writings and lectures, Protestant missionaries offer excellent access to stereotype development and institutional pressures in the nineteenth century.[2] These missionaries provided white Christian societies, the governments, and secular academic research institutions in Canada and the United States with lasting impressions of the native groups. The missionaries mattered because, unlike racial theorists and policymakers of the time, they dealt with natives on a daily basis, recording their own actions and attitudes toward natives along with their perceptions of native attitudes, culture, and societies. Additionally, Protestant missionaries on the western frontiers of Canada and the United States were moderately well educated and began their missionary endeavors with the specific and well-articulated goal of changing the Indians. Their means and motives of assimilation and conversion were clear and direct. In their writings, seventeenth-, eighteenth-, and nineteenth-century concepts of Indians converge, the realization of the inaccuracy of these concepts emerges, and economic and political tensions surface that threatened the missionaries' plans. Missionaries depicted what the white Christian public in Canada and the U.S. wanted to believe about Indians and the economic and political rewards given to those who validated this view.

Throughout the nineteenth century, Protestant missionaries produced copious reports, studies, and works of fiction about Indians and the western frontiers of Canada and the United States. They wrote for the benefit of missionary societies, church groups, government officials, the general public, and future missionaries, and to stimulate financial support for the missions. These documents reveal how Protestant missionaries, forced by financial and political pressures, expanded their missionary role to include advising government and otherwise serving as secular authorities on the natives.

To many, perhaps particularly those in the United States, the conclusion that the two countries possessed similar attitudes toward Indians seems commonsensical. Canada and the United States seem to share so many cultural and political similarities that similarities seem more common than differences. As Robin Winks summarizes, "Canadians are basically like Americans, except that it is colder and snows more often in Canada and that Canadians have a monarchical and parliamentary system of government. At bed rock, Americans think the Canadian experience is not all that different from the experience of the United States."[3] Whereas many Canadians see the United States as a crude imitation of themselves, many Americans see Canada as an informal annex of the United States.

Comparative scholars, though, present the two nations as distinctly different. Historians and other scholars portray the Canadian frontier as a kinder, gentler frontier, with little or no bloodshed between whites and natives as settlement progressed.[4] Scholars credit this difference to everything from the North-West Mounted Police to Commonwealth status to the Hudson's Bay Company. And to many, this difference is due to a higher institutional and attitudinal level of respect accorded by the Canadians to the native population. Many of these scholars, while basing their works on strong secondary sources, speak only in general and impressionistic terms, rarely applying their impressions to actual case studies, as will be done in this book. Despite this failing, these scholars do represent basic attitudes about differences between Canada and the United States. Particularly when discussing native/white relations on the frontier, the consensus of the few comparative scholars and commentators points to Canada as a calmer frontier. Seymour Martin Lipset states, "Although native people have been badly treated on both sides of the border, Canadians have shown them more respect than have Americans."[5] Paul Sharp, a pioneer in the field of comparative history, provides a blunt example of this when he states, "On the American side, this conflict [between whites and natives] was continuous, with unceasing guerrilla warfare punctuated by occasional formal military campaigns. To the north, the lack of population pressure permitted a more orderly development."[6] Robin Winks, in his essay collection on the relevance of Canadian history, puts it more glibly. In Canada, "there were few colorful Indian wars and relatively little bloodshed, and, while the Indian was not well treated, he did survive near or even on his ancestral lands."[7] Lipset points out that "on the American frontier, the quality of law enforcement often depended on local police authorities who reflected the value of the frontierspeople, including their prejudice against Indians and their lack of understanding for legal procedures incorporating the guarantees of due process."[8] Winks echoes this sentiment, stating, "Long before Canadian settlers had pressed into the western lands, both the common law and the specific regulations of that powerful semi-feudal, chartered company—the Hudson's Bay Company—had been placed upon the land."[9] These authors imply that Americans put race first and justice second. Lipset continues along this line by quoting Robert Thacker, who reported that Indians in Canada were impressed when they saw whites punished for crimes against Indians. This pleasantly surprised the Indians, according to Thacker, as "their previous experience [with American whites] had taught them to appreciate such impartial justice."[10]

Thus, when examining native/white relations on the nineteenth-century frontiers in Canada and the United States, scholars portray the two frontiers very differently. The Canadians appear as law-abiding protectors of justice on the western frontier. Many of the scholars' descriptions, by avoiding the use of race in the elucidation of Canadian policies, clearly suggest that Canadians were color-blind. This suggestion inevitably leads to the conclusion that Canadian racial attitudes, like their actions, policies, and institutions, were more balanced and accepting of the "other." On the other hand, descriptions of the U.S. frontier portrayed it as bloody and focused on racial issues concerning native groups. The racial attitudes toward Indians identified in the works of American historians Brian Dippie, Robert Berkhofer Jr., Reginald Horsman, and Bernard Sheehan, among others, appear to be an inherent part of the character of U.S. society.[11]

On the surface, Canada and the United States do appear to have some fundamental differences. At the beginning of the nineteenth century, the two countries seemed distinct. Canada remained a British colony, ruled by a multilayered British/Canadian government. The nineteenth-century western Canadian frontier stretched from western Ontario, across the prairies, north into the Arctic, and west to the Pacific Coast.[12] The British Parliament wrote laws covering certain issues, while the local colonial government wrote other laws. The Hudson's Bay Company controlled the western half of Canada from the prairie provinces through British Columbia, struggling at times with the United States for control of the Pacific Coast. In 1867, Canada became a confederation. It remained part of the British Empire but now was governed by self-rule. The Hudson's Bay Company relinquished the western lands to government control. After an uprising of the Métis, the new Canadian government established the North-West Mounted Police to maintain peace on the western frontier from Ontario to the Pacific Coast.[13]

In contrast, the United States remained free of other empires during the nineteenth century. Its western frontier, from the Mississippi River to the Pacific Coast, lacked any clear governing body like the Hudson's Bay Company. Much of the frontier regulation in the United States fell to the Army. In the mid-nineteenth century, just before Canadian Confederation, the United States suffered through the Civil War, dramatically changing eastern and southern politics and economics. After the Civil War, Congress utilized the Army to pacify the western frontier.

Canada and the United States also appear to differ when it comes to Indian/ Canadian government relations. The presence of the Hudson's Bay Company shaped Canadian Indian policy in the first half of the nineteenth century. The Company demanded a stable frontier for the Indians and removed squatters and other interlopers from its territory. After Confederation, the Canadian government focused on drawing up reserve treaties with the western tribes, excluding British Columbia. Most of these treaties and their terms were enforced by the North-West Mounted Police. Furthermore, the Canadian government attempted to make some concessions to the desires of the Métis population.

The U.S. frontier, on the other hand, was completely unregulated, with settlers often arriving before treaties with the Indians were signed and policies set. The government used the Army not as a peacekeeping force but as an occupier, meant to herd the Indians onto reservations. The U.S. government and the Army failed to enforce most of the treaties in the West and preferred to deal with Indians as one amorphous group on whom the government declared war. And the U.S. government failed to recognize any difference between full-blood natives and those, like the Métis in Canada, who had one European or American parent and one native parent. Thus, the two countries, in a brief overview, appear to have significantly different frontiers and Indian policies during the nineteenth century, which suggests that their racial attitudes were disparate also.

Initially, Protestant missionaries and their sponsoring societies in Canada and the United States appear to be different as well. Missionaries in Canada were Anglican, Presbyterian, and Methodist, while those in the United States were Presbyterian, Baptist, and Methodist. Additionally, each country produced its own missionary societies. In the United States, some denominations, like the Baptists, had two or more missionary societies associated with them. In spite of denominational and national differences, missionaries in Canada and the United States shared some important experiences. Both suffered through dramatic institutional shifts as sponsorship changed hands from missionary societies to the governments to secular, scholarly institutions. Protestant missionaries in both countries relied on these three institutions for financial and political support. Canadian and American missionaries also relied on public approval and assistance to continue with their work. Missionaries from both Canada and the United States wrote works that added to the growing nineteenth-century body of literature on the Indians, shaping impressions of the western frontiers and the natives who inhabited them.

This book examines Protestant missionaries on the frontiers of Canada and the United States in order to explore how two very different countries produced such similar attitudes toward one group. Did Canadian actions and policies match Canadian words and racial attitudes as they supposedly did in the United States? Did Canadian institutions, such as the government and the missionary societies, reward missionaries who pursued conversion or those who employed racial stereotypes? How did institutional responses shape and institutionalize missionary attitudes? Finally, were the Canadian and U.S. frontiers and their institutions and attitudes different? By comparing two fundamentally dissimilar frontiers whose institutions responded differently to one crisis (the Indian Problem), this book expands the discussion of institutions, attitudes, and race into a world context, exploring the uniqueness of both Canada and the United States.

To achieve this, the chapters are structured in an alternating manner beginning with chapter 2. Chapters 2, 4, and 6 examine the general history of three distinct time periods (1820–1850, 1851–1880, and 1881–1900, respectively) within Canadian and American frontier history as well as the changing relationships between missionaries and their sponsors. These chapters are meant to set the stage for readers unfamiliar with the frontier history of either country. These even-numbered chapters demonstrate how different Canada and the United States were in a general sense. Chapters 3, 5, and 7 examine the attitudes that missionary authors express in their writings during the three time periods mentioned above and how these attitudes reflect their changing relationships with sponsors and the policy changes on the frontiers. These odd-numbered chapters illustrate, at least within the realm of missionary attitudes toward the Indians, how similar they were.

Chapter 1 provides a history of the missionary societies, their goals for their missionaries, and their strategies for achieving these goals at the beginning of the nineteenth century in Canada and the United States. Chapter 2 examines early racial theories of the eighteenth and nineteenth centuries, the concept of the "noble savage," the differences between the early Canadian and U.S. frontiers and how these differences combined with missionaries' preconceptions to shape their early reactions and responses to the Indians. Chapter 3 studies how the differences between Canada and the United States shaped the first stage of missionary work—translation—to produce similar results. Chapter 4 details the shifting relationships between the missionary societies, their missionaries, and the governments within a general context of the changing frontiers in Canada and the United States. Chapter 5 discusses the individual missionaries' attempts to find funding after the missionary societies removed their financial support. Chapter 6 studies the breakdown of the relationship between missionaries and the governments as the pressure to pacify the western frontiers increased. Chapter 7 addresses the last stage of missionary work as missionaries attempted to draw support from the public by working closely with academic institutions. Though these chapters follow a rough chronology to help move the comparison along, missionary attitudes and interactions did not fit neatly into chronological stages. Thus, the book displays shifts in attitudes and policies as they become layered and multifaceted.

The research is based on the diverse private papers of more than eighty nineteenth-century Protestant missionaries, the newsletters and publications of nine nineteenth-century missionary societies, and approximately one hundred works of fiction and nonfiction published by Protestant missionaries and their children on life among the Indians. These sources cover roughly eighty years, from the 1820s until 1900, of image creation in Canada and the United States.

Missionaries produced much written material telling of their experiences, opinions, and pleas for help and support. In addition to annual reports, missionary societies published guides to recruiting missionaries, guides to the field, atlases, and handbooks on missionary life in various parts of the world and on life on the Canadian and U.S. western frontiers. The governing bodies of these missionary societies exchanged these pamphlets, handbooks, and mission accounts, making the Canadian and U.S. missionary societies and their missionaries colleagues in the foreign field.[14]

The most revealing resources available on Protestant missionaries are personal papers. Missionaries published their diaries, letters, and autobiographies, in hopes of raising financial support for their missions, or in some cases, to support themselves in retirement. Diaries present the intimate details of missionaries' lives, including their most private opinions and feelings about their work. There exists an obvious difference between published and unpublished diaries. Missionaries often edited diaries meant for publication or rewrote them using information they did not have earlier.[15] Unpublished diaries often expressed opinions that could not be stated otherwise and were not meant for public consumption. By comparing published and unpublished diaries by the same missionary, the researcher gains a more in-depth understanding of the missionary's true intentions and beliefs.

Letters pose a similar problem of audience and authenticity when they are published while the author is still alive. A researcher needs to remember that the author or publisher intended these letters for a certain audience and that the average reader read only this work and not all the others produced during the author's life. The provenance and address of a letter can alter the content drastically. A letter to a sister may differ considerably from one to a fellow missionary or to a missionary society board.

Although autobiographies and biographies differ from letters and diaries in that they were written during retirement, away from the field, most missionaries based their autobiographies on the diaries, letters, and reports they sent back to their sponsoring missionary society. Some, such as Stephen Return Riggs, who worked for the American Board of Commissioners for Foreign Missions among the Sioux of Minnesota, actually included excerpts from their letters and diaries. Many biographies about missionaries were penned by children and grandchildren, which affected the way the missionary was presented. In some cases, when a missionary died of disease or misadventure in the field, the sponsoring missionary society solicited memorials about the person or commissioned a biography to glorify his or her work. These works often employed extremely broad and colorful language, creating a distorted image of missionary life. It is easy to see why the bulk of the data used in this study is drawn from the personal papers of the Protestant missionaries in the nineteenth century, although the limitations of such papers must be kept constantly in mind.

In their publications, the missionary societies printed excerpts of letters from missionaries, ran editorials by board members, listed the assets of the various missions, recorded personnel, births, deaths, and marriages, and provided yet another outlet for missionary articles. These official publications provided a broader view of the missionary's world. First, missionaries read these publications, keeping up with what their brethren pursued elsewhere in the field, or in many cases, what relatives were doing. Protestant churches in Canada and the United States, as well as some in England, supplied official publications to their congregations to inspire them to support the missions, invariably providing a window into the world of the missionary for congregation members and helping them define the exotic entity known as the Indian. These publications also circulated through the hands of nineteenth-century government officials and scholars, providing them with information and impressions about the frontiers of Canada and the United States. Finally, missionaries and teachers utilized newsletters in education or as proper reading for young ladies. In those cases, the letters sent in were heavily edited by the creators of the newsletters. Additionally, some missionaries published the same letter or account in several missionary newsletters and some missionary newsletters reprinted items from other denominations' newsletters. In as many cases as possible, the original letters have been compared with the printed and distributed text. Many of these works have survived in divinity school collections and in some cases, the boards and their publications are still active.

Another method used by missionary societies to inspire and instruct was the publication of missionary handbooks, Sunday school books focusing on missionaries, and guides outlining how to conduct missionary society meetings. Whereas the handbooks and outlines of meetings targeted adult audiences, the Sunday school books targeted a younger audience. By the late nineteenth century, small picture books abounded that detailed the adventures of missionaries. Some simply memorialized brave missionaries who died in the field. Others were short and simple anthropological studies of different cultures. Still other children's stories told about the good works being done by the missionaries. Some of these stories contained myths and legends about the Indians, with strong Christian overtones. From the illustrations of Indians in loincloths and feathers to the text describing the conversion of Chief Running Bear, these works laid the basis for many of the images repeated in popular culture.

The missionary handbooks and outlines aimed to attract young adults and others who might decide to enter the mission field, or at least support it. Some of these materials, like William Rankin's *Handbook and Incidents of Foreign Missions of the Presbyterian Church, U.S.A.*, described the hardships missionaries faced and the people with whom they worked. Others, like *The Great Commission,* an inspirational text published in 1842 and aimed at Protestant missionaries, outlined how a mission should be set up, which verses from the Bible applied to the heathens, and what steps helped civilize the Indians. Many of these early works originated in England and were transported and reprinted in Canada and the United States, providing a link between the missionary movements in England and North America. Unlike the diaries, letters, storybooks, and autobiographies, these works were written by outside authors, who were often female, and officials of the missionary boards.

Missionaries produced the majority of dictionaries, translations, and anthropological works on Indians in the nineteenth century. Men like Stephen Return Riggs, Myron Eells, Samuel Hinman, Bishop William Carpenter Bompas, Edward Francis Wilson, and John Maclean became the ethnographers, anthropologists, folklorists, and lexicographers of the nineteenth century. All wrote dictionaries and translations for publication, not just for missionary use but also for the enjoyment and enlightenment of the general white population. They often published in hopes of supplementing their personal income as well. Stephen

Return Riggs lamented how slowly his translations sold until the Sioux Uprising of 1862 stimulated brisk sales. Dictionaries and other ethnographic tools helped define the Indian for the Canadian and U.S. public.

The ethnographies, lexicographies, and anthropological handbooks assembled by the missionaries provided the Canadian and U.S. governments with information that helped shape native policy. In some cases, such as that of Marcus Whitman, who fought for keeping the Oregon Territory out of British hands, or George and John McDougall, who negotiated treaties for the Canadian government, the missionaries worked with or for the various governments.

The last records utilized for this study were works by authors of secondary texts about the interactions between missionaries and Indians. These authors wrote biographies and histories based on missionary accounts, editing them carefully to project certain images. Authors such as Augustus Buckland and Beatrice Batty manufactured laudatory tomes recounting the adventures of the missionaries and the success of their missions. Many of these volumes imitate the authoritative tone of the missionaries' own books, and despite never having seen an Indian, the authors present themselves as experts on the subject. Authors like Buckland and Batty drew much of their research from missionary accounts and records and interpreted them within the context of Indian/white relations of the authors' time.

Missionary sources often remain virtually untouched, unanalyzed, and unused by researchers. The Duke Divinity School library (and other libraries as well), where much of this research was completed, is filled with gems such as Belle M. Brain's works on missionary fund-raising. Canadian archives also revealed diaries, reprints, and editorials previously unused by researchers. Obviously, these sources do not provide the Indians' side of the story.[16] But they do provide a glimpse of what the missionaries saw, felt, comprehended, and struggled with, as well as how these issues were presented by missionaries to the literate Christian public, government officials, and scholars.

Finally, studying Protestant missionary documents presents many challenges to the twentieth-century lay reader. Many missionaries published their works with an eye toward raising money, gathering political support, and recruiting new missionaries. The authors assumed that their audience accepted certain concepts about the heathen Indians and the need for radical social and cultural change. But these meanings may not be clear to the contemporary lay reader.

The terms "Christianity" and "civilization" appear repeatedly throughout this book. Where possible and relevant, the terms have been separated according to the ideas of assimilation, education, and conversion. Their usage here is defined by nineteenth-century ideas. Overwhelmingly, though, the terms surface interchangeably in quotes and in the text as their meanings intertwined in the minds of missionaries.

The following quote from the *Montreal Weekly Witness* illustrates this problem: "The Indians of the North-West are rapidly becoming a law-abiding and self-supporting people—in a word Christianized and so civilized."[17] To the contemporary reader, Christianity and civilization may appear to be separate concepts. Christianity is one specific set of moral and social beliefs and practices. Civilization represents a broader-based identity built on such notions as a common history, a common language, interconnected urban centers, and a complex infrastructure. Seen in this light, Christianity—or for that matter any other religious doctrine—is a subsidiary component of the broader civilizations.

This difference between Christianity and civilization did not exist in the minds of nineteenth-century Protestant missionaries and their white audiences. For them, civilization was synonymous with Christianity. As the missionaries entered the frontiers, they planned to convert the natives *and* to help them adopt Canadian and American societies' dress, habitation, manners, and customs. This required the natives to renounce their own religions and civilizations. Because Protestant missionaries firmly believed that they were acting in the best interests of the native groups, they foresaw few problems with this transition. After all, "as far as the temporal welfare of man is concerned, the history of the past demonstrates that even the worst form of Christianity is preferable to the best form which heathens ever know."[18]

Protestant missionaries associated with Christianity all that they considered good in the world. To them, this religion "humanized the dreadful art" of war where it could not "sheathe the sword." It "found the servant or slave and broke his chains. It found the poor—the mass of mankind—trampled under foot, and taught them to stand erect."[19] In this broad interpretation, not surprisingly, the missionaries considered modern European civilization the best exemplifier of Christianity.

Nineteenth-century Protestant missionaries recognized two types of civilizations: the historic and the contemporary. The historic consisted of ancient groups, such as the Romans, the Jews, and the Egyptians.[20] These groups laid the foundation for the missionaries' Christian civilization. The missionaries' definition of a contemporary civilization intertwined the concepts of "Christianity," meaning belief in a Christian God and His divine son Jesus Christ, and "civilization," denoting the acceptance of white manners, customs, language, history, and religion. As far as nineteenth-century Protestant missionaries were concerned, it was impossible for "these pagan nations" to be "converted and made humble Christians without first civilizing them."[21]

The term "Indian" also represents intertwined and interdependent concepts. Throughout the nineteenth century, as missionaries observed and wrote about Indians, they failed to distinguish between different groups, often applying the term "Indian" broadly. They created a monolithic image of natives, mixing traits from the cultures of plains groups, mountain groups, and others into one definition. All native cultures, religions, and languages became lumped under the term "Indian," creating confusion and stereotypes through the end of the nineteenth century. This word came to mean everything from a half-naked man astride a horse, tomahawk in hand, surveying the plains, to a drunk, bedraggled man living around a fort or town. These stereotypes ignored important cultural and individual differences.

Though native groups and nations who reside in the United States have attempted to reclaim the term "Indian" from its derogatory connotations, the majority of non-"Indians" still associate the term with negative stereotypes. Native groups who live within the Canadian borders refer to themselves as "First Nations," "native peoples," "natives," and by tribal or national names. Groups within U.S. borders use the terms "Indians" or "Native Americans," as well as tribal or national names. At the present time, though, no universal term exists to replace "Indian." Since this book examines both Canada and the United States and compares historical images to current realities, it became necessary to choose a term illustrative of all the native groups. Hence, throughout the book, the word "Indian" describes the historical concept and stereotypes, and the term "native" appears in reference to various cultural groups.

CHAPTER ONE

The Great Commission

THE WORDS and actions of Protestant missionaries open an important window into issues of race in the nineteenth century in Canada and the United States as well as other parts of the world, such as India, Africa, and China. Individual missionaries, who actually dealt with the native populations, did not act or form racial stereotypes alone; they played a part in a complex institutional structure that included the sponsoring missionary societies who had chosen them, the publishing groups associated with the missionary societies, and a fund-raising and fiscal infrastructure that supported them. At the beginning of the nineteenth century, these elements together created an active Protestant missionary movement on the western frontiers of Canada and the United States.

Of course, Catholic and Protestant missionary movements that focused on Christianizing the Indians had existed prior to the nineteenth century. From the sixteenth century onward, Catholic missionaries spread across North America seeking to convert and assimilate the natives there.[1] Beginning in the seventeenth century, Protestant missionaries, in the form of the New England Puritans, followed the Catholics into the field of conversion of the North American natives.[2] The early Protestant endeavors were followed by missionary societies that sought to convert and civilize not just the natives of North America but also the heathens throughout the world. In the late eighteenth century, they expanded their efforts into western North America.

Analyzing the images of North American natives that nineteenth-century missionaries presented to Protestant congregations in Canada and the United States requires an understanding of the corporate structures and strategies that shaped the nineteenth-century missionary movements and the missionaries' view of the Indians. Nineteenth-century missionary societies rose out of the Protestant missionary efforts of the eighteenth century, and the earlier efforts provided both the structure and theory behind much of the missionary work in the nineteenth century. This established structure, coupled with a new breed of missionaries, influenced how missionaries viewed the Indians, and these views in turn shaped the stereotypes that the literate Christian public had of the Indians in both Canada and the United States.

THE FOUNDING OF MISSIONARY SOCIETIES

Initially, British Protestant missionary societies led missionary efforts in the North American West.[3] Among the missionary societies based in England, the Church Missionary Society, founded in 1801, and the Wesleyan Methodist Missionary Society, founded in 1813, emerged as leaders in the field of mission work. The accomplishments of these groups inspired the founding of American Protestant missionary societies in the 1810s:[4] The American Board of Commissioners for Foreign Missions in 1810, the Baptist Missionary Union in 1814, and the Missionary Society of the Methodist Episcopal Church in 1819. They sent missionaries into the field not only in North America but in India and Africa as well.[5] As *The Great Commission* declared in 1842, "the accession of the American Churches to the Missionary enterprise was another and glorious stage in its progress."[6] In the 1830s, American Protestant missionaries started work among such varied native groups as the Cherokee in Tennessee and Georgia and the Nez Perce in Washington Territory, in an effort to emulate the British missionary societies. By the end of the nineteenth century, Protestant missionaries from U.S. and Canadian subsidiaries of English missionary societies covered the area west of the Mississippi River, north of the present-day states of Texas, New Mexico, and Arizona, and southwest of the Arctic circle.[7] Though the British government competed with the United States for territory in the West, particularly on the Northwest Coast, the U.S. and British missionary societies did not contend with each other for the souls of the natives. Denominational rivalry for missions and money existed among the missionary societies from each country, but throughout the nineteenth century, missionaries themselves still communicated with each other across denominational and national lines, sharing stories, impressions, and knowledge about native groups.

In addition to the major missionary societies mentioned above, hundreds of smaller Protestant missionary societies and associations sprang up throughout the nineteenth century.[8] They tended to be small, localized groups founded in an effort to raise money for one specific mission. Most of these groups lasted only a few years and relied on voluntary staffs and fund-raising organizations usually associated with one congregation. This book does not discuss these smaller groups. It focuses exclusively on the large missionary societies that had paid staffs, directed publishing projects, hired missionaries, and engaged in national and international fund-raising efforts. These corporate Protestant missionary societies had the means and the motivation to shape Canadian and U.S. public images about Indians and mission work.

From the beginning, the large missionary societies had several goals. Initially, they wanted to convert the Indians, but soon their focus expanded to include conversion of whites on the frontier as well. In fact, as historian Robert Pierce Beaver aptly states, "more and more the frontier settlements came to be stressed."[9] Missionary societies came to realize that to convert Indians they must be surrounded by Christian whites. Therefore, frontier missionaries needed to work with both the native and non-native populations to create a Christian frontier.

The major missionary groups all hoped to Christianize the heathens of the world, and the desire to do so shaped the structure of the missionary societies. The Church Missionary Society and the American Board of Commissioners for Foreign Missions as well as other missionary societies wanted to set up missions in Palestine, Africa, India, and China, and for this they required financial and spiritual support from the Christianized Indians and whites in North America. If these two groups could not provide financial and spiritual resources, then the missionary societies would end up proselytizing only in North America.[10]

In light of their larger goal of establishing world missions, the founders of the missionary societies imagined that by following certain procedures related to recruitment, teaching, and work with missionaries, their missions would produce self-sufficient, Christian groups of Indians. First, the missionary societies would recruit and ordain white men of piety and education to go out into the world. Though missionary societies eventually allowed white women to enter mission work in significant numbers as helpers, teachers, and spouses, the missionary societies consistently envisioned men as the leaders in the mission field.[11]

According to the missionary societies' plans, as restated in *The Great Commission,* after arriving at his mission, the missionary would engage in one of two activities before beginning the conversion process.[12] Either he would translate the Bible into the language of the natives or he would teach the natives English.[13] Then, he would establish a school and teach them how to read the Bible and other Christian religious works,[14] the result of which would be conversion, and consequently, the pacification of the frontier. As a native congregation grew, outstanding converts would be trained as ministers and teachers and would lead their own people toward Christianity and "civilization,"[15] for missionaries hoped that during the conversion process, the congregation would reject their own traditions and adopt Protestant values. Simultaneously, the missionaries would study and catalog the world of the natives so that white Protestant congregations could gain an understanding of non-Christians, their societies, and their transitions to Christianity.[16] The missionary societies envisioned Indian converts settling on the land, becoming farmers, and adopting Euro-American ways.[17] Through their hard work, the native converts could then support the church, both financially and spiritually, and hire native ministers.[18] Eventually, the native converts would be able to sponsor missions of their own, and the original missionary would move on to another group to begin the process anew.[19] This idealized structure for success reflects the missionary societies' primary emphasis on turning Indian groups into self-supporting Christian communities who could then aid in the conversion of other heathens.[20] Though the majority of the missionary societies started with missions that focused on the Indians in Canada and the United States, their overarching goal was worldwide conversion. In order to maximize their achievement, they developed a corporate structure to coordinate and fund these efforts.

THE STRUCTURE OF MISSIONARY SOCIETIES

Unlike small voluntary missionary associations,[21] whose efforts were guided by volunteer boards of parishioners and who rarely recruited missionaries and never trained them, large missionary societies were run by boards consisting of ministers, businessmen, and politicians who oversaw the many activities of the organization. The boards set policy, negotiated with the governments in their mission areas, sponsored publications, and directed fund-raising. The missionary societies recruited, hired, and trained their own missionaries. At the height of the missionary movement in the mid-nineteenth century, both the Church Missionary Society and the American Board of Commissioners for Foreign Missions employed several hundred missionaries worldwide. Additionally, all of the large missionary societies either owned publishing companies or had ties with printers, which allowed them to print and dispense information on their own.

The creation of corporate missionary boards and societies helped centralize fund-raising efforts, which furthered the goal of world mission work. The large corporate missionary societies relied on funds from a wide variety of sources. They looked to governments in Canada and the United States for financial support. They also raised money within white Protestant communities through such activities as penny societies, and Sunday school and congregational fund drives. They sent missionaries on lecture tours and marketed their publications to increase public awareness of and interest in missionary work around the world. Finally, they planned on raising money from the congregations of converted natives to support future missionary work. Very few, if any, of the missionary societies had endowments and most planned their budgets around the belief that within twenty to thirty years, they would be out of business and everyone in the world would be Protestant Christians.

The missionary societies dealt in large amounts of money. If one excludes world missions, the amount of money spent on Indian missions alone is sizable. In 1824, the U.S. government reported that 41 mission schools run by 11 missionary societies (including three small localized ones and the various Catholic orders) spent $170,606, not including government grants or annuity payments.[22] Between 1826 and 1842, according to Robert Pierce Beaver, a historian of American Protestant missions, the Baptist Missionary Union in the United States—one of the smaller missionary societies—spent $131,888 on Indian missions, with $72,184 coming from government grants and the rest coming from fund-raising efforts.[23] This translates into over $3,500 a year spent solely on the few Indian missions the Baptists supported. Between 1843 and 1864, the year the Baptists left Indian mission work, they spent $139,750 on Indian missions, with $70,275 coming out of their own fund-raising efforts and the rest coming from government grants.[24] These amounts are not unusual. In 1842 John Harns reported in *The Great Commission* that the annual income of the British missionary societies was £505,000, "of which about £400,000 [was] contributed by British Christians, and the remaints [sic] by the Christians of America."[25] As is discussed in this book, costs continued to rise throughout the nineteenth century. Beaver reports that in 1876 the expenditures for eight western missionary societies in the United States totaled $93,096.[26] As the missionary societies added more missions worldwide, costs continued to spiral upward. Eventually, these rising costs forced the missionary societies to change their structure and their relationships with their missionaries.

From the 1820s until the 1850s or so, building costs represented the largest expenditure facing the missionary societies when starting new missions among the Indians. Missionary societies paid for materials and the work of constructing

schools, churches, and missionary residences. Construction often involved trans-
porting lumber and tools to the mission site, which also added to expenses. As
the nineteenth century progressed and the missionary societies established fewer
new Indian missions, construction costs decreased, though other costs quickly
replaced them. Missionary societies paid the salaries of not only the missionaries and teachers, but also carpenters, blacksmiths, and farmers sent to teach their
skills to the Indians. In time, the British and American governments and eventually, the post-Confederation government in Canada took over some of these
costs. Finally, the missionary societies also paid for teaching supplies: paper,
tracts, textbooks, and Bibles for the converts. As early as the 1850s, the missionary societies began to hint that the Indians should pay these expenses themselves,
but as few did, the missionary societies continued to pick up the costs. Always
hopeful that the Indian converts eventually would be able to help support missions elsewhere in the world, the missionary societies persisted in producing
publications that would encourage native groups to give them financial support.

Because of the great costs of the world missions that missionary societies
supported, they needed constant infusions of money from the public. The missionary societies provided an overarching structure for their missionaries' lives
and placed pressure on them to generate funds from their work to support other
missions. Missionary societies required reports, pamphlets, and other descriptive materials to generate interest in the missions and inspire devotion to the
cause. The missionary publishing houses encouraged missionaries to write pieces
that would enlighten congregations and induce them to provide funds for mission work.

The first Protestant missionaries in the eighteenth century had published
numerous tales of martyred missionaries and struggling Indians, an example
used to provide impetus to the nineteenth-century missionary movement. For
nineteenth-century missionary societies and their missionaries, these earlier accounts were a structural model of how to dispense information through publications by showing images of how conversion and assimilation worked on the
North American frontiers. As historian Richard Slotkin states, "the missionary
tracts [produced by the earliest missionaries] were most often printed in London
or for the British book trade; they were addressed to English audiences, since the
Puritans wished to quash criticism of their lagging efforts in this field."[27]

Nineteenth-century missionary societies followed this same path, shaping
their newsletters for the literate Christian audiences and attempting to stave off
criticism of their efforts. As early as the 1820s, missionary societies created their
own publishing houses in order to better distribute information. Missionary so-

cieties praised missionaries who did translation work, and strove to make those works available to both literate white Christians and the Indians. In 1829, the *Report of The American Board of Commissioners for Foreign Missions* stated that the board had published 1,000 copies of Samuel Worcester's translation into Cherokee of a hymnbook and the Gospel of Matthew.[28] By 1834, the American Board boasted that "the whole amount printed in the Cherokee language by the Board is about 21,500 copies of books and tracts, embracing about 1,513,800 pages."[29] Just three years later, the American Board bragged that it had published 11 religious tracts in Choctaw in one year.[30] Considering that there was an average of 229,000 Presbyterians in the United States at the time, these Cherokee publications feasibly could have reached one Presbyterian in ten.[31] In addition to religious tracts and translations, all of the major corporate missionary societies published newsletters and magazines for their white congregations. These newsletters had large circulations. In 1860, 16,241 copies of *The Missionary Herald,* published by the American Board of Commissioners for Foreign Missions, circulated each month, potentially reaching as many as 292,000 Presbyterians.[32] These publications shaped future Protestant missionaries' and white congregations' perceptions of the Indians.

In the corporate context, Protestant missionaries maintained close ties with the missionary societies and the Christian public that they had left behind.[33] Missionaries wrote reports to their sponsoring board, describing the people with whom they worked, the conditions, and the country, all with a view toward raising money and spiritual support for the missions. Additionally, most missionaries returned from their missions every few years to do lecture tours aimed at Protestant congregations and potential missionaries and designed to raise and maintain interest in the missionaries' cause.[34] During these trips, many took the opportunity to publish autobiographies and collections of letters, as well as dictionaries, Bibles, hymns, and poems in indigenous languages. With the help of the missionary societies, all of these materials were spread through ladies' clubs, Bible study groups, seminary classes, Sunday school classes, and sermons, thereby continually shaping the Christian public's impressions of Indians.

Missionary authors provided Canadian and U.S. congregations with some of their earliest glimpses of native culture on the Great Plains and beyond. Untrained for detached observational work, the missionary writers defined native cultures through their own experiences. They functioned as nineteenth-century anthropologists, ethnographers, government agents, and reporters of the frontier and native life. With the aid of the missionary societies, the missionaries published their observations, circulated them among white congregations in Canada and the United States, and used them to influence attitudes toward natives and their work among them. It is the wide dispersion of their imagery that made the Protestant missionary view of North America so influential in its time and makes it important to us now.

The development of corporate missionary societies drove policies toward native groups of the West in addition to providing information about them. These missionary societies chose their missionaries, demanded information from them, and distributed this information in hopes of maintaining financial support from their white congregations on the East Coast. Most importantly, perhaps, the missionary societies created policies that shaped how missionaries attempted to change the natives and the frontier. Based on the primary goal of converting the Indians, missionary societies began to tailor their policies and strategies to the Indians. Though these policies were not unique to the missionary societies, as government polices often mirrored them, they significantly influenced how missionaries acted on the frontier in relation to the native groups they encountered.

STRATEGIES FOR MISSIONS

A combination of racial theory and information from the early Christian groups, such as the Puritans and small localized missionary societies, helped the corporate nineteenth-century missionary societies shape their basic Indian policies and vision of missionary work. Corporate missionary societies based their strategy for successful missions on three beliefs. First, many of the early missionary society leaders believed that the Indians were an endangered race.[35] Second, missionary leaders believed that the Indians must be assimilated into Canadian and U.S. societies to protect them from extinction and unchristian whites. Finally, they felt that farming would provide Indians with sustenance and financial support in the future. Protestant missionary handbooks repeated these principles to inspire the missionaries. As *The Great Commission* stated in response to the prospect of Indians farming, "it is important that if they have been accustomed to roam from place to place they should *renounce their wandering habits and adopt a settled abode.*"[36] The corporate missionary societies openly propounded these ideas, garnering support for them from their governments and congregations. Individual missionaries, in turn, fashioned their missions around these beliefs, becoming agents on the frontiers for the missionary societies.[37]

While most missionary society leaders agreed that the extinction of the Indians was inevitable, many disputes arose over the cause of their endangerment. From the 1820s until 1900, missionaries argued whether or not white intrusion led to a significant reduction in native populations.[38] Nineteenth-century missionaries and their sponsoring societies saw themselves as the solution to this problem. Only they could prevent the Indians from being wiped off the earth by bringing them the gospel. *The Great Commission* declared that missionaries and the gospel saved the Indians from extinction: "If in some instances, heathen tribes are indebted to Christian missionaries for their discovery, in still more, probably have they been saved, by the same agency, from *extinction*."[39] In the United States, after the government removed Chickasaw annuities from missionary control, the missionaries moaned that the Chickasaw would "be wasted away."[40] Thomas Crosby of British Columbia portrayed the Indians as a fading species to heighten the importance of his own role on the frontier and claimed, in his autobiography of 1914, that he and other missionaries worked "among a decaying race, almost all swept off into eternity by the white man's fire-water and debauchery."[41] Missionaries recognized that extinction might occur and sought to prevent it through the introduction of Christianity and assimilation of the Indians into Canadian and U.S. societies. At the same time, the imminent extinction of the Indians developed into an integral part of missionary authors' depictions of the Indians. These portrayals helped missionaries and missionary societies blame other whites for the native groups' fate. And the belief that whites had helped endanger the Indians allowed Protestant missionaries to play on white guilt to elicit support for their missions.

Many missionary authors pointed back to Puritan stories of the disappearances of Indian tribes and nations as evidence of their eventual extinction. John Eliot, one of the most famous of the Puritan missionaries, created praying villages and worked hard to convert them, only to see most of his converts die of disease and warfare. Canadian W. H. Withrow, in his 1895 compendium on North American native groups, described Eliot's work in translation as a "worn and meagre volume" and the "only vestige of a vanished race."[42] But the nineteenth-century missionary societies deemed him a success for his conversions and translation efforts. As Withrow clearly illustrates, Eliot also advocated the idea that native groups could not survive without Christian intervention, yet faced extinction because of uncontrolled white intervention. The missionaries' firm belief that contact between Indians and non-Christian whites hurt the Indians' chances for survival and for becoming "civilized" inspired guilt in Canadian and American Protestant congregations, which often led them to support native missions. Saving the native groups from extinction exemplified Christian concepts of love and charity, and ensured missionary participation in the settlement of the frontier. The possibility of the Indians' demise became an integral part of missionary society fund-raising and publishing efforts and played a role in their strategies for converting them.

Protestant missionaries and their missionary societies also employed the concept of the native groups' extinction to enhance their own positions on the frontier. First, missionary societies expanded their goals to include Christianizing whites on the frontier as well as Indians. Second, many missionaries suggested that the steady reduction of the Indian population should help make their work more effective. John Booth Good, an Anglican missionary in British Columbia, stated in 1865 that as the old generation of Indians died off, they would "be succeeded by others speaking our [the whites'] language, adopting our habits and possessing our faith."[43] But while convincing the public and the government that native groups were likely to die off, missionaries also pleaded for government intervention that would support their policies of preservation through assimilation. The Methodist Episcopal Church begged the U.S. government in 1854 to "throw over the scattered remnants of our Indian tribes its protecting aegis, and the Christian sentiment of this country should speedily demand it."[44] Missionaries secured their position on the frontier by portraying natives as fading yet salvageable, and thus in need of Christian intervention.

But for the missionary societies and their missionaries, saving the natives meant preserving only certain aspects of their identity. In 1853, the American Board of Commissioners for Foreign Missions declared that "the position which we wish to establish is this: a part of the Indian race may be saved from extinction. Not that they will always retain a distinct nationality."[45] This statement suggests that Indians would continue to exist physically, but not culturally. John Maclean, a Methodist Episcopal missionary in Manitoba who later became an anthropologist, echoed these sentiments. In his classic work of 1896, *Canadian Savage Folk,* he wrote that "the time may soon come when the Canadian Indian of Ontario and Quebec has ceased to be an Indian in his belief and civilization."[46] Missionaries sought to save only Christianized, civilized natives from extinction, which meant they needed to assimilate Indians into Canadian and U.S. Christian societies in order to save them.

The plans of the missionary societies delineated several steps in the process of assimilation. First, missionaries needed to bring native groups "under the influence of the Gospel."[47] Next, the missionaries were required to teach the Indians about civilization, which "tends, in a variety of ways, to create a demand for the *institution of laws*."[48] This institution of laws and the process of civilization was supposed to lead to "all the more useful among the arts and trades of civilized life."[49] Missionary societies meant this procedure to transform natives from pagan, unproductive Indians into productive Christians.[50]

Whether following this plan or not, missionaries expected a certain level of assimilation from native groups. Myron Eells, a second generation Congregationalist missionary who wrote scholarly pieces while serving the American Board of Commissioners for Foreign Missions on the coasts of Oregon and Washington, asserted in the 1880s that "if the Indian in time is to become an American citizen,—and that is the goal to be reached,—he must speak the English language, and it is best to teach it to him while young."[51] Assimilation included not only learning English, then, but also meant adopting Euro-American dress and habits. In 1868, Canadian missionary Egerton Ryerson Young congratulated a native group that had "once lived in vice and ignorance, the slaves of superstition" for becoming "well-clothed and educated; and not only theoretically educated in the plan of salvation but most of them enjoying the knowledge of sins forgiven."[52] Basically, missionaries expected Indians, as Young wrote in his journal, to "be like the white."[53]

For missionary societies, the creation of native ministers represented a great success and furthered the ultimate goal of worldwide conversion. If native congregations produced native ministers, then they reproduced the experience of the white Protestant missionaries and became self-sufficient.[54] As John Harns described in *The Great Commission*, missionary societies sought eventually to replace white missionaries with native ones. Harns declared that if the missionary societies did not intend "to furnish the nations with an adequate supply of preaching from our own land, and for generations to come, the heathen must be rendered independent of Christendom for their religious instruction as soon as possible. And in no other way can this be done than by taking the necessary steps for raising up a native ministerial agency."[55] Myron Eells echoed these sentiments when he stated in 1886 that "since I have been here I have worked with the idea that in time the Indians ought to furnish their own ministers and support them."[56] By creating a native ministry, missionary societies and their missionaries believed that they encouraged native communities to both spiritually and financially support their own Christian interests. The converts would pay for their own minister, church, land, schools, and supplies, freeing up capital for the missionary societies to spend on other heathen groups. Also, missionary societies saw converted native communities as a future market for their religious tracts and pamphlets, as well as a source of financial support for other missionary endeavors.[57] The missionary societies wanted native groups to become not only the colonial spiritual substructure but also the economic support for the Anglican, Baptist, Presbyterian, Congregationalist, and Methodist churches in western Canada and the United States as well as China, India, and Africa. Large expenditures to North American missions were preventing expansion to other parts of the heathen world, as budgets were stretched to the limits. By developing self-sufficient missions, the missionary societies sought to establish financial support for their work and to demonstrate success at assimilating the North American native groups into Christian societies.

Assimilation underlay everything missionaries attempted and became an important strategy for achieving worldwide conversion. By the end of the nineteenth century, it was an imperative. As Miss Weagart stated in an 1888 article, "they [natives] must walk in the white man's path or perish."[58] By the 1870s, missionary societies, and the governments in their tacit approval of missionary policies, had begun to present assimilation as the only alternative to extinction.[59]

Assimilation did not come cheaply, as the missionary societies would eventually discover. From the beginning, missionary societies planned for native groups to pay for their own assimilation. As early as 1840, Reverend John Smithurst felt that his greatest difficulty was "to make them [Indians] provide for their temporal wants." He found that "when converted into civilized and rational beings their new condition brings with it a number of wants which they have no means of supplying."[60] Beginning in the 1850s, though, as missionary societies reduced money to their missionaries, native groups' self-support became crucial. Missionary societies and the pre-Confederation Canadian and U.S. governments thought that hunting was the Indians' only means of sustenance, and this lifestyle did not generate enough wealth for Indians to purchase assimilation in the form of Bibles and missionary tracts.[61] Therefore, natives needed to support themselves in a manner acceptable to the missionaries, not by hunting. Eventually, farming appeared as the solution to this problem, and was deemed a good strategy for creating self-sufficient Indian missions.

For Protestant missionaries, farming was the most obvious way for native groups to become economically self-sufficient because it built on their links to the soil. Missionaries, who believed in the noble savage as a man of nature, saw Indians as a vital part of nature and recognized their connection to the land. This bond was described by the Bishop of Saskatchewan in 1883: "These Indians have some excellent qualities that will well repay the labour of cultivation. . . . They acquire a familiar knowledge of the objects of nature with which they are surrounded."[62] To the missionaries and the missionary societies, farming seemed like the perfect solution to the Indians' economic problems. Agricultural pursuits would allow natives to remain part of nature, yet would teach them self-sufficiency and a work ethic approved by the missionaries (because it was more conducive to financially supporting missionary work).[63] Few other professions offered such benefits.

Most importantly, farming kept the Indians in one place, making them easier to reach and more available to conversion. According to historian John Hines, many missionaries entered the frontier with "the Bible in one hand and a reaping-hook in the other to convert the heathen to Christianity, the hunter to agriculture."[64] Missionaries in both the United States and Canada expected their governments to support these efforts at making Indians into farmers. As John Booth Good pleaded in 1870, "the Government would confer a great favour by surveying off to them a proper reserve, so that they may know where to build and farm undisturbed by white intrusion."[65] Both the U.S. and pre-Confederation Canadian governments supported the switch to agrarianism, without getting directly involved in its implementation, by supplying land, tools, and in some cases, farmers.

Missionary societies, motivated by their beliefs about the Indians' future, formulated strategies that they thought would lead to successful Indian missions and, in turn, successful worldwide missions. They laid out a basic plan for assimilating the Indians and saving them from extinction that included Christianity, education, and agrarianism. They fully expected their missionaries to succeed quickly (within about twenty years), producing literate Christian Indians who read and purchased publications and wanted to help spread the gospel to other groups. But the success of this "great commission" relied on the individual missionaries' skills and ability to implement the plans.

THE MISSIONARIES

After trying several professions, Stephen Return Riggs entered into missionary work with his wife, Mary, in 1837 among the Sioux of Minnesota. Sponsored by the American Board of Commissioners for Foreign Missions, they spent almost fifty years in the field, translating, converting, and fulfilling other duties of the job. They survived the Sioux Uprising of 1862, the subsequent trials of the Dakota participants, and the removal of their band of Sioux to Dakota territory. In 1880, Stephen reminisced about his experiences in the West, recalling his first inclination to become a missionary: "Early in my course of education, I had considered the claims upon the Christians, and upon myself personally as a believer in Christ; . . . the decision had been reached that . . . I would go somewhere among the unevangelized."[66] A visit by Dr. Thomas S. Williamson, another missionary to the Sioux in Minnesota, prompted Riggs to request the American West, rather than China, his original choice. Riggs claimed that Williamson's "representations of the needs of these aborigines," coupled with "the starting out of [Marcus] Whitman and [Henry Harmon] Spalding [the first missionaries to Oregon Territory] with their wives to the Indians of the Pacific coast," attracted him westward.[67]

Riggs represents an average Protestant missionary to the nineteenth-century North American West. Lecture tours, tales of famous missionaries, or revivals inspired many to join the move west. Like Riggs, several chose North America by default or as an afterthought. Initially, they all would have preferred the more prestigious fields of India, China, or Africa. As religious historian Martin Marty points out, "Recruits for native missions were scarce. More glamour was associated with work in Burma, than in the midst of despised and hateful local non-whites."[68] Also like Riggs, the typical male missionary had an education, consisting of some high school and a little college or seminary work. Products of their times and their nationalities, Riggs and his fellow Protestant missionaries entered the frontier either with romanticized ideas or none at all about how to transform native societies into civilized (meaning Canadian or American), Christian ones. Under the aegis of the missionary societies, missionaries entered the western frontiers with the goal of cultural change.

As their first requirement, Canadian and U.S. missionary societies demanded educated men and women as their missionaries. Canadian missionary societies expected a more standardized level of education, assuming that most missionaries would join the movement with some education. Their missionaries, according to anthropological historian George W. Stocking, "were often self-educated men of artisan origin."[69] The Anglicans of the Church Missionary Society wanted only the most highly educated, requiring missionaries to have attended a seminary or church college.[70] The British Presbyterians and Methodists called for some seminary education or training in another field, such as law, before joining the ranks of their missionaries.[71]

In the United States, the Baptists required the least amount of education, viewing it as "non-essential, perhaps even harmful." According to historian Tetsuo Miyakawa, some western Baptists felt "it was sinful to try to educate a man called by God since He never called an unprepared person."[72] American Methodists (both in the Methodist Episcopal Church and the Methodist Episcopal Church, South), though requiring some education beyond simple reading skills, did not believe that missionaries needed the seminary education that the Presbyterians and the American Board of Commissioners for Foreign Missions believed they did.[73] All missionary societies, however, demanded some degree of literacy, believing that the Bible embodied the sole standard of faith and piety.[74] Literacy allowed for Bible study, and the Bible was the primary measure by which the missionaries would judge and change the Indians.

All missionary societies also required piety of their missionaries. The handbook for Presbyterian missionaries stated disapprovingly that some young men who asked about becoming missionaries lacked "one essential quality for this work, to wit, the impelling power of the Holy Ghost."[75] Missionary societies searched for men, and in some cases women, who expressed a willingness to sacrifice something for their work.[76] This expectation eventually changed, when a missionary shortage emerged in the 1850s. Canada was the least-desired destination, and missionary societies began to let less-educated missionaries, such as Anglican William Duncan and Methodist Thomas Crosby, fill empty positions there.

In Canada, nineteenth-century Protestant missionaries represented a sizable group of workers and explorers. Between 1820 and 1900, several hundred missionaries, predominantly male, worked on the western Canadian frontier. Though British missionary societies and their Canadian subsidiaries recommended that missionaries be married, they did not recognize women as active participants on the frontier as much as their U.S. counterparts did. Single female missionaries on the Canadian frontier were a rarity until the latter part of the nineteenth century. Male missionaries, most of whom came directly from Britain, usually worked alone.[77]

Almost a thousand missionaries and their families worked on the U.S. frontier during the nineteenth century.[78] Most of them were American-born, and more than sixty percent of the missionaries were women. Fully half of these women were single and unrelated to other members of their mission.[79] In fact, women entered the U.S. frontier consistently during the nineteenth century.

Men and women entered missionary work with different backgrounds and for different reasons. Men tended to come from the merchant class, and those headed to western North America, while literate, were not nearly as educated as the men sent to India, Africa, and elsewhere.[80] Male missionaries sent west often spoke only English. Those sent to India and Africa had completed seminary work and often had professional training as lawyers, doctors, or teachers. Also, many of the male missionaries who headed to the less-coveted North American frontiers had pursued higher education because it was a requirement for becoming a missionary, not because they had a great desire to do so.

Women in Canada and the United States became missionaries under different circumstances. Those who left behind records were highly educated, many speaking French or other languages, and several had been trained at Mount Holyoke Seminary. Mary Riggs, who worked among the Dakota with her husband, had "not only the advantage of the common town school and home culture, but [of being] a pupil of Mary Lyon [the founder of Mount Holyoke] . . ."[81] These women generally came from more privileged backgrounds than their male colleagues, and were often not used to even cooking for themselves, much less to dealing with conditions on the frontier. They picked the West as their first choice, partly because they perceived it as safer than other places and partly because until the mid-nineteenth century, other sites were not open to single women and only marginally to married women.

Missionary societies provided men and women the opportunity for contact with natives. Though some missionaries spent their lives on the frontier, most returned to white society after a few years, taking with them impressions and ideas that stayed with them for the rest of their lives. A few, such as Julia Wright McNair and Egerton Ryerson Young, became novelists; their fictionalized experiences provided the public, as well as future missionaries, with images of the frontier. Whether fictionalized or not, missionary writings successfully sold distinct impressions of Indians to literate Christian Canadian and U.S. audiences. Excerpts from missionary works were continually reprinted and quoted in other works, influencing the image of the Indian for generations to come.

Both male and female missionaries entered the frontiers with limited resources. They possessed only piety, education, and a plan presented to them by the missionary societies. Though a few eighteenth- and early nineteenth-century missionaries had already worked with native groups, missionary societies mythologized their experiences, using them to bolster their own ideas about the conversion process. Eighteenth-century publications portrayed Indians as "noble chiefs" and "wretched savages" willing to convert. Unfortunately for the future missionary societies and individual missionaries, these early accounts focused on tribes in northeastern North America, and were a poor model for missionaries in western Canada and the United States. Many Northeastern Indians had converted to become part of a community, since often their own had been destroyed through disease, war, and removal.[82] The Puritans and other early missionaries had worked with a disenfranchised native population, unlike that of the West. In effect, the motivational rhetoric inherent in the first organized missionary endeavors—the image of heathens ripe for conversion—was later popularized in published accounts. The missionary societies passed on this image to missionaries on the western frontiers, providing them with a sense of purpose and hope.

Nineteenth-century Canadian and American missionaries were like cogs in a large machine. While they pursued the missionary societies' goals, the missionary societies acted as liaisons with congregations and governments, and supplied missionaries with policies, financial and spiritual support, a plan for conversion, and a structure for communication. Missionary societies could do only so much for their missionaries, though. On the frontier, missionaries had to cope with their own preconceptions about the Indians, with the sometimes frustrating government policies designed to deal with them, and with their own responses to the Indians they encountered. Missionaries, while prepared spiritually, were often unprepared for the rigors of cultural conflict.

CHAPTER TWO

Noble Savages and Wretched Indians

M ISSIONARIES ENTERED the North American frontiers with images of the "noble savage" dancing in their minds, only to encounter what they began to call "wretched Indians." While missionary societies provided an institutional structure and financial support for their missionaries, the missionaries entered their fields in western North America with ideas absorbed from Canadian and American societies, among them popular eighteenth- and nineteenth-century perceptions about Indians. Additionally, missionaries, even when not working with or for the different governments, operated in areas controlled by government policies, including Indian policy, which differed greatly between Canada and the United States. These two factors, preconceptions and policy, shaped how missionaries reacted once they arrived at their missions.

THE NOBLE SAVAGE

Protestant missionaries from Canada and the United States entered their work in nineteenth-century North America as distinct products of their societies. For hundreds of years, Western theologians and scientists had been developing racial concepts, even though most of them had never encountered Indians or the "other" in terms of race. These racial attitudes and stereotypes had trickled down to the missionaries, but most of them had little constructive information about the people they planned to convert.

From the seventeenth century to the nineteenth century, theories about the origins of Indians, Africans, and other groups were based on a combination of Biblical theory and accounts from travelers. Historians such as Robert Berkhofer Jr., Reginald Horsman, Francis Jennings, Roy Harvey Pearce, Bernard Sheehan, William Stanton, and Ronald Takaki have examined these theories.[1] While their studies help illuminate the elaborate racial concepts that emerged during the seventeenth, eighteenth, and nineteenth centuries, they focus predominately on the creation of the theories. Few if any of the studies examine how racial theories affected the missionaries, explorers, or traders and trappers who interacted with the Indians. Analyzing how these ideas appeared in the works of the missionaries who dealt with Indians on a daily basis reveals that the missionaries entered their fields with watered-down versions of many of these theories and when the natives failed to fit the theories, they altered or combined the theories to reflect the situations they encountered. Examining how missionaries interpreted the ideas of European and American scholars and theologians also suggests how educated people in Canada and the United States felt about these same theories, since both groups were literate but not necessarily intellectual.

For the first two hundred years of interaction between Indians and the Canadians and Americans, three groups tried to explain the existence of Indian societies and how they fit into the Biblical explanation for the origin of man. The earliest attempts came from theologians who combed the Bible for clarifications of how Indians and societies in North America could be so different from and yet so similar to those in Europe. As North America became more settled, a second group of theorists appeared. They consisted of observers who used their limited contact with the Indians to add to the theoretical literature. Men such as George Catlin, various Puritan ministers, and colonial governors who spent limited time with the Indians provided first-hand evidence to bolster racial theories about a shared origin for mankind and competing theories on how differences between groups such as the Indians and Europeans occurred.[2] Their works became the basis for the efforts of the last group, the scientists. These scholars combined Biblical theory with scientific methods in attempts to prove or disprove theories about the origins of the Indians and other groups. By the late eighteenth and the beginning of the nineteenth century, scientists who studied the origins of man emerged as the definers of race and ethnicity.

The works of these three groups share several characteristics. All of them used the Bible as the basis for much of their evidence and argument, even the nineteenth-century scientists. They all sought to explain the differences between the inhabitants of the "conquered" world and the people of Europe and its settlements. Finally, they exhibited a desire to fit the Indians into their own preconceptions of the world. By trying to place the Indians into the Eurocentric history of mankind, they could justify the Biblical accounts of a common origin for all men.

By the late eighteenth century and early nineteenth century, Western theologians, observers, and scientists worked from the Mosaic explanation that all mankind descended from Adam and Eve. This idea came to be called the monogenetic theory and implied that all men were created similarly and were alike despite surface differences such as language and culture. According to this theory, because all humans shared the same origins, they must also share similar basic traits. Out of this belief in the monogenetic origins and the similar traits shared by Indians and Europeans grew the idea of the noble savage.

The Indian as the noble savage represented a free, natural man unhindered by the rules of society, and thus surrounded by a more unfettered environment.[3] The representation of the noble savage, who embodied the basic elements of humankind (like honor and familial love) in an unstructured manner, reiterated monogenetic beliefs in a singular creation by suggesting that Indians and Europeans were fundamentally alike. Traits like honor and familial love coexisted in the noble savage without the hierarchical structure of church and state imposed by the Europeans. But if the noble savages descended from the same lineage as the Europeans, why did they seem so different? One theory held that their environment had shaped the noble savages differently. Another explanation was that the noble savages represented a fallen society. These two theories competed for dominance until the 1840s, when the debate shifted to possible genetic differences between Europeans and Indians.

Because the noble savages possessed the same basic characteristics as all other humans, European intellectuals and missionaries assumed that when confronted with the prospect of conversion to Christianity, Indians would respond like Europeans and their North American counterparts. This belief provided justification for such diverse groups as the Puritans and the trading companies to "aid" the Indians through religious or economic conquest. As Herbert Malchow summarizes, "Educated Europeans of the early Enlightenment inherited a view of foreign peoples that was a mixture of fantasy and hearsay, often used to expose the venality of European life, as in Montaigne and Montesquieu, . . . to administer a crude justification for economic penetration and religious conquest."[4] The noble savage was thought of as the ideal of mankind without institutions, in his natural state, awaiting the proper environment in which to be shaped and raised. If missionaries could simply surround the Indians with the right environment, the Indians would respond as whites did and quickly become productive citizens.

This idea of the noble savage as the natural state of man became a tool with which Enlightenment critics could condemn European society. They could point to the Indians and declare the extravagances of Europe to be unnatural. In addition to being used as a basis for criticism and as a recruiting tool for missionary societies, Indians served another purpose as well. European and American religious leaders, politicians, and philosophers used this "inferior" group to point out the dangers of not being part of a "superior" society. Ronald Takaki states: "English culture-makers and political leaders had associated [both Indians and blacks] with the instinctual life; and in the very way they identified peoples of color, they were defining themselves as men of 'civilization.'"[5] Civilization was not a given. A lack of religious belief, a lack of belief in the monarchy, and a lack of "civilized" behavior could reduce any "superior" society to the "inferior" level. The Indians provided a vivid example of what that reduction would mean.[6] Thus, though the racial theorists began to think that the Indians could change, they continued to represent the idea of a fallen society. This theory was a prominent one until the early nineteenth century.

The idea of the noble savage prospered in the minds of writers in the eighteenth and early nineteenth centuries.[7] Explorers and travelers, who did not deal with natives on a daily basis, praised their "natural" life. As whites drove natives from the east coast of North America onto the plains and prairies of the West, writers romanticized the Indians' existence. As Gaile McGregor explains,

> Pragmatic realities notwithstanding, the literati were not the only ones who rallied to the bedside of the almost forgotten noble savage during this period [the nineteenth century]. Indeed, as soon as the great American public considered itself safe from all the various threats that the Indian had formerly embodied as a social reality, the movement to rehabilitate him as a symbol became both fashionable and respectable. Scientists, historians, politicians all hastened to espouse the popular cause.[8]

Fiction writers such as Melville and Cooper portrayed natives as noble savages in their works, reinforcing the idea in the minds of Protestant missionaries and the literate public. These works followed a set formula, which Roy Harvey Pearce identifies:

> The Indian is described for what he is, a noble savage. The coming of the white man is described for what it is, the introduction of agrarian civilization. And the Indian is shown dying or moving west, often with a vision of the great civilized life which is to come after him, occasionally with the hope that he himself can become civilized.[9]

In Canada and the United States, the idea of the noble savage continued to be reinvented as the frontier and its native population receded westward. The figure of the noble savage became an important tool for recruiting more missionaries, and this image and its mutations persisted in missionary publications throughout the nineteenth century. After all, if missionaries did not believe the natives had redeemable qualities, why would they join the movement?

By the end of the eighteenth century and the beginning of the nineteenth century, as Europeans and Americans came into more prolonged contact with different native groups, the monogenetic theory came under attack.[10] If all men descended from one point, how did different skin colors, cultures, and languages emerge? Racial theorists had explained away the differences between Europeans and the North American Indians by claiming that climate and environment shaped one's skin color, habits, and intelligence, but in the 1830s and 1840s, scholars began to look for biological explanations for the diversity of humans. Competing theories emerged as the nineteenth century progressed. Scientists began to propose genetic explanations for the existence of different races.[11] They suggested that some humans are simply genetically inferior to others, breaking the hold of the monogenetic thesis that all humans came from one lineage. Some theorists used Linnaeus's work on plants as a scientific model for explaining race, suggesting that humankind consisted of many species with varying degrees of intelligence and civilization, distinct physical features, and different origins. Based on this reasoning, skin color began to represent the presence or absence of certain inherent characteristics like leadership ability and complexity of thought. According to Reginald Horsman, science conveniently provided Anglo-Saxons with "a confident explanation of why blacks were enslaved, why Indians were exterminated, and why white Americans were expanding their settlement rapidly over adjacent lands."[12] As this new theory emerged, though, many, particularly those outside the intellectual communities, stubbornly clung to the monogenetic theory. Others suggested that this diversity originated with the Tower of Babel and the multitude of languages created there, again reaching back to the Bible for theory. And some combined these ideas, as science and theology were comfortably intertwined during this time. In any case, the majority of scholars based their theories on evidence supplied by others. They pored over firsthand descriptions of Indians and Africans. They corresponded with explorers, consulates, and missionaries asking for bones and skulls. They based their theories on all kinds of accounts, and so shaped public perceptions of Indians and influenced both missionary societies' and governments' policies concerning the Indians.

According to historian Ronald Takaki, during the eighteenth and nineteenth centuries theories about Indians moved from viewing them as a fallen society to seeing them as genetically inferior.[13] Throughout this transformation, a layering effect occurred. New theories never replaced old; they simply caused the mutation and alteration of older theories. In some cases, new theories ended up bolstering the popularity of older ones.[14] By the early nineteenth century, those in the eastern half of the United States as well as European societies and their colonists in Canada no longer saw the Indians as noble savages held down by their environment, but associated their skin color and behavior with racial inferiority.

Protestant missionaries believed in the idea of the noble savage, and so they assumed that Indians would see the logic and superiority of Christianity and convert as many whites had. As John Booth Good recalled, "I presume that we all start with *beau ideal* pictures of our cherished anticipation, our fancy ever busy conjuring up pictures of the richest coloring and the noblest design. . . ."[15] As Good admits, many missionaries entered the field with a rather optimistic, if unrealistic, portrayal of the Indians in mind after reading early accounts of Indians as noble savages. To missionaries who planned to quickly convert the Indians and change their environment, these images also painted Indians as rational beings, in the European sense, able to quickly assimilate and understand Christianity. Indeed, if all humans began alike and became divided only by environment, then Indians possessed within themselves the ability to accept Christianity. But Protestant missionaries ignored the most fundamental aspect of the concept of the noble savage: that he represented freedom—from church, hierarchy, and the state.[16] Instead of malleable Indians, they encountered a range of peoples who preferred their own cultures and religions to those of Protestant missionaries and their societies.

CANADIAN AND U.S. POLICY: THE EARLY YEARS

Many of the theories about Indians, in vaguer forms, simply trickled down from missionaries into the public understanding and into the minds of policymakers. But national and regional differences also determined how theories circulated. When missionary societies began to send missionaries into the North American West in the 1820s, the Indian policies of Canada and the United States differed. Both countries' policies treated the Indians as inferior, but on different grounds.

The pre-Confederation Canadian government viewed the Indians as inferior due to their environment, whereas the U.S. government believed in the genetic inferiority of the Indians. Both policies reflected racial theories of the time.

On the Canadian western frontier, Protestant missionaries had to deal with the legacy of French Catholic missionaries, who had been there during the two previous centuries when the French had controlled western Canada and shaped Indian/white relations. The French developed an economic relationship based on trade with the natives and therefore "could not afford to permit their sense of superiority to become overbearing."[17] But the economic relationship did not prevent them from adopting a policy of civilization and assimilation. They hoped the Indians would "adopt a sedentary life" and "cultivate the soil," thereby providing "a more stable supply of food for the young colony" as well as making the natives easier to control.[18]

By the early nineteenth century, the Hudson's Bay Company had expanded into western Canada and taken the place of the French and smaller English and American trading companies.[19] The Hudson's Bay Company continued many French economic policies toward the Indians, in part because it absorbed and utilized the French traders and trappers and their trading systems. It too treated the natives as economic partners and sought to create a stable and calm frontier for business purposes. The Hudson's Bay Company established common law and regulations. More importantly, it controlled the distribution of land and slowly allowed settlers into its territories. Like John West, an early missionary to Manitoba, most Protestant missionaries entered the prairies and British Columbia through the grace of the Hudson's Bay Company rather than under the auspices of the missionary societies or the pre-Confederation Canadian government. This permission had less to do with the Company's belief in the conversion of the Indians and more to do with its financial interest in the territory. By treating the Indians as partners and surrounding them with a stable and controlled economic environment, the Hudson's Bay Company appeared to accept the idea of the noble savage and of the concept that environment shaped humans.

Between 1820 and 1850, the pre-Confederation Canadian government passed laws that helped stabilize the frontier controlled by the Hudson's Bay Company. In 1837, a committee presented a report to the British Parliament stating, as historian Olive Dickason summarizes, that "unregulated frontier expansion was disastrous for native peoples."[20] In an effort to rectify this problem, in 1839 Parliament passed the Crown Lands Protection Act, in which the ownership of native lands was transferred to the Crown. This change meant two things: settlers could not squat on Crown lands and Parliament denied native groups any political rights based on land ownership. Natives in Canada had the right to use the land but they did not own it outright—it existed in trust only. The British government held it in protective trust to prevent its dissolution. The passage of this law demonstrates one of the basic late-eighteenth- and early-nineteenth-century ideas about race: inferior groups needed to be protected. By placing the land in trust, the pre-Confederation Canadian government hoped to protect natives from white land speculators, preserve a protective land barrier around the natives, and prevent exposure to less desirable aspects of Canadian society. This legislation would effectively keep native groups from moving around, so that they would be available for proper instruction and socialization by the Protestant missionaries.

The pre-Confederation Canadian government continued to pursue protective Indian policies from the 1840s onward. In 1842, the Bagot Commission, after reviewing the operations of the Indian Affairs Office, came to three conclusions.[21] First, continuing French policy, the commission decided that the Indian Affairs Office should encourage the development of native agriculture. Second, schools should be developed to help Indians assimilate into Canadian society. Finally, the commission declared that religious instruction should be supported by the state. This report laid the basis for the next hundred years of native policy in Canada. It also, in three phases, set about changing native environments to a British Canadian one.

In addition to these policies, though, western Canada lived under British, Canadian, and native laws. Many of the laws that regulated land under the Hudson's Bay Company originated in England. Canadian law originated in eastern Canada, far from the Hudson's Bay Company and the Indian frontier—the area it supposedly regulated. And native law, or the custom of the country, regulated land from western Ontario to the Pacific Coast. The complexity of laws, combined with a growing Métis population (the Métis population in Manitoba and the North-West Territories expanded as more non-natives moved into the Canadian West) and a fading fur trade, made western Canada in the 1830s, 1840s, and 1850s an intersection of different institutions, cultures, and regions rather than a result of outright conquest.

Canadian policy, then, driven by the desire of the Hudson's Bay Company to maintain the fur trade, centered around the idea of creating a stable frontier. Governments and institutions needed to be monitored to prevent conflicting policies from affecting the Indians. It is this focus on stability that has provided historians with the idea of a kinder, gentler Canadian frontier.

During this same period, the 1820s through the 1850s, the United States seemed to have incongruous Indian policies. On the one hand, Congress provided money, through the Civilization Fund, for the education and "civilizing" of the natives.[22] This discretionary fund allocated $10,000 annually for the president to grant to benevolent associations, which included missionary societies.[23] On the other hand, the Indian Removal Act of 1830 removed some of the more assimilated tribes, like the Cherokee, to Indian Territory.[24] This act seemed to set the tone for nineteenth-century American Indian policy. As the white population pushed west in the 1840s, the U.S. government continued removing native groups, including nonassimilated ones, further west, disrupting the missionaries' work.

The removal of the Cherokee, Choctaw, and Creek tribes in the 1830s affected the relationship between missionaries and the U.S. government. As Samuel Francis Smith, a nineteenth-century historian of the American Baptist Missionary Union, declared, "The nomadic habits of the Indians, the legislation of the United States, often transferring their possessions from one place to another under color of treaty stipulations, were always a bar to continuous work among them."[25]

From 1826 to 1838, the Cherokee fought against removal. During their fight, Protestant missionaries who worked with them repeatedly published articles in missionary newsletters, pleading on behalf of the Five Civilized Tribes (i.e., the Cherokee, Chickasaw, Choctaw, Creek, and Seminole). Wrote one missionary in 1829, "The people of the four southwestern tribes; viz. the Cherokees, Creeks, Choctaws, and Chickasaws; are greatly agitated and distressed, by the apprehension that they shall be compelled to remove beyond the Mississippi." The author pointed out that these groups felt their claim to land had "been many times recognized and guaranteed by the United States." And these groups considered "any public measure, which tends to deprive them of the right of self-government, or of the possession of their country, as being, in their nature, cruel, unjust and oppressive."[26] Removal of the Cherokee, Choctaw, Creek, and Chickasaw was a direct attack on the work of the missionaries, who felt they had clearly succeeded in assimilating these groups. Removal implied that assimilation was not enough to protect the Indians from the whims of the U.S. government. For roughly ten years after the removals of the Five Civilized Tribes, Protestant missionaries and missionary societies, especially the American Board of Commissioners for Foreign Missions and those missionaries who worked with the Tribes, distrusted the U.S. government and their actions toward the Indians. Removals cost missionary societies money, and damaged, at least temporarily, any trust established between the missionaries and the natives.[27] In 1831, the American Board of Commissioners for Foreign Missions hoped to be reimbursed for $11,000 worth of buildings lost to them when the U.S. government removed the Cherokee.[28] The American Board of Commissioners for Foreign Missions believed that the government owed them for disrupting and devaluing their work. However, within ten years criticism had all but disappeared. After all, if missionaries were to continue with their work, they needed both financial and political government support. Thus, with some trepidation, missionaries supported U.S. Indian policy as they continued to rely on government land and money.

In 1819, Congress created the Civilization Fund. The Civilization Fund is an example of the idea of superior cultures aiding inferior ones, and the attempts of the U.S. government to "improve" on the environment. The Indian Removal Act, though, appears to contradict these attempts. The Indian Removal Act authorized the president to exchange land in the western part of U.S. territory for land held by the Five Civilized Tribes. The bill provided money for reimbursing the Indians for their eastern land, for the cost of removal, and for protection of the Five Civilized Tribes in their new homes.[29] On the one hand, these provisions suggest that the U.S. government hoped to protect natives from the less desirable aspects of society by moving them out of the path of white settlement. Political leaders in the United States justified conquest of the Indians and expansion into their lands as part of the process of leading the Indians to a higher society.[30] But, since the government aimed removal efforts of the 1830s at the most assimilated groups — those that had supposedly begun the climb to a superior society — policymakers seemed to believe that natives were an obstacle to the progress of civilization and a threat to peace and security. Removal also implies that the government viewed Indians as genetically inferior and dangerous to the white population. While the Cherokee and other Civilized Tribes had clearly succeeded in changing their environment, their progress seemingly mattered little in the decision to remove them west.

The United States, without an institution like the Hudson's Bay Company to regulate the frontier, expanded explosively across the Mississippi River and along the West Coast from the 1820s through the 1850s. Viewing the trans-Mississippi West as free, open land, settlers, traders and trappers, and businessmen flooded the prairies and the Pacific Coast. No treaties protected these native western lands, allowing for unregulated settlement. The government attempted to avoid native/white conflicts by simply removing all natives into Indian Territory. But by the end of the 1840s, it became clear that avoiding conflict would not be possible. As settlement and squatting ran unchecked, tensions rose between the settlers, the government, and native groups. Reginald Horsman concludes: "In dealing with the Indians . . . the United States began to formulate a rationale of expansion which was readily adaptable to the needs of an advance over other people and to a world role."[31] Though the government still supported some assimilation efforts after the removal of the Five Civilized Tribes, it worried less about creating a stable environment for the development of the Indians and more about clearing the Indians from the path of white settlement.

It is clear, then, that early-nineteenth-century Canadian and U.S. Indian policies were fundamentally dissimilar. While both attempted to assimilate the Indians, they measured the success of such efforts differently. Canadians continued to pursue assimilation and clung to the notion that more stable surroundings would help the Indians become members of Canadian society. The Hudson's Bay Company continued to treat Indians as economic partners, adding them to the trading society of the West. The U.S. government, after first supporting and funding assimilation, ignored its results and began to focus on removing the natives from the path of western expansion. The government directed its first removal efforts in the 1820s and 1830s at the Five Civilized Tribes, whom the missionary groups had praised for their progress, meaning that tribe members had adopted English, sent their children to missionary schools, and attended churches.

One would expect Canadian Protestant missionaries to have been more committed to and better prepared for the task of assimilation, since their government clearly believed in it more strongly than that of the United States. Ironically, as seen by accounts of first contact between missionaries and Indians, Protestant missionaries in Canada and the United States had remarkably similar views toward Indians, despite the different attitudes of their governments.

ELEMENTS OF FIRST CONTACT

Though the majority of western North American Protestant missions began during the period from 1830 to 1870, the time of first contact cannot be established for missionaries in either Canada or the United States. For Protestant missionaries and the natives of western North America, first contact was a process that began in the 1620s and continued through the end of the nineteenth century.[32] In this book, the term "first contact" refers to the first time a missionary encountered the Indians with whom he was to work. It does not discuss the event of Indian first contact; most of the Indians in this study had already encountered Europeans by the nineteenth century.[33]

As successive waves of Protestant missionaries spread across North America, they met many native groups about whom they knew little except for the generalizations they had heard from others. From the 1820s until the 1870s, as they expanded, Protestant missionaries came into contact "with a very different group of Indian cultures, far more nomadic and barbaric, far less sophisticated in their forms of government, far more brutal to captives than the eastern tribes."[34] Thus, the stereotypes that existed in the 1820s and 1830s became quickly outdated and constantly updated as missionaries entered new parts of the West and met new groups of Indians.

The process of first contact differed between Canada and the United States. From the 1830s to the 1850s, Canadian missionaries worked their way north and northwest from Ontario, moving west to the Red River Settlement of Manitoba, north into the North-West Territories, and eventually into the Arctic Circle.[35] During this process they encountered native groups from the Eastern Woodlands, Sub-Arctic, and Plains cultures who differed politically and socially from the natives missionaries had encountered previously. In the United States, from the 1830s to 1850s, Protestant missionaries jumped to the Washington/Oregon territories, moved up the Mississippi River, and followed eastern Indians, like the Five Civilized Tribes, as the U.S. government removed those groups to Indian Territory west of the Mississippi. U.S. missionaries reportedly dealt with several distinct cultures—including the Columbia Plateau, the Eastern Woodlands, the Plains, and the Southeastern cultures—unlike those supposedly encountered by Canadian missionaries. Given the fact that Protestant missionaries in Canada and the United States worked with a wide variety of native cultures, their writings should portray different pictures of native cultures, societies, and their willingness to convert.

After the 1850s, both Canadian and U.S. missionaries continued to come into contact with new groups of natives. As the process of first contact went on, missionary settlement in North America differed between the two countries. As Robin Winks points out, Canadian settlement moved more north than west, while movement in the United States was definitely east to west.[36] Bishop William Carpenter Bompas provides a perfect example of the Canadian northward trend. An Anglican who was originally sent in the 1850s to what is now central Manitoba, he continued to drift north in search of noble savages untouched by white intrusion and ready for conversion. He ended his forty-year career just inside the Arctic Circle. Though the main drive in Canada was northward, some missionaries came *from* the West. Men like Thomas Crosby and William Duncan, an Anglican missionary from the 1850s to the 1890s, came into British Columbia from the Pacific Coast.

In the United States, Protestant missionaries steadily encroached upon the Great Plains from the east, though they had initially skipped this region, going around it to the West Coast. The activity of Stephen Return Riggs illustrates this pattern of east to west movement. He began his career in Minnesota in the 1830s and followed the Sioux band with whom he worked when the U.S. government moved them west into the Dakota Territory. His mission became a springboard for other Protestant missionaries into this region.

The contrast between the patterns of missionary settlement in Canada and the United States is significant. In different orders, the Protestant missionaries in the two countries worked with a wide variety of native groups and cultures. One might expect missionary accounts of the Northern Plains groups in Canada to deviate from the descriptions by U.S. missionaries of natives on the Columbian Plateau. Thus, one might anticipate the assorted descriptions of Indians in missionary accounts to eventually eliminate the idea of the noble savage. It is reasonable to expect that Protestant missionaries who began their careers in the second half of the nineteenth century would have been prepared to encounter diverse Indian groups that defied past stereotypes of the noble savages and "fallen races." As individual missionaries in both countries encountered different native groups, one might expect diverse descriptions to emerge from their writings, emphasizing the differences between the groups as well as the differences between each native group and the concept of the noble savage. This difference failed to emerge as Protestant missionaries clung to the idea of the noble savage throughout the nineteenth century.

First contact differed over time as well as over space. The noble savage stereotype suggested to the missionaries that the Indians shared rationality and other characteristics with them, and that the native groups were redeemable and worthy of conversion. Protestant missionaries continued to search for the noble savage in the new groups they encountered even into the early twentieth century. Missionaries compared the habits and cultures of Indians in the 1890s with those of groups from the 1870s or 1880s to try to prove that the newer groups came closer to the model of the noble savage. As late as the 1890s, missionaries such as E. J. Peck, who worked in the Yukon with the Inuit, discovered groups that defied the traditional definition of the "Indian" as "noble savage." Thus, this definition evolved throughout the nineteenth century to include such changing concepts as heathenism, cannibalism, and idolatry.[37] Consequently, any discussion of the definition of first contact must be comparative through time and geography. One would expect that the stereotype of the noble savage would have faded as new, detailed information from previous missionaries became available about native groups. Unfortunately, for both the missionaries and the natives, this did not happen.

Other differences in first contact existed between Canada and the United States, particularly from 1820 to 1850. In Canada, many of the early Protestant missionaries went west with the support of an additional sponsor, the Hudson's Bay Company, and followed the few settlers allowed west of Ontario. The Hudson's Bay Company, concerned about its white employees, allowed the missionaries into its territory to work with the white population but did not encourage their work with the Indian population. The early Protestant missionaries to the Selkirk community at Red River—John West in 1820, Robert Rundle in 1840, and John Black in 1851—followed the few white settlers that the Company allowed into the area. Except for John West, whom the Hudson's Bay Company hired to minister to both white and Indian congregations, most missionaries ministered to the natives only and used the white settlements to launch themselves further into the frontier.

From 1820 to 1850, Protestant missionaries in the United States proceeded west with only the sponsorship of their missionary societies and the permission of the U.S. government. They neither faced the stresses nor reaped the benefits of answering to a third institution. Many Protestant missionaries moved west ahead of white settlers or in several cases brought white settlers with them. In some instances, missionaries abandoned their mission to become settlers themselves, something that rarely happened in Canada.[38]

One other major difference regarding first contact existed between the two countries—the role of women. Most Canadian missionaries entered the field as single men, though by the mid-nineteenth century their missionary societies were encouraging them to marry. In the United States, though, early missionaries often brought their wives. In fact, many missionary societies strongly encouraged it. Of the Marcus Whitman party headed to Oregon in the 1830s, all the men were married.[39] Missionaries to the Five Civilized Tribes in the 1820s and 1830s—men like Cyrus Kingsbury, William Potter, and Ard Hoyt—also began their careers with their wives beside them.[40]

The lack of women on the Canadian frontier and the seeming preponderance of women on the U.S. frontier are due to missionary society attitudes about women and the safety of the frontier, the needs of the missionary societies, and concepts of Christianity and civilization. Issues of safety often dominated the debate over whether to send women onto the frontier. Until the late nineteenth century, the Church Missionary Society in England and Canada required single men to "ascertain their fitness to the climate and the [missionary] work, and also acquire the language before receiving permission to enter the state of matrimony."[41] The fact that the Church Missionary Society expected the men to scout out the condition of the frontier before taking wives suggests that the Society had concerns about the men's survival. Additionally, the Hudson's Bay Company had ruled against sending white women to its forts, based in part on an incident in which white women were caught in frontier warfare between the French and the British. The Company also viewed white women as a distraction, preventing traders and trappers from doing their duty.[42] These examples show that Canadian institutions worried about the safety of women on the frontier, thus explaining the low number of female missionaries, particularly single ones. It was not until the last quarter of the nineteenth century that missionary societies began encouraging their missionaries to take wives.

U.S. missionary societies also worried about women's safety, but only outside national borders. The missionary societies wanted to include women in their missions because they felt strongly that women aided in conversion. The American Board of Commissioners for Foreign Missions noted in 1825 that native girls under female missionaries "made rapid improvement, in various departments of domestic industry, and exhibit traits of character well worthy of cultivation."[43] *The Presbyterian Church* reminded one of its conferences in 1893: "Brethren of the ministry, did not some of you learn more theology from your mothers and elder sisters than from your theological professors?"[44] U.S. missionary societies also thought that women would provide a calming influence on the frontier. Belle M. Brain, in her inspirational 1904 text, *The Redemption of the Red Man*, described a successful female missionary who, "through her benign influence, induced the Nez Perces to give up their wild life and adopt more civilized ways."[45] U.S. missionary societies thought the benefits of having female missionaries outweighed the risks to the women themselves. In light of this belief, the missionary societies allowed married and even *unmarried* women to work for Indian missions from the 1840s onward, though they still balked at sending single female missionaries abroad without the protection of a husband.[46]

Canadian and U.S. missionary societies had different visions of Christianity and civilization and the process that would bring these ideals to the natives. Protestant missionaries in Canada sought to instruct the natives in the specifics of Christianity, while missionaries in the United States tried to teach by example. Missionaries in the United States aimed to provide a living example of the joys of a Christian family on the frontier. These different approaches necessitated different roles for women and determined the number of females needed for the success of the missions.

Missionary societies in Canada and the United States never intended to provide an endless supply of white missionaries to the frontiers, as they believed that Indians would one day take over the missions. The Canadians may have felt that men unencumbered by wives and families could become acclimated to and thus facilitate change in native cultures more quickly, which would, of course, accelerate their move to the next group of natives. The U.S. Protestant missionaries acted on the principle that presenting a Christian family would be attractive to the family-oriented natives. Martha Ramsay, a missionary to the Creek Indians in the 1850s, provides an example of the role of female missionaries on the U.S. frontier, for she "soon entered with alacrity upon the duties of directing the household affairs of the mission school, instructing the Indian girls in the useful arts of domestic life and preparing suitable clothing for the boys."[47] Missionary societies also assumed that conversion on the frontier would follow the course of the various Great Awakenings, spreading through the women and sparking the missionary spirit.[48] As John Harns declared about female missionaries in *The Great Commission:* "Here female piety has recovered and displayed anew the glory which it won when it wept at the cross, and was at the early sepulcher."[49] Or as proclaimed in an address to the General Assembly of the Presbyterian Church in 1880: "We stand in wondering gratitude at what our eyes see on the decennial year of women's work for woman. Shall we call it an inspiration? Shall we speak of it as of a rushing, mighty wind, that fills all the house; that sweeps away debts and losses, and bears to famine-stricken mission fields the sound of abundance of rain? . . . not woman's work for woman, but woman's work for the heathen world."[50] Clearly, missionary societies in the United States saw women as a strong addition to the conversion process, while Canadian missionary societies viewed women as a potential hindrance, particularly in the early years.

Thus, the Canadian and U.S. missionary frontiers in the West varied on several issues, from the native groups to the institutions that influenced the missionaries to the role of women. Protestant missionaries in the two countries encountered different cultural groups of natives. Within each country, individual missionaries experienced first contact at different times. Many early Canadian missionaries went west and north with the Hudson's Bay Company overseeing their work. Many American Protestant missionaries entered the frontier with wives and daughters as helpmates.

Both Canada and the United States produced early Protestant missionaries to the Indians who exemplified the distinctiveness of each country's frontier. Two men—John West and Marcus Whitman—illustrate the societal and institutional differences between Protestant missionaries in Canada and the United States. They also represent examples of typical first contact experiences.

John West began his missionary work as a single man in Canada in the early 1820s. The Hudson's Bay Company sent him to the Selkirk colony in the Red River District of Manitoba to minister to both the white and the native populations. The Church Missionary Society sponsored him, meaning they ordained him and supplied him with tracts, but did not provide financial support; the Hudson's Bay Company contributed that. In addition to serving the native and white congregations, West established a school for natives in hopes of training future native leaders, and more importantly, native ministers. West quickly gained the animosity of the Hudson's Bay Company when he began advocating for the development of a school system for natives that would cover the area from the Red River to the Northwest Pacific Coast. Many at the Company feared that education would interfere with the fur trade. Eventually, the Hudson's Bay Company withdrew sponsorship of West for advocating education over white settlement and commerce.[51] Without financial backing for his work—the Church Missionary Society did not step in—the mission closed. Even though the Society would not financially support West, it continually used his biography as an inspirational tool for recruiting new missionaries.[52]

In the United States, Marcus Whitman entered missionary work in Oregon Territory with his wife and two other couples in the 1830s. The American Board of Commissioners for Foreign Missions ordained and sponsored him, and he had permission from the U.S. government to enter the British-controlled territory. Whitman's mission had two goals: conversion of the Indians and settlement of the territory by U.S. citizens. During the early nineteenth century, these two goals were not seen as contradictory. As Reginald Horsman points out, "Even at the end of the 1820s, when a shift in emphasis was gaining momentum, the drive for Oregon was interpreted as the planting of the seeds of improvement and progress for all mankind."[53] Whitman's belief that a delegation of Nez Perce came to St. Louis after the Lewis and Clark expedition to request the Great Book of Heaven (the Bible) provided the catalyst for his first goal of conversion.[54] His fear that the British would take Oregon Territory and spread east motivated him in the pursuit of his second goal. In order to help preserve Oregon Territory for the United States, Whitman eventually brought 300 families into the territory. Tensions arose between the missionaries and the American Board of Commissioners for Foreign Missions because the three sets of missionary couples fought constantly. Eventually, the American Board of Commissioners for Foreign Missions recalled one of the missionaries, Henry Harmon Spalding. In 1847, the Cayuse killed the Whitmans, several other missionaries, and many of the white settlers. Though the native population probably revolted as a result of the pressure caused by a smallpox epidemic and the increasing presence of white settlers, Henry Harmon Spalding blamed it on a "popish plot" (to overthrow the Protestant missionaries) involving French priests. Congress blamed the British trading companies for stirring up the natives.[55] The mission ended for a time. Whitman became a martyr for the American Board of Commissioners for Foreign Missions and for the U.S. government. The U.S. government also established a garrison on the site of the mission to protect the white settlers.

These two men are examples of the dissimilar experiences of Canadian and U.S. missionaries on the different frontiers. First, the two men found sponsorship in different types of organizations. The Hudson's Bay Company, an economic and political institution, sponsored West, while the American Board of Commissioners for Foreign Missions, a missionary society, sponsored Whitman. Each missionary developed ties with two distinct institutions—West worked with the Hudson's Bay Company and the Church Missionary Society, and Whitman worked for the American Board of Commissioners for Foreign Missions and the U.S. government. Both men worked with natives under different political and social circumstances. West worked around the fort at Red River with Indians who were necessary if unequal trading partners with the Hudson's Bay Company. Whitman worked with several Columbia River Plateau native groups whose contact with whites had been confined mainly to French and English traders and trappers. West's and Whitman's different marital statuses also illustrate the contrast between the U.S. and Canadian missionary movements. West, like most Canadian Protestant missionaries of his time, entered his career as a single man, while Whitman started out as a married man.

The Hudson's Bay Company contracted West to work with the existing white and native, but especially with the white, congregations, while the American Board of Commissioners for Foreign Missions contracted Whitman to work with the native congregations (though he began to minister to a white one over time). These disparate experiences led to different tensions for each man: West fought with the Hudson's Bay Company over creating schools for the natives, and Whitman fought with the natives over bringing in settlers. The fact that the Hudson's Bay Company dismissed West because education might disturb its fur trade exemplifies the basic differences between the two frontiers. The Canadian frontier was controlled by the Hudson's Bay Company's desire to create a calm, stable atmosphere for economic development—the education of the native population was seen as a threat to this status quo. Whitman's troubles stemmed from an entirely different problem. He sought to surround the natives with a white settler population, providing them with a proper environment and securing new property for the United States. Finally, though both became remembered and canonized for their early efforts, the circumstances connected with the end of their careers illustrate the differences between the Canadian and the U.S. frontiers. The Hudson's Bay Company fired West over a difference of opinion about native policy and his responsibilities, but the Cayuse killed the Whitmans. Thus, Canada seems to have had a calmer, less bloody, less destructive way of dealing with the native population frontier than the United States.

As the cases of West and Whitman illustrate, the Canadian and U.S. missionary frontiers were distinct in many ways from the 1820s through the 1850s. Though both West and Whitman came from white Protestant societies that embraced racial theories of the Indians' inferiority, their countries focused on different aspects of the theories. Canadian institutions tended to treat the Indians as inferior but worthy of change. They assumed that the environment had negatively affected the Indians and their cultures. U.S. policymakers focused on removing the Indians. Though assimilation efforts continued after the 1830s, the removal of the Five Civilized Tribes suggests that the government still viewed Indians as a threat to American civilization. As the two governments responded differently to Indians, so did the missionaries. Through their own work, West and Whitman demonstrated the effects of these national biases. Thus, we have seen examples of how different Canadian and U.S. institutions were on the issue of early Indian/white interaction. But were the attitudes of Canadian and American missionaries different?

EFFECTS OF FIRST CONTACT

Despite their differences, Protestant missionaries in Canada and the United States shared one important feature in addition to their goal of conversion. The years 1820 to 1850 were a honeymoon period for the missionaries in both countries. The missionary societies acted as liaisons between the missionaries and the governmental institutions that granted them permission and funding for their work, so the Protestant missionaries had little direct contact with any of these institutions. Also, missionaries entered their fields completely confident about their missions. Mary Riggs, one of the first female missionaries among the Sioux of Minnesota, expressed her hopes for the future as she traveled toward her mission in 1837. For her, it seemed "desirable that [white] Christians in these villages of the Upper Mississippi should become interested in the missionaries and the missions among the northern Indians, that their prejudices may be overcome and their hearts made to feel the claims those dark tribes have upon their sympathies, their character, and their prayers."[56] Unlike later missionaries, who had access to more information about the difficulties of the frontier and more institutional pressures, missionaries like Mary Riggs entered the West secure in the knowledge that they simply had to bring God's word to the heathens.

The concept of the noble savage continued to flourish in both countries in different forms as seen in nineteenth-century missionary writings about first contact. Missionaries throughout the century had strong reactions when the Indians they met did not fit with their image of the noble savage. Some missionaries actively debunked the concept, while acknowledging its importance. They reacted against the idea of the noble savage upon realizing that the natives they met failed to fit neatly into the categorization. Missionaries like S. M. Irvin, who worked from the 1830s to the 1860s with the Iowa Mission of the American Board of Commissioners for Foreign Missions, and John Booth Good, who ran a school for the Thompson natives in British Columbia in the 1860s, openly criticized the romanticism of writers who had described Indians and had not had direct contact with the natives. Irvin expressed his disappointment upon first meeting natives and finding his preconceptions shattered:

"From traditions, . . . I had fixed in my mind an idea of his appearance. The picture was badly drawn and on the 10th day of April, 1837, it was taken down and well corrected or rather reconstructed. . . ."[57] Likewise, Good felt that "the pen of genius and the inventive narrative of exciting romance may invest these ancient dwellers of the western world with attributes of attractive interest in their natural state of lawless freedom and mere instinctive existence . . ." But as far as he and other missionaries were concerned, "these bright tinselled embellishments of fiction would be rudely discoloured by a better, . . . closer acquaintance with the subject of their themes, and that it is 'distance which lends enchantment to the view.'"[58] Both Irwin and Good, like other missionaries, found their preconceptions shattered by their first contact with natives. By discounting the romanticized, fictional accounts of the noble savage as inaccurate and championing their own more realistic version of the Indians, these missionaries began to lay the groundwork for their role as authorities on the Indians.

It is important to note the differences between Irvin's and Good's experiences in order to better understand the similarities. They worked with two distinct groups of natives, and twenty years separated their experiences. They also maintained contact with different institutions. Nevertheless, they both railed against the broadly painted romantic images of Indians common to the literate public. Missionaries like Irvin and Good recognized the dangers in romanticizing the natives as noble savages. Accepting the idea of the noble savage only hindered the process of conversion and civilization because missionaries had to deal with the conflict between the image and reality. If they assumed that Indians and whites came from the same racial origin, they often assumed Indians would react like Canadians and Americans to the introduction of Christianity. When that failed to happen, missionaries rejected their previous beliefs about Indians, as Irvin and Good did. But it was not easy to disabuse Canadian and U.S. authors and their audiences of the image of the noble savage. Not only did Good acknowledge the image as a force to be reckoned with in the 1860s but later missionaries also acknowledged the power of this representation. As late as the beginning of the twentieth century, some missionaries continued to refer to the image of the noble savage. H. A. Cody, who worked for the Anglican Church in the Yukon Territory from 1900 to 1910, persisted in stating that natives there "are not the type of Indian one reads about in such works as the 'Last of the Mohicans.'"[59] And in 1904 *The Redemption of the Red Man,* a work based on second-hand information, still referred to the Indian as having been "characterized as the noblest type of heathen man on earth."[60] Thus, throughout the nineteenth century, Protestant missionaries found themselves confronting their own preconceptions about the noble savage as well as the biases of the literate public in Canada and the United States. In spite of the different frontiers the Protestant missionaries confronted in the two countries, they consistently reacted in similar ways to their first contact experience.

Not all missionaries rejected the idea of the noble savage. Some attempted to use it to their advantage. Just as monogeneticists argued that all of mankind stemmed from the same beginning, some missionaries, hoping to emphasize the simplicity of converting the natives, attempted to keep the model of the noble savage alive. In 1854, a poet in the Methodist Episcopal Church, South, wrote of the Indian,

> Free as were his mountain breezes
> Once he roamed, the son of Kings
> Boundless was his rude dominion
> When he drank his native springs.[61]

After a visit to the Stanley mission, which was on the English River in present-day Saskatchewan in 1883, Bishop Mclean of the Anglican Church declared that "these Indians have some excellent qualities that will repay the labour of cultivation."[62] Announced an article in *The Foreign Missionary* in 1883, "In natural gifts of mind and heart, some of the noblest specimens of manhood that have ever appeared on this continent were of pure Indian blood."[63] By adhering to the idea of the noble savage, missionaries maintained both the natives' redeemable qualities and the illusion that Indians remained willing to convert and become civilized. These attempts to uphold the natives as redeemable crossed national and denominational lines, suggesting that all missionaries understood the importance of showing how valuable their work on the frontier was.

Whether they saw the noble savage as a destructively romantic image or as an important reminder of the common threads that natives shared with Canadians and Americans, missionaries commented in their writings on the power of this image, and on the experiences that shaped their impressions of the native. The noble savage became a launch pad for analysis and interpretation of the various native groups.

The thought of working with Indians usually excited missionaries. John Booth Good recalled:

Here then it was I first found myself in contact with the aborigines of the country who from my earliest years had been the object of my solicitudes and dreams. Could it be possible we had brought with us a talisman that would transform this repellant mass and would indeed the Gospel of God prove itself a power by which they should sooner or later be "turned into other men?"[64]

Good, after anticipating his mission for years, found himself confronted with "this repellant mass" which he had hoped to transform into "other men" just as West and Whitman had before him. Missionaries headed to the field envisioning the Indians and conversions of their dreams.

All missionaries expressed shock and disappointment that the natives failed to meet their expectations. In a Methodist Episcopal Church, South, report of 1855, an anonymous author reported that "the poor Indian now needs instruction in almost everything necessary to his very existence."[65] Good bemoaned that "truly in their then semi-civilized and more than half brutalised condition, a sadder or more disheartening spectacle, morally as well as physically one could scarcely disclose."[66] He had imagined a rather different scene, where "in the foreground of such a vista there stood our ever with me the 'proverbial noble savage,'" who however "wildly and grotesquely clad it may be, and fierce in deed and mien, yet Nature's noble man withal, lord of the soil . . ." Good had believed that this noble savage would be "capable, under the Divine aid and blessing of becoming wise unto salvation, and of being radically transformed by the renewing of His unenlightened mind under happier influences with changed surroundings."[67] Good's distress illustrates the contrast between the native of missionaries' preconceptions and the native they encountered. Good acknowledges that the definition of the "noble savage" combines the "wild and grotesque" Indian with the Indian who is "lord of the soil." He reiterates that the noble savage image conveys the probability of saving the natives, which justified his own presence on the frontier. Good clearly elucidates the crushing effects of the Indians' true condition on himself and other missionaries.

In nineteenth-century Protestant missionaries' minds, the commonalities of humankind as represented by the noble savage focused on a rationality which recognized Christianity and the missionaries' civilization as superior to other forms. The noble savage image suggested an uncultured Indian awaiting the mold of white Protestant Christian society. Invariably, when missionaries met their first natives, the idea of wild but noble men vanished, as did hope for quick conversions. As Good wrote, "How great the shock of surprise, and how sobering the actual contact, is mine to tell."[68]

Good's experience also illustrates how the paradox between image and reality in first contact persisted. Though he was not the first Protestant missionary in his area, which he entered in 1861, he still maintained the same preconception of the Indians that John West and Marcus Whitman did. Though racial theory evolved considerably during the nineteenth century, missionaries heading to the unconverted frontier remained fixated on versions of the noble savage and quick conversion. Missionaries who entered the frontier after 1850 came from the Christian reading public, meaning that they had access to missionary newsletters, handbooks, sermons, and other missionary publications. These materials exposed them to current accounts of the Indians, but appear to have done little to change their stereotypes of the Indians. One might expect the second generation of missionaries in the 1850s to have begun their careers with views of the Indians that differed from their predecessors, just as the views of the racial theorists and authors of fiction changed during the nineteenth century. But new missionaries still expected very different Indians from the ones they encountered, apparently having gained no insight from the flood of information available to them.

Most missionaries both intentionally and unintentionally continued to use terms associated with the image of the noble savage. Some missionary authors and lecturers used words like "proud" or "noble" to describe the Indians while presenting evidence to the contrary from their observations of native actions. Mary C. Greenleaf, an American missionary to the Chickasaw in Indian Territory from the 1830s to the 1850s, wrote her autobiography in 1858 as an inspiration for future missionaries. Demonstrating her understanding of the ideas that potential Protestant missionaries on the U.S. East Coast harbored, she described the father of one of her wards as "a very noble looking man."[69] Over fifty years later, Canadian missionary Caroline Tate, who worked among the coastal natives in British Columbia, employed similar language when she addressed an audience in Cincinnati, Ohio. She also used familiar terms, but in a subtly derogatory manner, when she recalled that the natives at Port Simpson in British Columbia "were a proud race," who "would point to their totem poles with arrogant pride. Tell you of their noble ancestry, of their prowess in war, of the tribes they had conquered and the Slaves they had taken."[70] She presented this pride as false, implying how silly it was for natives to be proud of their ancestry. In recalling the incident several years later, her words still conformed to the noble savage image. As a Canadian speaking in the United States, Tate's use of the noble savage image provides enlightenment on the way the development and staying power of the concept intersected in the two countries. She appears to have assumed that invoking this image would strike a chord in her American audience. Whether or not it did is unknown. But for a Canadian Protestant missionary on the cusp of the twentieth century, the image of the noble savage still appeared to be useful. Tate demonstrates the universality of this image in Canada and the United States and their similar attitudes toward Indians, despite the two countries' very different institutional and frontier histories.

Just as Tate used the word "pride" in a less than complimentary manner, other Protestant missionaries belittled different characteristics. "Clever" became "shrewd"; "proud" became "haughty."[71] Qualities that one admired in a Canadian or American became unfavorable in a native.[72] Reverend John Douse, who worked with the Mohawk, characterized them in 1834 as "a very shrewd and haughty people, looking with contempt on the other Indians." Though some had converted, Douse maintained that "the unconverted are miserably wretched, and lost in drunkenness and poverty."[73] Douse divided the Mohawk into "good" and "bad" groups. Missionaries appeared to base improvement of one's status on economic gains, as illustrated by Douse's contrast of "large and good farms" to "drunkenness and poverty." Even when Protestant missionary authors began to abandon the image of the noble savage, the vocabulary that invoked this image remained part of their descriptive arsenal.

Protestant missionary writers expressed their frustration with the discrepancy between the noble savages they expected and the Indians they encountered. They came armed with the idea that their missions would be successful, based on their understanding of the frontier and the noble savage. As John Maclean described in 1896, "When Catlin, the artist, travelled among the Indians, he found the Sioux a fine-looking body of men, well dressed in their deerskin garments, a noble type of nature's gentlemen."[74] The Indians of earlier missionary and artist accounts implied a willing and, by European standards, "rational," audience for the gospel. Instead, the missionaries found native societies uninterested in their teachings and overwhelming in their "need" for salvation. As a result, if a native group failed to conform to the image of the noble savage, the missionaries deemed them "wretches" and "disappointments."

Protestant missionaries in both Canada and the United States realized they needed to reshape their expectations if they wanted to maintain public support for their missions. They needed to inform institutions such as their missionary societies and governments, as well as supporting members of the literate Christian public, of these new views of the Indians. Protestant missionaries in both countries came to view themselves as those most qualified to become authorities on the frontier and the Indians.

DEGRADATION BY WHITES

A new image of the Indian began to compete with that of the noble savage. By the late 1840s and 1850s, as Canadian and U.S. Protestant missionaries came to accept that the natives had failed to meet their expectations, many attempted to describe the natives as they "found" them. Their writings now portrayed the natives as "wretches" to the literate Christian public. Herbert Malchow gives an example of this phenomenon when discussing abolitionists in Britain during the 1820s and 1830s. He states, "While the intention of the evangelical abolitionists may have been to portray the black slave as 'a man and a brother,' the actual effect of their propaganda . . . was to reiterate an image of the Other as a special kind of childlike, suffering, and degraded being, rarely heroic, that became part of the common coinage and popular culture."[75]

William Duncan, who worked with the Tshimshian of British Columbia from the 1850s to 1887, proclaimed in an early diary entry, "I cannot describe the condition of this people better than by saying that it is just what might be expected in savage heathen life."[76] An unnamed missionary to the U.S. Kansa cried in 1846 that "of their condition mentally and morally, we are assured, from what we have seen, that they are the most wretched people we ever knew."[77] Although these statements could mean that Protestant missionaries accepted the idea that environment shaped a racial group's abilities, a more practical explanation is that missionaries used the wretched Indian image to illustrate the need to send more missionaries. Richard Slotkin describes how "the missionaries discussed [the Indians'] character and religion solely to establish their aptness or inaptness for conversion."[78] It seemed obvious to Protestant missionaries that the Indians needed religious, social, and economic help, and as Slotkin observes, the Indians' "fatal weaknesses tempted [the missionaries] to prove their strength."[79] While the image of the noble savage implied that the natives had redeemable qualities, the image of the wretched Indian demonstrated the need for Christianity and civilization, thus providing Protestant missionaries, and in some cases their missionary societies, with an argument to use when seeking support. Protestant missionaries found that the image of the wretched Indian resonated with several audiences. For East Coast theorists, it provided fodder for the discussion of monogenetics versus polygenetics. For monogeneticists, this image demonstrated the rapid slide of Indian societies. For polygeneticists, it highlighted the inherent difference between Indian and European societies, suggesting separate origins. It also appealed to the literate Christian public as an example of heathens who clearly needed Christianity.

In the 1830s and throughout individual missionaries' first contact, in their rush to shock, many missionaries described the natives in such horrific terms that they scared supporters and general audiences away. Martin Marty points out that "a stream of letters to the sending agencies and other folks back home would describe the obvious evils [of the Indians]. . . . These evils would be formalized and exaggerated through repetition. . . ."[80] Also, because missionaries rarely used tribal names but instead used the term "Indian" to refer to all groups, their writings firmly established the idea of all natives as wretched.

Contact with the various native groups forced Protestant missionaries to reevaluate their ideas about the Indian and the noble savage. If missionaries abandoned the idea of the noble savage, then they relinquished the notion that natives were redeemable as Christians. To admit that the Indians were unredeemable was to give up their justification for being on the frontier. Replacing the image of the noble savage with that of the wretched Indian forced missionaries to rationalize the continuation of their work so they would not lose financial support. If missionaries could prove that the Indians' heathen environment had made them wretched, then they could argue that a Christian environment would save them. Suddenly, the secondary goal of the missionary societies—the conversion of the white population who already lived on the western frontiers—became important to the missionaries in the field. These whites, mainly traders and trappers, had failed to provide a Christian environment, the missionaries argued, thereby hastening the Indians' slide into wretchedness.[81] By placing the blame for the fall of the noble savage firmly on the shoulders of these degraded whites, the missionaries also tugged at the heart and purse strings of East Coast Christian audiences and the missionary societies. After all, their white brethren were responsible for the destruction of the idyllic life of the noble savage.

For Protestant missionaries, including those who worked for the Hudson's Bay Company, traders and trappers embodied all the reprehensible elements of Canadian and American societies. Historian Roy Harvey Pearce states, "By the same token, it was obvious that the frontiersman was an agent of cruel destruction."[82] Traders and trappers swore, drank, fought, and deserted white moral standards to cohabit with native women. In some cases, they cheated the natives out of money and encouraged them to fight one another. The degeneracy of their lives overwhelmed and horrified missionaries, and illustrated the fall of "superior" societies. John West declared that "The repeated Blasphemy" of his white guides and the trappers he encountered "was truly horrible, I had hoped better things of the Scotch from their known moral and enlightened Education, but their horrid imprecations proved a degeneracy of character in an Indian country."[83] Samuel Pond, one of the first missionaries to the Dakota in Wisconsin and Minnesota, wrote to his brother, Gideon, in 1833, that the traders and trappers were "nearly as ignorant" as the Dakota—a rather damning statement considering how missionaries viewed intelligence as an aspect of race.[84] In the eyes of the missionaries, traders and trappers no longer represented the superiority of Canadian and American societies.

Contact between missionaries and both isolated native groups and those at trading posts, helped shape the missionaries' perceptions that uncontrolled white influence had ruined the noble savage. West compared the isolated Indian groups with those at trading posts: The Cree who lived around the trading post at Red River, unlike the "Eskimo" in Hudson's Straits, "presented a way-worn countenance, which depicted 'suffering without comfort, while they sunk without hope.'" To West, "the contrast was striking and forcible . . . the mind with the Idea that the Indians who knew not the corrupt influence and barter of Spirituous Liquors at a Trading Post were far happier than the wretched looking group around me."[85] West clearly believed that white traders and trappers were the cause of the corruption of the noble savage. Sherman Hall, an American Board of Commissioners for Foreign Missions missionary to the Ojibwa in Michigan and Wisconsin in the 1840s, echoed West's sentiments. He found that "they are, indeed, wretched as they now are; but they are in danger of becoming more so, in consequence of their increasing intercourse with white people."[86] In the 1880s, Alfred James Hall, an Anglican missionary to British Columbia, similarly bemoaned the problem. He "found these Indians in a very wretched condition. The progressive colonization up the coast, instead of advancing the Natives in the place, gives them more facilities to sin, and early death follows in many cases."[87] Interestingly, this quotation appeared in both *The Church Missionary Intelligencer and Record* and *The Church Missionary Gleaner* in 1879. Obviously, Alfred James Hall meant to illustrate to readers that white influence without Christianity deprived the natives of a civilized future.

By blaming the unchristian whites for the current condition of natives, missionaries justified their own existence and importance on the frontier.[88] Without their influence, the Indians would be ruined.[89] Missionaries believed themselves to be undoing the damage done by their fellow white men. Perhaps John Maclean voiced the societal evolution of the Indian best when he stated in 1889:

> The advent of the white men, and the influences of encroaching civilization of the white race have wrought many changes upon the natives, so that we can no longer gaze upon the ideal Indian, as depicted for us in the pages of Fennimore Cooper and Catlin. The days of the bow and arrow, buffalo skin lodges, and ornamental native dresses are past, and in their stead there are plain matter-of-fact Indians, facing the stern reality that soon, very soon, they will be doomed to earn their bread by the sweat of the brow.[90]

Maclean clearly lists the developmental stages of the image of the Indian: "the ideal Indian," or the noble savage; "the influences of encroaching civilization of the white race," or the degradation of the Indian; and the Indian "doomed to earn their bread by sweat of the brow," or the converted and civilized Indian. Though as late as the 1880s Protestant missionaries hoped to create peaceful, hardworking farmers out of native groups, they recognized, some with regret, the passing of the romantic noble savage. Instead, as early as the 1820s Protestant missionaries in both countries began to focus on understanding the wretched Indians with whom they now worked, preparing them for salvation and civilization. They also began to introduce the idea of the wretched Indian to the literate Christian public to help bolster their own position on the frontier.

Roy Harvey Pearce states, "The idea of savagism had destroyed the convention of the noble savage by subsuming it, by showing that savage nobility was part of man's earliest nature and that it was integral with the savage ignobility of nature."[91] He bases this statement on an intellectual shift that happened with East Coast writers, who saw savagism as an inherent part of nature. The shift was easier for missionaries: false constructions of the noble savage fought the grim reality of frontier Indian life. Missionaries adjusted their view of Indians not because they suddenly accepted "savage nobility" and "the ignobility of nature" but because to be able to survive on the frontier and complete the task at hand they had to face the Indians as they existed.

Protestant missionaries in Canada and the United States began their work with the idea of the noble savage and certain racial theories about monogenetics firmly in mind. But, as evidenced by the contrary Indian policies of Canada and the United States, these two nations interpreted the racial theories quite differently. Put simply, in the early period, Canada tried to isolate and protect the Indians while the United States tried to remove them. The two countries also managed their frontiers in different ways. Canada's frontier was regulated by a multi-layered government and the Hudson's Bay Company, and was characterized by closely controlled white settlement. The U.S. government provided some support for missionary work on its frontier, while it concentrated on removal of the Indians and allowed uncontrolled white settlement. Missionary societies in Canada and the United States acted differently as well. Canadian missionary societies, in conjunction with the Hudson's Bay Company, sent primarily single men north and west. U.S. missionary societies sent married men to the Midwest and the Pacific Coast, in conjunction with government policies. One might expect these distinct structures and situations to have produced different missionary attitudes toward the Indians in each country. But both Canadian and American Protestant missionaries dealt with the preconceived image of the noble savage and wrestled with disappointment when the Indians weren't what they had expected. In the end, missionaries in both nations began to utilize the wretched Indian image to justify their work on the frontier.

CHAPTER THREE

Speaking in Tongues

M ISSIONARY SOCIETIES required their missionaries to begin the business of conversion and civilization as soon as they arrived at their destination. In the idealized plan of the missionary societies, teaching natives about Christ took precedence over anything else. To do that, missionaries needed to be able to communicate with the Indians. To this end, they had to either learn the native language or teach the Indians English. Once the missionaries made this choice, they needed to decide which alphabet to use, and what to translate or teach. As the difficulties of the translation process became apparent and the procedure stretched from weeks to months to years, missionaries struggled to communicate this to the missionary societies and the Christian public. The translation process, which continued throughout the nineteenth century as missionaries encountered new groups of natives, became the first area of tension between missionaries and the missionary societies.

Many Protestant missionaries published translations and dictionaries in order to aid future missionaries. These writings show us how the demands of the missionary societies shaped the development of the wretched Indian image from the 1820s to the 1850s, and how that image interacted with and eventually dominated the noble savage image by the beginning of the 1850s. The language studies and exercises created by the missionaries furnish subtle clues to their new attitude toward the Indians and reflect their frustration with the goals set for them by the missionary societies.

Throughout the nineteenth century, missionary societies continually pressured missionaries to translate and create religious texts in Indian languages. Missionaries approached translation with the idea that it would be a relatively simple process. The existence of some eighteenth-century dictionaries of Indian languages proved that it could be done. Despite the fact that missionaries in Canada and the United States dealt with different cultural and linguistic issues, their frustrations about the translation process are remarkably similar.

Protestant missionaries arrived in North America in the nineteenth century armed only with education and piety. Their education permitted them to read the Bible and accounts of the frontier, but the missionary societies required more of them. Missionary societies wanted their missionaries to teach reading, instruct natives in the gospel, and learn all they could about the Indians. Canadian and U.S. missionaries accomplished all of these goals to varying degrees. However, their educations had not prepared them to become translators and cultural interpreters. The problems that the missionaries had with translation and the pressure that missionary societies placed on them to succeed helped to shape missionaries' views of native societies.

THE IMPORTANCE OF TRANSLATION
AND LEARNING NATIVE LANGUAGES

In 1879, Samuel Francis Smith explained the continuing importance of translation. "Hymns were printed in Shawanoe, Delaware, Ottawa, Otoe, and Ojibwa as well as in Cherokee so that these barbarous tongues were consecrated to the high praises of God."[1] Smith implies that the simple act of singing about God, even if it was in a "barbarous tongue," moved one that much closer to being saved. For the missionary societies, learning the native language was a means to an end. The Church Missionary Society, the American Board of Commissioners of Foreign Missions, and the Baptist Missionary Union, among others, impressed upon their workers the importance of learning the native language and translating the Bible into that language. Stephen Return Riggs remembered that before he and his wife left the United States for Minnesota Territory in the 1830s, "it had been impressed upon us by [American Board of Commissioners for Foreign Missions] Secretary David Greene that whether we were successful missionaries or not depended much on our acquiring a free use of the language."[2] Comments by Bishop John Horden of Moosonee, an Anglican who spent almost sixty years in northern Canada, clearly illustrate how important learning Indian languages was to the future of Christianity. In 1892, at the end of his career, Horden described completing translations into various Indian languages of the books of Judges, Ruth, and Samuel I and II as well as working on a translation of the rest of the Old Testament. He also planned to "revise, probably rewrite" his version of the Old Testament, "which has been in print several years." He saw his translation work as "the crowning work of my life, which will continue to call souls to Christ for generations after I have been called to my rest."[3] Horden obviously viewed translation as his most important contribution to mission work. Missionary societies believed that if the missionaries could learn the native language, then they could surround the Indians entirely with a Christian environment and thus convert, assimilate, and civilize them.

Many of the men sent onto the North American frontiers were not as well educated as their counterparts sent to China, India, and Africa. For men like William Duncan in British Columbia, Edward Francis Wilson in Ontario, and Stephen Return Riggs in Minnesota and Dakota Territory, education and conversion intersected. They had learned to read as adults, using the Bible, which had led to their own conversion. Basing their plans for conversion of the natives on their own experiences, they expected the same results with their Indian audiences.[4] Once the native groups could read the Bible, missionaries and the missionary societies assumed natives would convert and adopt both civilization and a civilized language—English.[5] Anna Eliza Robertson, a missionary to the Creek, expressed this idea as late as 1895 when she wrote to the *Oklahoma School Herald,* pleading for more translators. She spoke on behalf of the "other Indians of our country, who have never known the joy of reading even one verse of God's word, and never can know it, except through the work of a translator. . . ."[6] This belief in the power of the gospel was the basis for two characteristics of the nineteenth century missionary movement. First, missionaries assumed that natives would react and relate to the Bible just as Canadian and American converts had. They failed to recognize that men like Duncan, Wilson, and Riggs were adult converts who had been raised in a Christian society. Thus, when they had "converted" they simply joined the majority in the predominating culture.

Canadian and U.S. missionary societies saw an intertwining of civilization and Christianity. They considered the Bible both a product of civilization and a means to achieve civilization. As historian David Baird states, "[translation of the Bible] meant that salvation, civilization, and English-language literacy remained merely different facets of the same Christian message."[7]

Until the end of the nineteenth century, at which point the majority of Indian languages had been translated and emphasis had shifted to teaching natives English, Protestant missionaries frantically tried to acquire a working knowledge of the local native language as soon as they arrived at their new post. Many missionaries experienced a feeling of despair as they attempted to learn these languages. Abraham Cowley, who served in Manitoba for the Church Missionary Society, entered missionary work with only seven years of primary schooling and two years at the Church Missionary Society College in Islington, England. He and his wife Arabella arrived in Red River in 1841. Twenty-two years later he lamented that "in regard to my learning the language it seems some times almost an impossibility for me ever to preach to them in their own tongue, but still I feel determined God been [*sic*] my helper to pesevere [*sic*]."[8] And Cowley was not alone in his plight. Bishop John Horden described how his successor, Jervois Newnham, worked at learning Cree: "He has been indefatigable in the study of the Indian language, in which I assist him two hours daily . . ." Though Newnham appeared to be a quick study, "conducting our Indian services, reading the whole church service," the daily lessons delayed other duties.[9] Protestant missionaries in the United States experienced as much frustration as those in Canada. In 1822, Reverend Daniel Butrick, a missionary to the Cherokee in Tennessee, wrote to the American Board of Commissioners for Foreign Missions that he "has found the perfect acquisition of the language much more difficult than been [*sic*] supposed."[10] A report to the same board in 1829 stated that "the principal labor of Mr. Worcester [the father of Anna Eliza Robertson] is devoted to translations." But, the report continued, "to translate the Scriptures into Cherokee, or any other language, indeed requires great care, caution and diligence."[11] Isaac McCoy, a Baptist missionary in Kansas and Oklahoma in the 1840s, shared Butrick's and Cowley's regrets. "When I first went into the wilderness as a missionary, I set about the study of the Indian language, but circumstances had denied me the opportunity of acquiring such a knowledge as would enable me to address the natives on the subject of religion without an interpreter."[12] Like many before and after them, these missionaries assumed that an "inferior" culture would have a simple language. They failed to grasp the complexity of learning and translating languages until they entered their fields. To the missionaries, this predicament was just another example of the Indians' inferiority and backwardness. Not only were the Indians different from the missionaries' preconceived ideas, but their languages failed to lend themselves easily to translation.

Distanced from and unsympathetic to missionaries' feelings of futility about learning native languages, the missionary societies continued to pressure them to acquire a working knowledge of native languages without preparing them to achieve this goal. As late as the 1880s, missionary societies still charged their missionaries with the responsibility of learning native languages. Before J. William Tims headed for his mission in the North-West Territories in 1883, the Church

Missionary Society gave him certain instructions. They wrote that they hoped Tims would regard it of "necessity to acquire the Indian languages." He was to "let no day pass without the acquisition and the use of Indian words and phrases." The Society demanded that he "pray and long unceasingly for the time when you will be able first to say a few words concerning the Saviour and afterwards to pour out from a full heart the story of His redeeming heart." They warned him not to rely on an interpreter, a plan with "deep imperfections." Finally, with an eye to civilizing as well as converting, Tims was to "aim also at being able to speak freely and familiarly on all topics with the Indians around you."[13]

These explicit instructions emphasized the significance of being able to spread the gospel through the native language, even if the communication was rudimentary. The Church Missionary Society oversimplified the situation and exposed its ignorance by using the term "Indian" to refer to the natives, implying one people and one language. Institutional assumptions about the importance of translating and the ease with which missionaries could translate and learn native languages created unattainable goals for the missionaries. Once they discovered the difficulty of their task, the missionaries' frustration boiled over into their translations, resulting in negative portrayals of native languages and culture.

The Church Missionary Society tried to dissuade Tims against the use of interpreters, who were often non-Christians or, worse to some, Catholics. For missionary societies, using interpreters greatly diminished the reliability of communication. Finally, the instructions of missionary societies stressed the ability to discuss all subjects, especially those concerning civilization, in the native language. The content of these instructions is further evidence that Christianity and civilization were intertwined concepts for the missionary societies and the missionaries.

The Church Missionary Society's demands were echoed in the orders of other missionary societies. In 1842, an article in *The Foreign Missionary,* a publication of the American Presbyterian Church, announced that "as soon as the missionary has learned the proper native language, it becomes his duty to preach the gospel."[14] The assumption seemed to be that missionaries made it a priority to learn the language. Presbyterians apparently felt strongly about this point, as a similar statement appeared in the same newspaper in 1878 in a column titled "Instructions to Missionaries": "First among such things the *committee would desire to lay stress on the acquisition of the language of the people to who you are sent.*"[15] After all, "the *mother tongue* has more power in it, with those who speak it, than any other language can be found."[16] Bishop William Hobart Hare, a former missionary and Episcopalian of the Niobrara district in Nebraska, also believed in the benefits of linguistic skills. He cheerfully announced in his annual report in 1883 that "most of the clergy have an admirable zeal and patience, acquired the language of the Indians, a pre-requisite to successful Missionary and pastoral work among them. . . ."[17] Hare asserts that missionary work could not proceed without language skills, emphasizing the importance of learning the local language.

Fluency in the heathen language aided missionaries in their quest to civilize the "savage" Indians. As the instructions of the various missionary societies stated, with the ability to converse on all subjects the missionary could "enlighten" the native groups every moment of the day. Many hoped to repeat their own experience of education and conversion with the natives, converting them to Christianity and assimilating them into Canadian and American societies. As Robert Berkhofer Jr. pointed out, to nineteenth-century missionaries, "the only good Indian was a carbon copy of a *good* white man."[18]

Missionary societies based their goal for translation on the experiences of one of the first missionaries. Portrayals of John Eliot created a myth of simple assimilation and conversion. In Samuel Drake's 1837 version of Eliot's mission, Eliot came, he translated, he converted and assimilated the natives. Drake's depiction of Eliot's success as simple built on the idea of the noble savage who quickly saw the rationale and superiority of Christianity. Throughout the nineteenth century, both missionaries and authors of secondary texts repeated such parables and myths, hoping to inspire emulation among their colleagues. Even into the twentieth century, authors asserted that simply reading the Bible helped natives assimilate key elements of Canadian and American societies. According to one author, in 1917 studying the Bible taught natives "more correct ideas concerning marriage," "a strong desire to have their children educated like the whites," "a disposition to raise the condition of their women," to stop "idolating their prophets, and the medicine bag," and a "growing sense of the sinfulness of murder, drunkenness, implacable enmity and revenge."[19] The persisting message was that if simply reading the Bible led to the conversion of Canadians and Americans, then it should do the same for the Indians.

Protestant missionaries employed other means besides the Bible and lectures in their crusade to convert and assimilate Indians. With the financial support of their missionary societies, missionaries also printed tracts and hymnbooks in Indian languages. Missionaries designed these works to subtly teach what they considered to be civilization. Since most Protestant Christian readers saw no line between Christianity and civilization, lessons about behavior directed at the non-Christian Indians appeared to be acceptable. Compared to the lessons directed at Protestant Christian audiences, the messages in these tracts and hymns were blatant. But to the non-Christian native who knew very little of what hymn text looked like or what Christianity entailed, these lessons and dictums seemed to be a legitimate part of Christianity. They could not differentiate between scripture and behavior suggestions. Missionaries titled their works in ways that successfully blurred the lines between Christianity and civilization.[20]

Myron Eells's *Hymns in the Chinook Jargon Language* served just this purpose.[21] Eells parlayed his language skills into an official position with the Smithsonian in his latter years. Because of his extensive translations of hymns and tracts into Chinook Jargon, ethnographers considered him an expert on the language. Because of the language skill demonstrated by these works, certain missionaries became known as authorities on the Indians. Eells's hymnal, first published in 1878, stressed assimilation. Few of the hymns resemble those found in a traditional hymnal designed for white congregations. One hymn, titled "Sunday," urged:

> Come here—*i.e.,* to church
> To-day
> Do not work
> To-day
> Do not beg
> To-day
> Do not trade
> To-day
> Do not play
> To-day
> Get the talk
> To-day.[22]

This hymn did not spread the gospel. Instead, it attempted to discourage behavior that the missionaries considered disrespectful and unchristian. Yet these words unmask missionaries' stereotypes of Indians. Two activities banned by the hymn—begging and trading—are bad habits supposedly acquired from whites, thus invoking the image of the wretched Indian. And the use of "playing," as opposed to "working" or "hunting," illustrates that missionaries assumed that Indians had childlike behavior.

Some Protestant missionaries wrote hymns about concepts that the natives considered significant. J. E. Middleton based his "Moon of Wintertime" upon native religious concepts in combination with Christianity and it became a standard Presbyterian hymn.[23] But the majority of hymns that Protestant missionaries wrote for natives dealt not with Christianity but with civilization. As Myron Eells explained, so many hymns written for white Protestants did not translate directly into native languages. In *Ten Years of Mission Work,* published in 1886, Eells declares, "The expressions, syllables, words, and accent did not agree well enough for [the native language] is made up some simple sentiment, repeated it two or three times, fitted it to one of our tunes, and sang."[24] The fact that he employs "some simple sentiment" and repeats it suggests that he saw Indians as children who could learn only in small doses. And the attempts at changing illicit behaviors through hymns represent an effort to create a stable Christian environment for the Indians. Hymns condemning prostitution, gambling, begging, native religion, and liquor abound in missionary societies' records. A hymn called simply "Whiskey" illuminated the problem of drinking.

> If we drink whisky [*sic*]
> Whiskey will eat up our money
> If we drink whiskey,
> Whiskey will eat up our things
> If we drink whiskey,
> Whiskey will eat up our lives
> If we drink whiskey,
> Whiskey will eat up our souls.[25]

A lack of working knowledge of Indian languages combined with the belief that Indians existed in a childlike state led the missionaries to create simple, repetitive songs. These hymns tended to focus on behavior rather than theology, implying that theology remained beyond the grasp of the Indians' intelligence.

TRANSLATION EQUALS CIVILIZATION

For the missionary societies, translation was just the first step in the process of civilization and assimilation. But this step served two purposes: exposing natives to the Bible in their own language and providing the means to teach them English. *The Great Commission* said of missionary translators that *"an Uphilas, a*

Patricius, and a Cyril of earlier times has given to the people a written language." [26] Missionaries also needed to "devote every moment of their leisure, which could be spared from their religious instruction, to their mental education" and teach the Indians "the alphabet of civilization" as well as the "alphabet of their own language." [27] Missionaries believed that their role imitated that of the ancient saints and philosophers who had battled "barbarous" cultures in the past and had assimilated these cultures with their own. The lesson from these past successes was that changing the language and environment of the Indians would change them into Christians. If previous groups could fall under the sway of the Bible through its translation, then so too could the Indians. With the charge to civilize the Indians, it became clear that just translating the Bible was insufficient. Missionaries had to offer intellectual enlightenment as well as Christianity and civilization. They needed to mold the native cultures into literate societies and not just oral ones, and eventually wean their converts from their native languages to English, the language of the civilized.

The use of the English language became a measure of how civilized a group of natives had become. The question was when and how did a Protestant missionary teach English to the natives? In many cases, particularly in Canada, missionaries usually taught English to the Indians only after gaining an understanding of the native language and converting the natives to Christianity. On the other hand, particularly in the United States, missionary societies generally considered teaching English and teaching the gospel in English a top priority that sometimes even took precedence over the missionary learning the native language.

Throughout the nineteenth century, different denominations in the United States argued about the sequence of teaching. In the early part of the century, the Presbyterians sided with the British missionary societies in Canada and demanded that their missionaries learn the native language first, translate the Bible, and *then* begin to teach English. [28] The Missionary Society of the Methodist Episcopal Church, South, pushed the teaching of English over translation. Their "grand aim is to lead the young into an entire abandonment of the language and whatever is distinctly Indian . . ." [29] Though they translated some works into native languages, most Protestant missionaries in the United States preferred to replace the works with English versions. The issue of the use of English versus translations draws attention to the debate over whether theology or behavior was more important to teach first. The Canadian groups and the Presbyterians in the United States believed that a Christian environment would transform the Indians. The other groups in the United States clearly felt that Christian behavior, as shown by the examples of the missionaries, would lead the Indians to Christ.

Even within the individual missionary societies, missionaries argued over the need to learn local dialects and languages and translate the Bible into them. In 1872, H. T. Cowley, a missionary to the Nez Perce in Washington, wrote to the secretary of the American Board of Commissioners for Foreign Missions to complain that Dr. Lindsey, another missionary in Washington, "spoke depreciatingly of your instructions in reference to my learning the Nez Perce language."[30] Some missionaries felt that if the native populace was to learn English anyway, then why spend time on the native language? Mary C. Greenleaf, a teacher and missionary to the Chickasaw, remembered that learning the native language was "of very little use, as the teaching is all in English."[31] Others pointed to various jargons, such as Chinook, as the perfect transitional languages between the native one and English.[32] Despite these debates, translation work continued uninterrupted.

Most Protestant missionaries saw the problem with teaching English in the fact that most native languages existed only in oral form. But, if a missionary learned the native language and created a written alphabet for the natives to read, he or she facilitated the learning of English. Natives mastered the art of sounding out words, using sounds not found in their own language, associating objects with words, and acquiring vocabulary. Both the syllabic alphabet, which consisted of a series of phonetic shapes, and the Roman alphabet helped natives hone these skills. Dr. Thomas S. Williamson, who helped translate the Bible into Dakota as a Congregationalist missionary to the Minnesota Sioux, realized the significance of his work to the future of the Indians. As he pointed out in 1869, "it has been well observed that our knowledge of words cannot be more extensive than our knowledge of things."[33] He quickly found that the Dakota had "no nouns corresponding to our words *time, space, color,* and very few [nouns] expressive of what we term abstract ideas."[34] These statements implied that the Dakota were less knowledgeable than the whites, and that because they had fewer words representing abstract ideas, the Indians could not think abstractly, making them inferior to whites. He also suggested that by learning to read works such as the Bible and *Pilgrim's Progress,* abstract concepts would be introduced to them.[35] Therefore, translation became tantamount to civilizing and aiding in the development of the Indian mind.

Translation made the work of future missionaries much easier. Prior to the early nineteenth century, the only translations of native languages concentrated on those in northeastern North America, fueling the preconceptions of Indians as noble savages. Most native languages west of the Mississippi River and Ontario and south of the Mason-Dixon line remained untranslated. Some Canadian trappers and colonial officials with the Hudson's Bay Company knew the languages but did not put them into written form. This lack of available translations greatly limited the information and field support that missionaries received before starting their missions. Before the mass missionary movement to the western United States, there were even fewer groups that could prepare the missionaries for the natives and vice versa. Early-nineteenth-century missionaries sought to rectify this situation by providing new translations and dictionaries. When Cyrus Byington, a missionary to the Choctaw, finished his dictionary in the 1830s, he hoped "it [would] be of much service in settling the orthography of the language and in facilitating the labors of those who may hereafter attempt to acquire a knowledge of it."[36]

Missionaries headed to the North American frontiers with few notions of the Indians and their culture, save the romantic idea of the noble savage. The governing boards of the missionary societies held even more antiquated ideas about the Indians, not having had direct contact with them. In spite of this lack of understanding, the missionaries were responsible for cataloguing and understanding the natives and their languages. The missionaries also needed to re-educate their governing boards about the reality of the frontier and the Indians.[37]

Translation provided ample opportunities to examine the natives, their customs, and their societies. On the most basic level, the process allowed missionaries to catalog the various languages and dialects of North American Indians. Archdeacon Farrar of the Church Missionary Society in Canada boasted about the missionaries' efforts in 1887: "They have given such an impetus to philology that the scholar may now have before him in his study the data of 200 languages."[38] Beyond the addition to philology, translation allowed missionaries to examine the cultures that created the native languages. The American Board of Commissioners for Foreign Missions, for one, encouraged such activity. In 1878, an article appeared in *The Foreign Missionary* exhorting the missionaries to study "the [native] language, which is only secondary in importance, and [make] *an earnest, diligent effort to get as thorough a knowledge as possible of the history, literature, religion, and habits of the people among whom your lot is cast.*"[39] Once missionaries fully understood natives' history, literature, and religion they could better replace it with white culture. This examination of culture and language ultimately allowed missionaries to justify their role on the western frontiers and establish themselves as authorities on the natives.

THE PROCESS OF TRANSLATION

Most missionaries lacked the education and skills to translate and struggled with the task, a fact even the missionary societies started to recognize. *The Foreign Missionary* declared that "the acquisition of language is no easy task, as outside of a few civilized tribes, there is no written language and no literature."[40] This statement is evidence that missionary societies eventually began to see translation as a difficult task. It also illustrates the link in their minds between language and civilization. According to the missionary societies, only tribes with a written language and literature were civilized. Despite the lack of direction and training from their missionary societies, missionaries in the field produced a wealth of dictionaries or lexicographies, and orthographies that served government agents and scholars for years to come.

The process of translation required several choices. First, the translator had to choose either the syllabic alphabet or the Roman alphabet. This choice depended on the missionary's goals. If the purpose was to translate the Bible, the syllabic alphabet was the more effective option. Since the syllabic system is phonetic, missionary translators did not have to decide how to represent sounds with letters. And because the sounds were familiar, the natives quickly learned to read their own language. Bishop John Horden, who was one of the most prolific translators in Canada, chose the syllabic method because he found it sped up the learning process. For similar reasons, Baptist missionary Isaac McCoy also employed the syllabic alphabet when working with the Choctaw.[41] This alphabet allowed missionaries to get the word of God directly to the Indians through their own language.

On the other hand, to choose the Roman alphabet was to prepare the Indians for the acquisition of English. If the natives learned English and became civilized, then the translation of the Bible was not as necessary. However, many native languages did not use all the letters of the Roman alphabet, and had sounds that were hard to represent with this alphabet. These two factors severely limited the quality of translation.

The decision to use the syllabic versus the Roman alphabet was split somewhat evenly along national lines. Protestant missionaries on the Canadian frontier employed syllabics more often, while those sent to the American frontier primarily used the Roman alphabet.[42] The goals set for the missionaries by their missionary societies dictated these choices. The Church Missionary Society and other English and Canadian missionary societies pushed for conversion first and translation of the Bible into the native language second. In the United States, several groups, particularly the Baptists and the Methodist Episcopal Church, South, demanded that the missionaries teach English to the Indians first, then convert them using an English-language Bible. Thus, Canadian and U.S. missionary societies wanted the same policies but wanted them implemented differently.

This difference is another example of the distinct attitudes of the two countries toward the Indians. Missionary societies in Canada expected their missionaries to simply instruct the Indians in Christianity. U.S. missionary societies wanted their missionaries to convert the Indians using themselves as examples and on the missionary societies' terms. The use of syllabics brought the gospel to the Indians immediately. The use of the Roman alphabet prepared the Indians to learn English, which was just one small step on the road to joining American civilization. Of course, not all missionaries in both countries fit the model. Those who fell outside of it were missionaries who made choices based on their field experiences and secretly set their own goals. The decision to use syllabics or the Roman alphabet set the stage for future troubles over ideas concerning assimilation and the destruction or preservation of native culture: Were missionaries to create Christian *Indians* or Christians in their *own* image? Syllabics made the Bible more accessible to the Indians, but failed to make native languages accessible to the missionaries, which made conversion more difficult. Using the Roman alphabet preserved the native languages even as policies sought to eradicate them.

The second choice in the translation process was which basic procedure to use for putting the native language into written form. Protestant missionaries essentially had two choices. They could try to learn the Indian language and create a dictionary at the same time. Or they could dictate to an interpreter, usually a trapper or a bilingual native. While Protestant missionaries in both countries produced dictionaries, U.S. missionaries usually completed them as their first priority, in order to facilitate learning English. Canadian missionary translators tended to produce dictionaries at the end of their careers. Since most Canadian missionaries sought to convert Indians early, it made sense for them to create dictionaries later.

Both methods had limitations. Learning an Indian language well enough to compile a dictionary often took years and hindered progress in converting the natives. In the early 1830s, Cyrus Byington of the Choctaw mission devoted most of his time during the period of a year and a half to the preparation of a ten-thousand-word Choctaw-English dictionary, and a fifteen-thousand-word English-Choctaw dictionary, sacrificing other work to complete it.[43] It is interesting to note that missionary society policies on women sometimes unintentionally led to a missionary's decision about which method to use. Compiling dictionaries took vast amounts of time and most Canadian missionaries entered the frontier without wives or other female help. They had to do all work themselves, and so did not have much time to spend on translation work. On the other hand, many American missionaries had wives or female missionaries who could apply "themselves to any domestic labors, which particularly need attention."[44] Over and over again, one reads of male missionaries in the United States who gave up all other activities to learn native languages and translate the Bible while the wives and single women took on other responsibilities like overseeing schools, Bible study, housework, and even farming.[45] Whether intentional or not, Protestant missionaries in the United States clearly had an advantage in pursuing translation work with the presence of women at their missions.

Many missionaries tried the other method and discovered how complicated using an interpreter could be. In the 1840s, Stephen Return Riggs employed as an interpreter a man he described as an illiterate, non-Christian trapper named Joseph Renville. Historian Gary Clayton Anderson identifies Renville as a Métis who had been exposed, if not converted, to Catholicism.[46] While a conversion to Catholicism would explain Renville's familiarity with French, it also exposes Riggs's prejudice toward Catholics and how he defined Christianity because Riggs identified Renville as a non-Christian when describing him.

In addition to the bilingual Renville, who also knew Dakota, two other missionaries, Dr. Thomas S. Williamson and Gideon Pond, had both learned to read French. Williamson read the Bible aloud in French to Renville verse by verse. According to Riggs, "Mr. Renville's memory had been specially cultivated by having been much employed as an interpreter between the Dakotas and the French." As he orally translated the French verses into Dakota ones, Riggs, Williamson, and Pond had to spell the Dakota words and match them with those in the English version of the Bible. This process proved difficult because, as Riggs wrote, "we, who wrote the Dakota from his lips, needed to have it repeated in order that we should get it exactly and fully." As a check against mistakes, the

Dakota was read by one of the three missionaries. After all, Riggs pointed out, "we were all only beginners in writing the Dakota language, and I more than the others."[47] Using this method, they compiled a translation of the Bible and a dictionary. Like all missionaries, Riggs discovered how slow the process of translation was.

Riggs's methodology left many places for mistakes in connotations and translation to occur. One problem was that the missionary's understanding of the Indian language was limited to the interpreter's knowledge of that language and English or French. Another source for potential errors lay in the differences between the original French and English versions of the Bible, as well as between a Dakota translation of French and one of English. Translating verse by verse also opened the door for misinterpretation as Riggs took certain words out of context for his dictionary. This method assumed that all languages have one word for one certain thing and denied that languages are fluid and part of a culture. But as Isaac McCoy, who used a similar process to talk to the Potawatomies, stated, "This was a poor way of conversing upon subjects of importance, but it was the best that circumstances permitted."[48] No matter what the pitfalls were, missionaries needed to learn native languages and make these languages accessible to other non-natives if their missions were to succeed.

After choosing an alphabet and method of translation, the third choice was whether to first create a dictionary or translate religious works the missionaries needed for their work. Many missionaries worked for years on comprehensive dictionaries of up to fifteen thousand words, which were eventually used by government agents and scholars.[49] These dictionaries made the native languages more accessible to future missionaries. Others translated only parts of the Bible and left it at that. These writers tried to portray the most important concepts of Christian theology in their work and approached conversion as a one-shot opportunity. Either the Indians accepted these concepts and converted, or they did not.

When Protestant missionaries attempted to translate religious works, they often limited their efforts to certain key words. They concentrated on terms such as "devil," "God," "heaven," "Hell," "love," "shame," and "spirit," frequently without much success.[50] When native languages lacked such words, missionaries deemed those languages substandard. Lamented Riggs, "There [were] times when the Dakota language seemed to be barren and meaningless. The words for Salvation and Life, and even Death and Sin, did not mean what they did in English. It was not to me a heart language."[51] Riggs portrayed the "Dakota" language as unemotional and cold by declaring it "not a heart language." With this interpretation, Riggs also insinuated that the Dakota themselves had these characteristics, and so reinforced both the noble savage and the wretched Indian stereotypes.

In the same work, *Mary and I,* Riggs also blamed the "Dakota" language for problems that he encountered in teaching. He declared, "Thus, the poverty of the language has been a great obstacle to the teaching of arithmetic. And the poorness of the language shows their poverty of thought, in the same line."[52] Like many missionary translators, Riggs believed that a savage language was an example of a savage, or poor, mind. Other missionaries presented similar pictures to the public. Disheartened by the gaps between the languages and frustrated by their work, missionaries often dismissed native cultures and languages as limited and not worth preserving. Like Riggs, they often presented a picture to the public that suggested that Indian cultures and languages were limited and unimportant. Since the missionary societies saw language and culture as intertwined, missionary reports like Riggs's shaped missionary societies' attitudes about the Indians, as well as future plans for the Indians and their conversion and survival.

Another problem with the translation of religious works was interpretation. Bishop John Horden struggled with the difficulties of interpreting Cree, despite having forty-two years' experience with the language and being as fluent in it as he was in English. As he wrote to his publisher in 1883, "I feel myself in a difficulty about this work; I wish to give my people the counterpart of the Original [Acts of the Apostles], but what is the Original?"[53] It was often hard for the translator to choose the word or phrase that best expressed the meaning. Denominational differences also muddled translation—an Anglican might interpret a passage of the Bible differently than a Methodist—leading to competing translations and confusion among the natives about which translation and belief was correct.

Once the Protestant missionaries completed their translation work, they faced a fourth and final choice in the process: how and where to get the accomplishments printed. There were two types of printing facilities available: ecclesiastical and secular. The ecclesiastical establishment consisted of agencies such as the Bible Society, the Society for Promoting Christian Knowledge, and the Congregational Sunday-School and Publishing Society that printed thousands of works for missionaries and their converts. These printing agencies then distributed the works not only to these two groups, but also to interested parishioners, laying the basis for a market for future publication efforts.

Printing was expensive and the market for dictionaries and hymnals in native languages was small. North American native peoples, unlike those in India and elsewhere, balked at paying for religious and orthographic works that they had not requested and did not want. This attitude discouraged many missionaries in their attempts at translation. Riggs saw himself as the saint who was "giving the entire Bible to the Sioux Nation," and he was disappointed when they did not react as he had hoped. He commented that "when we missionaries had gathered and expressed and arranged the words of this language, what had we to put into it, and what great gifts had we for the Dakota people" that the natives cried "what will you give me?" He responded that he came "not to preach Christ to them only, but to engraft his living words into their living thoughts so they might grow into his spirit more and more." To men and women like Riggs, "the labor of writing was undertaken as a means to a greater end." Riggs intended to "put God's thoughts into their speech, and to teach them to read in their own tongue the wonderful works of God, had brought us to the land of the Dakotas." But in the end, Riggs lamented, "they do not appreciate this."[54] Despite such disheartening receptions from the natives, missionaries continued to be the most productive translators of native North American languages in the nineteenth century.

In the early period (1820–1850) of Protestant missionary work in Canada and the United States, missionary societies paid for the printing of translated works. They assumed that native congregations would buy the translations and so the missionary societies would be reimbursed. But by the 1850s, it was clear that North American natives saw no need to buy these translated materials, and publication became too expensive. The financial constraints led some missionaries to form partnerships with non-religious institutions like the Royal Society of Canada, the Smithsonian Institution, and the Minnesota Historical Society. Alfred James Hall is an example of one who benefited from such a partnership. While finishing a manuscript in the 1880s on the Kwakiutl language, he was visited by Dr. G. M. Dawson of the U.S. Geological Society. Dr. Dawson "strongly advised" Hall "to complete the grammar, and suggested the Transactions of the Royal Society of Canada as a medium of publication."[55] In the United States, Stephen Return Riggs and Dr. Thomas S. Williamson found that the Smithsonian Institution would pay for the publication of their *Dictionary and Grammar of the Dakota Language.*[56] Thus began many fruitful alliances. From the 1850s onward, as tensions and financial troubles intensified between missionary societies and their missionaries, these new secular affiliations became increasingly important to maintaining support and ensuring a future for missionary work.

While publications from religious societies reached a limited, ecclesiastical audience, the secular, scholarly publishers exposed missionary translations to a wider audience that included scholars, politicians, and policymakers interested in the Indians. The exposure helped reinforce the missionaries' position as authorities on the Indians, and the new partnerships led to the publication of cultural studies and other works that influenced native policy during the nineteenth and twentieth centuries.

CULTURAL LESSONS WITHIN THE STUDY OF LANGUAGE

Though denominational and national differences existed, through the process of teaching natives about Christianity and civilization, missionaries also taught literate church members and future missionaries about natives. Expanding on the idea of the wretched Indian, missionary publications painted a picture of Indians as simple people with no imagination or thinking ability. Protestant missionary translators often implied or even stated that because Indian languages lacked Christian terms, the Indians lacked religion. This perception quickly expanded to include the Indians' lack of morals, direction, and intelligence. As many of these translations became standard works of instruction for government agency workers and anthropologists, the negative images became ingrained in the minds of the literate Christian public. These language and field studies became the new textbooks for Canadian and American societies on what was a western North American "Indian." Unlike previous works that focused on eastern North American natives, these new studies helped define the evolving image of the Indians. Missionaries' condemnation of Indian languages and culture in their publications created the impression that Indians were inferior. Descriptions of Indian languages as "barren and meaningless" and "peculiar" informed Canadian and American readers that these languages were not equal to English and other "civilized" European languages.[57] This idea expanded to include the inferiority of Indian cultures to European and American cultures, providing more evidence for the belief in Canadian and American superiority. Eventually, the words "barren and meaningless" came to describe Indian societies as a whole, and not only the languages.

Two works illustrate how embedded this negative image became into the minds of literate Canadians and Americans. While navigating the coast of British Columbia, Newton Chittenden visited the Queen Charlotte Islands where he met Mr. Harrison, a missionary to the Haida. Chittenden went away with the impression that "the Hydas [*sic*], with the exception of those who have embraced the Christian faith, have no forms of religious worship." Mr. Harrison, "*probably the best authority on the subject,*" had informed Chittenden "that there is no word in their language which signifies the praise or adoration of a Supreme Being."[58] Because Harrison failed to find a word equivalent to "God" in the Haida language, he proclaimed them devoid of religion. He passed this perception on as fact to Chittenden, who then relayed it to the government. Incidents such as this one illustrate how the power of missionaries' opinions helped establish false images of North American Indians, which led to serious consequences for both the missionaries and the natives as the century progressed.

Such statements were apt to be repeated for years to come in publications ranging from Protestant missionary newsletters and annuals to scholarly books. In 1837, a report of the American Board of Commissioners for Foreign Missions ran a description of Indian languages by Dr. Thomas S. Williamson. He noted that the ideas of "joy," "grief," "courage," and "cowardice" "seem not to be found in the mind of a Dakota, and can with difficulty be made to enter there."[59] He clearly portrayed the Sioux as having limited minds, with few emotions or morals. Williamson's partner, Stephen Return Riggs, echoed similar thoughts in 1869 when he wrote, "The language of *every heathen people,* as ignorant and degraded as the Dakotas were, will present on the surface much that is impure and vile. The Dakota language was not an exception."[60] By using words such as "impure" and "vile," Riggs confirmed to Canadian and U.S. readers that Indians are lesser than whites.

Other authors produced equally damning descriptions. As early as 1831, in one of her many books about her mission visits, Sarah Tuttle attempted to astound her readers by saying, "You can scarcely conceive the *poverty* of the Osage language, it being almost entirely destitute of words by which to convey *moral sentiments.*"[61] Like Riggs and his use of the term "poverty," Tuttle implied that a people whose language lacked "moral sentiments" must also lack such sentiments themselves. These sweeping condemnations of Indians and their languages continued well into the latter part of the nineteenth century, and was repeated by authors of secondary texts. In a history of missions written in 1880, S. C. Bartlett, president of Dartmouth College, stated that "language was troublesome to the missionaries. It not only abounded in clicks, and gutturals, and unprecedented compositions, splitting a verb with a pronoun or a preposition, but, like other heathen languages, it was sadly defective for the utterance of religious ideas."[62]

Protestant missionaries usually first noticed the lack of religious terms equivalent to those in Christianity, because their primary purpose was conversion. Mary Riggs, in her dictionary, noted that a long list of words did not have Dakota equivalents: "aborigines," "adultery," "amen," "bible," "communion," "destiny," "heaven," "hell," and "devil." However, she did find several Dakota words for "sin."[63] While the preponderance of words for "sin" probably had more to do with previous Sioux exposure to Catholic priests than with any fault of theirs, Mary Riggs and her Congregationalist audience doubtless interpreted it as another sign of the inherent inferiority of Sioux culture. And in British Columbia in 1880, John Booth Good complained that the Thompson tongue failed to contain a word for "Holy."[64] Again, the lack of an important Christian word became a sign for the deficiency of Indian culture as a whole.

Portrayals of Indian cultures as "backwards" or "barren," had deep repercussions on the missionaries' work. If missionary societies and their congregations perceived natives as beyond hope, then financial and institutional support would cease. Therefore, to avoid being recalled, some missionaries tempered their portrayals of native languages just as they had when they first encountered the Indians. Missionaries began to present these languages to their missionary societies and governments as watered-down versions of ancient, more "sophisticated" languages such as Greek and Hebrew. In addition to reinforcing the idea that Indian societies might be fallen ones, these comparisons helped explain the "deficiencies" in the Indian languages.

For example, John Booth Good praised the Thompson language as a "surprisingly rich, euphemistic and expressive tongue, abounding in abstract and metaphysical terms, with a superabundance of synonyms." But he also said this of the Thompson Indians: "They may thus have fallen from some previous state of civilization and come as a great wave of immigration from Eastern climes."[65] So, though Good sees beauty in this foreign language, he places it in an acceptable context. His explanation of a once mighty society having fallen could fit into either the noble savage or wretched Indian theory.

Bishop William Carpenter Bompas tried to liken Tenni to Greek to lessen its "barreness [*sic*]." Bompas, who was virtually a recluse in the North-West Territories from the 1880s on, spent the last twenty years of his life working on a translation of the Syriac Bible into classical Greek. He justified how difficult it was to convey "religious teachings, or to translate the Gospels, in a language so destitute of abstract expressions; but a careful examination of the Gospels in Greek will show that nearly every radical word is based upon some outward act or object." Thus, Bompas compared Tenni with Greek to prove that conversion still remained possible and probable. Bompas viewed the experience of translating the Bible as a positive one, as "fresh proof of the universal adaptation of the Gospel to the wants of every nation."[66]

In the United States, Anna Eliza Robertson matched Bompas's effort. She was born to the missionary Samuel Worcester, who had worked with the Cherokee and had sued the state of Georgia on their behalf. In 1850, she married W. S. Robertson, who became the principal of the Creek boarding school in Tullahassee.[67] As late as 1893, she was struggling to translate the Psalms from Hebrew into Creek. Like Bompas, she used Hebrew to draw parallels between Indian languages and ancient Judeo-Christian societies. She used her knowledge of Hebrew and native helpers, who aided her in understanding the connotations of words. Robertson also saw similarities between Creek and Greek. She commented, "First, in the order of words in a sentence it much more nearly follows the Greek than the English. And I think this will be found true of all Indian languages."[68] Furthermore, Robertson pointed out another complexity in translation—metaphors differ dramatically from one language to another. As she explained in an article in the *Oklahoma School Herald*, "For example, 'The face of the earth' or 'the mouth of the sack' seems a perfectly natural expression to a white man, but to a full Creek, literally translated, it is perfectly absurd."[69] Unfortunately, for every attempt like Bompas's and Robertson's to give credit to Indian languages, there were others that denied these languages any complexity of thought and sought to designate them as "heathen," "uncivilized," and wretched.

Some Protestant missionary writers openly rejected the idea of any connection between Indian languages and ancient languages. Reverend W. Arthur Burman, a missionary to the Sioux in Manitoba, declared their language one of "melody and grace," but dismissed any connection to Hebrew. He stated, "I am afraid if we are to seek for evidence of connection between the lost tribes and the Dakotas, we must not seek it in the language, but I think will prove but a poor foundation upon which to build any grand theory of a Jewish origin for our dusky neighbors."[70] Even into the twentieth century, Canadian and American authors—inspired by the writings of missionaries before them—viewed native languages and the Indians who spoke them as limited, simple, and unable to express abstract concepts.[71]

The language studies written in the nineteenth century by Protestant missionaries laid the groundwork for future investigations by anthropologists and linguists.[72] The missionaries' studies examined not only specific Indian lan-

guages but also the relationships between these languages. An 1825 report
to the American Board of Commissioners for Foreign Missions claimed that
"the Choctaw language resembles the Cherokee, inasmuch as they both have a
structure wonderfully complicated and artificial; but there does not appear to be
any other resemblance."[73] Charlotte Bompas, wife of Bishop William Carpenter Bompas and a missionary in Manitoba, declared that "the Indians all speak
Slave, a dialect akin to Chipewyan."[74] Though she was referring to the Indians
around the fort where she lived, her message implied that all natives spoke Slave
or a form of Chipewyan. Because the general public had only two basic concep-
tions of the Indian—the noble savage and the wretched Indian—they simply incorporated new information into those models. By using the term "Indian" instead of "Chippewa," Charlotte Bompas only furthered the preconceptions. Her
husband stated in 1877, "I think I am able to trace a very slight resemblance between the languages of the coast tribes and those of the interior, but the likening
is very distant and obscure."[75] Other missionaries were much more explicit in
their methods and conclusions. Alvin Torry, an American missionary who
worked in Ontario in the 1840s and 1850s, carefully divided the Indians into four
distinct groups. Each of these groups "spoke a distinct language having no
affinity to the other." He then subdivided the groups "into various tribes, each
speaking a separate dialect of their original tongue." Torry was surprised to discover, though, that "among all of the tribes a remarkable similarity in custom and
institution prevailed."[76] These descriptions portrayed native languages as related
and indistinct groups. Whereas native groups saw themselves as having separate
nations with different languages and customs, missionaries represented them as
one family called "Indians." These works almost invariably reinforced the images
of the noble savage and the wretched Indian, even though a variety of missionaries wrote them.

With support from the missionary societies, missionary publications on native languages reached into the thousands.[77] Missionaries often spiced up reports
to congregations in Canada and the United States with parts of their translations
of native languages. These segments were primarily chosen for practical reasons.
To raise money and to be able to entice a steady stream of new recruits, missionaries needed to stimulate the imagination of the white population through
any available means. The more complex and frustrating the language appeared,
and the more difficult the task of conversion looked, the more the public seemed
to admire the missionaries' efforts. Also, by demonstrating the complexity of

translation, missionaries tried to explain why their progress in conversion and civilization was so slow. Bishop John Horden tried this approach while trying to raise money for his mission in northern Ontario. He constantly sent snippets of translations into the British children's magazine, *The Coral Missionary Magazine*, in 1890. Often he picked versions of Bible verses or prayers. One such piece began: "Here are a few words of the Lord's Prayer. *Wayoosimegoyun Reshikok andayum; da Richeapetantakwut Rit isheneleasuwin.* That is as far as 'Hallowed be Thy Name.'"[78] In the 1830s, Dr. Thomas S. Williamson provided examples of the Dakota language: "A 'good heart' means simple *joy:* 'a bad heart' means *grief:* 'a hard heart,' *courage:* and 'a heart not hard,' *cowardice.*"[79] In these publications directed solely at white congregations, Horden, Williamson, and other missionaries used native languages to illustrate the frustration they endured and to demonstrate their expertise. They tried to educate the public about the difficulties of translation and conversion.

The differences between an oral culture and a literate one complicated the translation process for Protestant missionaries in the nineteenth century. Writing and literacy allow a certain freedom to express abstract ideas. Oral cultures often must rely on what exists physically. Native vocabularies that were oral until missionary intervention did not always contain exact equivalents of the English terms for abstract concepts.[80] Thus, many missionaries found native languages "barren and meaningless" because they lacked the ability to express, in simple words comparable to English, the concepts of "love," "peace," "joy," and "holiness."[81] The discrepancy between oral and written language, and the trouble it caused the missionaries, reverberated throughout their translations. It didn't help that missionaries looked for Christian concepts in a non-literate, non-Christian environment. Invariably, translation became frustrating or even impossible with such limitations. Without an understanding of the differences between orality and literacy, missionaries compared their own language skills with those of natives, which led them to draw unjust conclusions about Indians and their cultures.

Another factor that hindered missionaries' progress was the fluidity of language. While the English language is always changing, few missionaries recognized this. By not recognizing the fluidity of Indian languages, most missionaries further limited their understanding of them. Consequently, their conversion efforts were stymied. Some missionaries recognized this problem. Isaac McCoy stated, "The Indians being destitute of writings, and by their habits of obtaining subsistence often parted asunder in small bands, each of which may be the nucleus of a tribe, are subject to rapid mutations of language."[82] And Myron Eells complained that "no one person is competent to write a dictionary of the Chinook jargon, because it is so constantly changing and is used very differently at the same time in different localities."[83] Indian languages also frequently incorporated Spanish, French, and English vocabulary. Nineteenth-century missionaries often forgot that most tribes had encountered explorers from Europe for hundreds of years. Thus, for example, missionaries often recorded forms of "Dieu" as native equivalents of "God" without realizing that the Indians had adopted it from earlier French missionaries. Missionaries viewed these changing languages, especially ones that did not have words for Christian ideas, as inferior to English.

All of these problems with translation affected the documents that missionaries produced. They criticized native languages, deeming them backwards and useless. Even simple statements about which letters of the Roman alphabet were not used in the orthography of a particular Indian language often were misconstrued to mean that the language and its society were limited and unrefined. These discussions of language came to dominate conversations on all Indian culture, making it seem "barren and meaningless," and preventing constructive debate.

Protestant missionary translations quickly became widely used by government Indian agents, the military, traders and trappers, and settlers. Versions of translations appeared in scholarly publications. But they taught cultural lessons as well as the language to the reader. Canadian and American missionary translations portrayed native cultures as without morals, without imagination, and without cognitive thought. In reference to Lakota, an unidentified author declared in the 1837 *Report of the American Board of Commissioners for Foreign Missions,* "The language is represented as being peculiarly barren, as is probably the language of every people, whose character and habits of life are like those of the Sioux, of large classes of words which seem almost indispensable in communicating instruction in moral and religious subjects."[84] Or as John Booth Good wrote in 1880, "The retention and transmission of a tongue so perfect and highly organised is surely in itself a marvellous first and would infer possibly the original superior condition of those possessing it. They may thus have fallen from some previous state of civilization and come as a great wave of immigration from Eastern climes."[85] Both Canadian and American missionaries represented native groups as limited, destitute versions of ancient civilizations, who shared one language that had not changed through time. Missionaries imprinted these spurious ideas on the minds of future policymakers. Canadian and American societies readily accepted the depiction.

After Protestant missionaries in Canada and the United States recovered from the astonishment of their first contact with the Indians, their missionary societies required that they settle down to the business of conversion and civilization. The first step on this long road was for the missionaries to learn native languages, or for the Indians to learn English. Then the missionary societies expected the missionaries to be able to communicate with and teach the Indians.

Translation was the next step in Protestant missionary work. It laid the groundwork for the other steps at both a practical and cultural level. All the problems and issues that emerged during the process of translation, such as cultural misinterpretation, stereotypes, and funding problems, continued during the rest of the civilizing process. Additionally, the idea of missionaries as orthographic and ethnological experts began when they started translating and became more prevalent as missionaries took on more responsibilities.

The majority of missionaries sent to the North American western frontiers were ill-prepared for these first steps. Though the missionary societies wanted them to teach reading, instruct Indians in the gospel, and learn all they could about the Indians, most missionaries began their careers with only their piety and minimal literacy skills. Their education had failed to prepare them to become translators or cultural interpreters for the white, literate Christian public in Canada and the United States. Nonetheless, missionaries managed to fulfill these roles, albeit with varying degrees of success.

As missionaries became translators and cultural interpreters, they encountered problems with the Indian languages, such as the lack of religious terms and the metaphors that were incompatible with those in English, that frustrated their efforts. These frustrations shaped their views of Indian cultures, languages, and intelligence. Whether missionaries used their frustrations to argue for the noble savage or the wretched Indian or both, their opinions appeared both subtly and obviously in their dictionaries and translations.

Canadian and American missionary translators often implied, or in some cases boldly stated, that because Indian languages lacked Christian terms, the Indians themselves lacked religion. This concept was in contrast with the Tower of Babel theory expressed by monogeneticists. If Indians had the same origins as all other humans and had only been separated by the Tower of Babel incident, then how had they lost basic "religious" concepts, like sin? wondered missionaries. The apparent lack of religious terms in Indian languages quickly came to indicate also a lack of morals, direction, and intelligence in the Indians. In a way, these beliefs directly challenged the idea that a changed environment would produce changed Indians. That is, if Indian languages were inherently flawed, then nineteenth-century Protestant missionaries' logic suggested the Indians might be inherently flawed as well.

Protestant missionaries to western Canada and the western United States differed in three ways. First, Canadian missionaries generally learned the native language before they taught English to the Indians. On the other side of the border, missionaries usually taught English first. Second, Canadian missionaries employed the syllabic alphabet more often than did American missionaries. Both of these differences point to an important third distinction between Canadian and American missionaries. Missionaries in Canada attempted to teach Christianity first and then civilization, whereas U.S. missionaries focused on civilization and then Christianity.

Even though they pursued their goals in a different order, Canadian and U.S. missionaries experienced the translation process similarly and produced comparable stereotypes about the Indians through language studies. All missionary societies required their missionaries to learn native languages because they saw language proficiency as a vivid illustration of one's level of civilization. The majority of North American Protestant missionaries struggled with this task due to poor education, problems of interpretation, and failure to understand the fluidity of language. And intentionally or not, these frustrations appeared in their translations as embedded condemnations of native languages. Canadian and American missionaries made similar critical comments, which, when coupled with the missionaries' intimate knowledge of native languages, helped lay the groundwork for the perception of missionaries as authorities on the Indians.

A Protestant missionary's knowledge of native languages served several purposes. The ability to communicate in a native language allowed missionaries to teach the gospel to the natives through preaching and the singing of hymns. Additionally, Protestant missionaries could teach lessons on civilization through pamphlets and speeches in the native language. By creating a written form of the native language, missionaries facilitated the learning of English by introducing reading skills and abstract concepts, the last of which missionaries thought was previously unknown to the native groups.[86] Finally, native languages provided missionaries with the ability to examine the various native cultures in a more specific manner, leading to some of the first anthropological studies of the period.[87] More precisely, these projects entailed cultural studies, orthography, and the creation of a written language. It is through such studies that translation played a vital role in the creation of the Indians' image. The Canadian and American missionaries' publications on language helped define the literate Christian public's view of Indians.

The translation process extended from the 1830s until roughly 1900. Had it been limited to those first twenty years, missionaries' attitudes might have remained within the confines of the missionary societies. But since missionaries constantly encountered new groups and languages, the process of translation and image creation continued. And as the missionary societies withdrew financial support beginning in the 1850s, translations became one of the skills missionaries could offer in exchange for outside funding.

By the end of the nineteenth century, as more Protestant missionaries began to fictionalize their time on the frontier, a new image of Indian languages emerged. White Canadian and American society began to see them as quaint and imitated them. Despite the fact that these languages had continued to change and grow, the white concept of them had not. Hence, terms such as "Great Spirit" (God) and "Great White Father" (the president) continued to appear in both fiction and non-fiction.[88] Authors persevered in giving characters names like "Live Black Thunder," "Strong Arm," and "Little Snowbird," in spite of the fact that most natives were following western traditions and using English or French names.[89] The tradition of lampooning the Indians' style of speech continued into the twentieth century.

EGERTON R. YOUNG.

Egerton Ryerson Young in Native Attire. From the frontispiece of Egerton Ryerson Young's *By Canoe and Dog Train: Among the Cree and Saulteaux Indians* (New York: Abingdon Press, 1890).

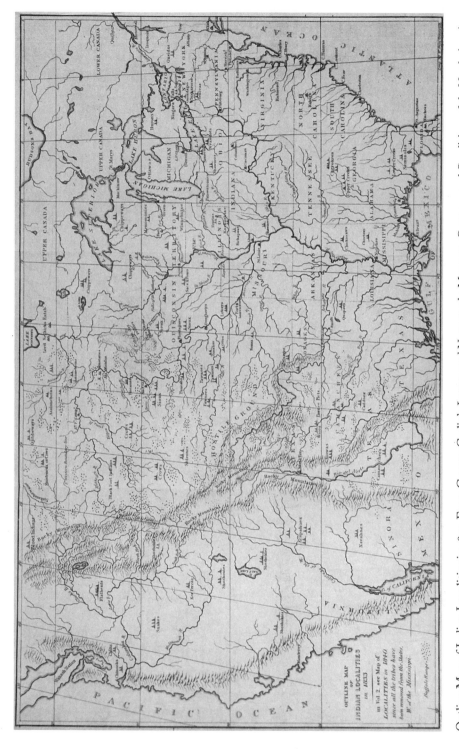

Outline Map of Indian Localities in 1833. From George Catlin's *Letters and Notes on the Manners, Customs, and Conditions of the North American Indians*, vol. 1 (New York: Wiley and Putnam, 1841). Courtesy of Cushing Memorial Library, Texas A & M University.

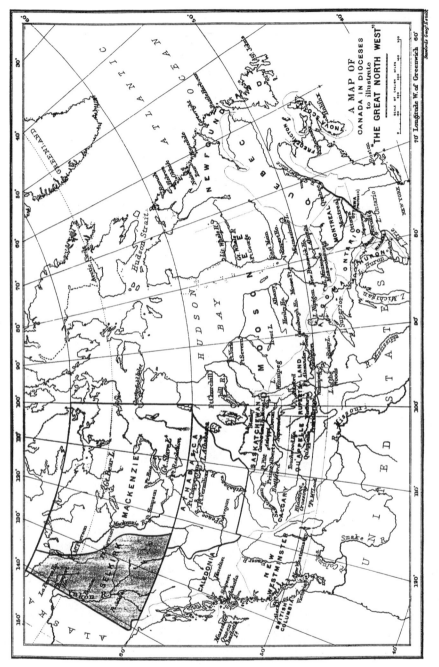

A Map of Canada in Dioceses to Illustrate "The Great North West." From William Carpenter Bompas's *Northern Lights on the Bible, Drawn from a Bishop's Experience during Twenty–Five Years in the Great North–West* (London: J. Nisbet, 1892).

206

Classic Illustration of the "Noble Savage." "Notoway," from George Catlin's *Letters and Notes on the Manners, Customs, and Conditions of the North American Indians*, vol. 2 (New York: Wiley and Putnam, 1841). Courtesy of Cushing Memorial Library, Texas A & M University.

Noble Chiefs: plate 133—Sho-me-cos-se; plate 134—Meech-o-shin-gaw; plate 135—Chech-o-hang-ha; and plate 136—Wa-hon-gawshee. From George Catlin's *Letters and Notes on the Manners, Customs, and Conditions of the North American Indians*, vol. 2 (New York: Wiley and Putnam, 1841). Courtesy of Cushing Memorial Library, Texas A & M University.

CREE SYLLABIC ALPHABET.

INITIALS.	SYLLABLES.				FINALS.
	ā	e	o	a	•
a	▽	△	▷	◁	o ow
wa	▽·	△·	▷·	◁·	X Christ
pa	V	∧	>	<	' p
ta	U	∩	⊃	⊂	′ t
ka	٩	ρ	ϱ	b	` k
cha	٦	ſ	J	∪	‾ h
ma	˥	Γ	⌐	L	᷎ m
na	᠊ᔅ	σ	ᣞ	ᓇ	ᑊ n
sa	٦	↶	↷	↳	⌒ s
ya	↶	↝	↯	↳	ᔐ r
					⸧ l

Cree Syllabic Alphabet. Found in Egerton Ryerson Young's *By Canoe and Dog Train: Among the Cree and Saulteaux Indians* (New York: Abingdon Press, 1890).

THE LORD'S PRAYER.

ᑲᑎᐯᔨᐦᒋᑫᐟ ᐅᑕᔭᒥᐦᐊᐤᐃᐧᐣ

ᓄᑕᓈᐣ ᑭᐦᒋᑭᓯᑯᕽ ᐁᐊᔮᔨᐣ,
ᑭᑕᑭᐢᑌᔨᐦᑖᑲᐧᐣ ᑭᐃᐧᐦᐅᐃᐧᐣ;
ᑭᑐᑌᓈᐃᐧᐃᐧᐣ ᑭᑕᐃᐧᐅᒋᐦᒋᐸᔨᐤ;
ᐁᐃᑌᔨᐦᑕᒪ ᑕᐃᐧᐃᐦᑭᐣ ᐅᑕ ᐊᐢᑮᕽ
ᑲᐃᓯ ᐃᐦᑭᕽ ᑭᓯᑯᕽ.
ᒥᔦᓈᐣ ᐊᓄᐦᐨ ᑲᑭᓯᑲᐠ ᑫ ᐅᐦᒋ
ᐱᒪᑎᓯᔮᕽ.
ᐁᑲᐃᐧᔭ ᐱᓯᐢᑫᔨᐦᑕ ᓂᒪᒋᑐ
ᑕᒧᐃᐧᓃᓈᓇ, ᑫ ᐃᓯ ᐁᑲ ᐱᓯᐢᑫ
ᔨᐦᑕᒧ ᑲᒪᒋᑐᑕᑯᐃᐧᔭᐠ;
ᒪᒥ ᐧᐊᓃᓂᓈᐣ ᑭᒋᐁᑲᒪᒋᑐᑕᒫᕽ;
ᐸᒋᑎᓭᐦᐊᒫᐃᐧᓈᐣ ᑲᒫᔭᑕᕽ:
ᑮᔭ ᑭᑐᑌᓈᐃᐧᐃᐧᐣ, ᒥᓇ
ᓲᐦᑳᑎᓯᐃᐧᐣ, ᒥᓇ ᑭᐦᒫᔨᐃᐧᐃᐧᐣ,
ᑲᑭᑫ, ᒥᓇ ᑲᑭᑫᐧ ᐁᒣᐣ.

The Lord's Prayer in Cree Syllabic Alphabet. Found in Egerton Ryerson Young's *By Canoe and Dog Train: Among the Cree and Saulteaux Indians* (New York: Abingdon Press, 1890).

Redeemable Savages. "Jonas, Samson, Pakan," found in Egerton Ryerson Young's *By Canoe and Dog Train: Among the Cree and Saulteaux Indians* (New York: Abingdon Press, 1890).

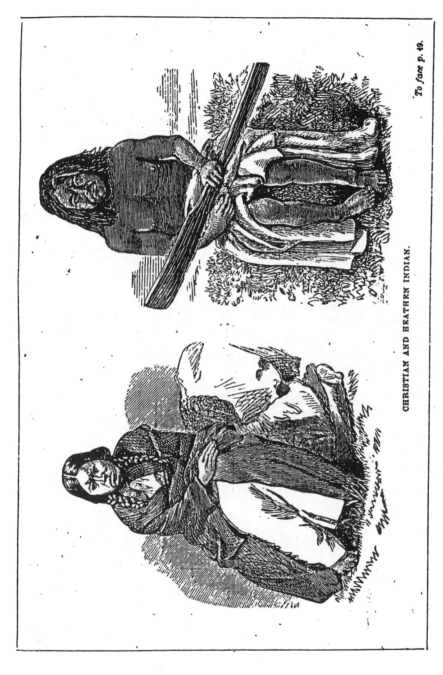

CHRISTIAN AND HEATHEN INDIAN.

To face p. 49.

Missionary Concepts of the Christian and Heathen Indian. Found in J. J. Halcombe's *Stranger than Fiction*, 3rd ed. (London: Society for Promoting Christian Knowledge, 1873).

INDIAN DOG-EATERS.

To face p. 16.

Indian Dog-Eaters. Found in J. J. Halcombe's *Stranger than Fiction*, 3rd ed. (London: Society for Promoting Christian Knowledge, 1873).

Canadian Savage Folk

The Native Tribes of Canada.

... BY ...

JOHN MACLEAN, M.A., Ph.D.

AUTHOR OF 'THE INDIANS OF CANADA,' 'THE WARDEN OF THE PLAINS,' ETC.

In one volume, 642 pages, fully illustrated and handsomely bound.

PRICE, - - $2.50

CONTENTS: SOME QUEER FOLK—IN THE LODGES—CHURCH AND CAMP—NATIVE HEROES—NATIVE RELIGIONS, RACES AND LANGUAGES—ON THE TRAIL.

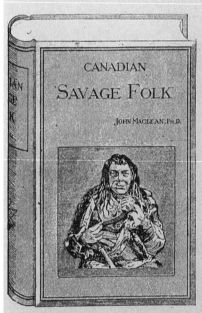

"There is no man in Canada, possibly anywhere, who has made a more careful, painstaking life-work in the study of the aboriginal races and all the writings extant relative to them, their traditions and history, than Dr. John Maclean. . . . While gleaning information from all the recognizedly authentic sources, Dr. Maclean, by his personal experience and individual knowledge, has added not only a vast amount of hitherto unpublished material, but has revivified and reset the old in the most attractive and readable form."—*The Week.*

"The whole ground is covered with a wealth of historic knowledge, while the style makes it as interesting as a romance. The author's familiarity with the subject, being for years a missionary in the far North-West, makes the work a thoroughly reliable treatise."—*Neepawa Register.*

WILLIAM BRIGGS, Publisher, Toronto.

Advertisement for *Canadian Savage Folk: The Native Tribes of Canada* by John Maclean. Note that his status as a missionary is not mentioned. Found in John Maclean's *The Warden of the Plains, and Other Stories of Life in the Canadian Northwest* (Toronto: W. Briggs, 1896). Courtesy of Cushing Memorial Library, Texas A & M University.

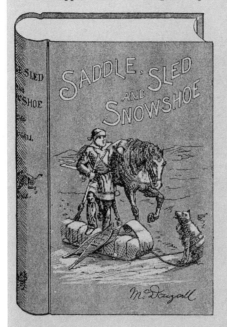
Advertisement for *Saddle, Sled and Snowshoe: Pioneering on the Saskatchewan in the Sixties* by John McDougall. Note that his status as a missionary is not mentioned. Also note the reference to "an heroic, muscular Christianity" in the review by *Canadian Home Journal*. Found in John Maclean's *The Warden of the Plains, and Other Stories of Life in the Canadian Northwest* (Toronto: W. Briggs, 1896). Courtesy of Cushing Memorial Library, Texas A & M University.

REV. EDWARD PAPANEKIS AND FAMILY.

Indian Missionary and his Family in Christian Dress. Found in Egerton Ryerson Young's *By Canoe and Dog Train: Among the Cree and Saulteaux Indians* (New York: Abingdon Press, 1890).

"IN MY TRUSTY SUIT OF MOOSE-SKIN."

Egerton Ryerson Young in Native Dress. Found in Egerton Ryerson Young's *Stories from Indian Wigwams and Northern Campfires* (London: Charles Kelly, 1893).

CHAPTER FOUR

Many Tender Tithes

A s many Protestant missionaries toiled on the frontiers of western North America, producing translations, dictionaries, and religious tracts, their sponsoring missionary societies began to reevaluate the importance of missions to the Indians. Just as many early missionaries were overcoming the surprise of their first contact experiences, they encountered a new shock. Beginning in the 1850s, missionary societies started to see the missionaries' work with the Indians as too unproductive and expensive. This apparent change of heart inevitably placed pressure on missionaries, and their perceptions and presentations of the Indians changed as they searched for new audiences for their publications and new sources of financial support.

MISSIONARY SOCIETIES AND
THE RISING COSTS OF CONVERSION

In the 1830s, missionary societies envisioned a simple model for conversion.[1] Missionaries would set up a mission, convert the local Indians, replace themselves with newly converted missionaries, and then move on to another group. This process would continually create new markets for missionary publications, and an ever-expanding base of tithing converts to support mission work. Thus, the Anglican, Presbyterian, Methodist, and Baptist missionary societies could achieve their goal of spreading the word of God to heathens around the world.

For most of the nineteenth century, North American missionary societies advocated this model of self-sufficient missions because of the relative success they had achieved with this model in India, China, and eventually Africa. These experiences and the reports of early travel writers to the North American West encouraged the missionary organizations to conclude by the 1850s that non-

Christian groups welcomed conversion.[2] They assumed that indigenous, non-Christian societies were static and completely prepared for a radical cultural transformation, and denied that such societies exercised any choice over their social and cultural destinies. What the missionary societies failed to comprehend was that missions in India, Africa, and China worked with fundamentally different populations than those in North America. Missions in these three regions had more in common with each other than any of them had with those in North America, and in many ways, these shared qualities led to more successful missions.

As well as having larger populations with which to work, India, Africa, and China presented fewer obstacles to conversion than North America. In India, Africa, and China, missionaries needed to learn fewer languages per capita to be able to spread their message effectively. In North America, missionaries encountered hundreds of languages, many previously unknown to Europeans and Americans. India and China had urban, settled populations, from among which Protestant missionaries could attract the poor and disillusioned. In contrast, North American missionaries worked with much smaller, more rural populations. In some areas, like the Plains, the native populations were nomadic and sometimes even moved to avoid missionary contact. Settled populations inhabited areas such as the Northwest Pacific Coast or could be found around trading centers, but these communities remained small and insular. Also, missionaries in India and China felt little or no pressure from the Euro-American colonial governments to calm areas for settlement.[3] Canadian and American missionaries often found themselves caught between recalcitrant native groups and demanding governments that wanted the native groups removed or assimilated so that whites could safely settle the area. This need to assimilate the natives made the production of self-sufficient native missions more urgent.

Finally, and most importantly, India and China contained large groups of alienated and isolated people, who had been denied political, social, and economic power. In India, the missionaries attracted alienated groups, such as the pariah caste and the Muslims.[4] Missionaries offered these groups—which were at the bottom or even outside of the caste system—conversion and education so that they could improve their social status. Accepting Christianity and learning English often led to jobs in the British colonial system. Becoming a Christian effectively moved one outside the caste system. By the mid-nineteenth century, the missionary societies assumed that their work was responsible for the converted groups' assimilation into colonial society and the network of government connections.

By contrast, the conversion process in western North America proved more difficult for the Protestant missionaries and less rewarding for the intended converts. The native groups missionaries in North America encountered were smaller and more numerous than those in India, Africa, or China. This meant even fewer alienated and isolated people who might seek assimilation into another society. Groups—such as Indian women—that missionaries often perceived to be alienated or isolated usually did not actively seek conversion in order to change their social status. In any case, during the early period of their work, from 1830 to 1850, missionaries had few, if any, direct ties to their colonial governments, and so conversion and education in Canada and the United States generally failed to result in jobs and higher status. Often they led to worse conditions instead, as converts had to give up social ties and their land.

Furthermore, Canadian and American Protestant missionaries' situations on the frontiers differed from those in India, Africa, and China in relation to the sponsoring institutions. Most early Canadian missionaries were sponsored by the Hudson's Bay Company, which rarely required the natives to convert in order to trade with the Company. Mission schools proved helpful for some natives and half-breeds who sought to advance within the Company, but such cases were infrequent.[5] On the whole, the economic relations of native groups and missionaries with the Hudson's Bay Company remained separate. On the other side of the border, U.S. Protestant missionaries' ties to the government focused on activities that inherently excluded native participation. For example, missionaries with direct connections to Congress sought to aid American citizens in the settlement of the western frontier, instead of protecting the natives who already occupied the region. These two processes failed to aid missionary societies in North America, leaving the missionaries with no economic rewards to offer the natives for conversion.

Perhaps as much as anything, the limited education of the Protestant missionaries sent to western North America hampered their progress. Throughout the nineteenth century, Canadian and American missionary societies used the western North American frontiers as a dumping ground for missionaries whom they could not place elsewhere. Africa, India, and China received the crème-de-la-crème of the seminaries. These men—like David Livingstone, a British doctor and missionary to Africa, and Adoniram Judson, an American missionary sent to India—sacrificed lucrative careers to become missionaries. They brought advanced education and experience to the frontier. Men like Marcus Whitman and Stephen Return Riggs in the United States and William Duncan and

Thomas Crosby in Canada became missionaries after failing at other professions. Seminary was their only education rather than an extension of it. They lacked any experience with a second language, leaving them ill-prepared for a population that often spoke little or no English.

That the missionary societies sent the least talented seminary students to western North America in the early years from 1820 to 1850 suggests that missionary societies believed the conversion process in this region would be relatively simple. Although this proved not to be the case, as the nineteenth century progressed, missionary societies not only continued to send less-qualified candidates to the western North American frontiers but also reduced manpower. By sending less-qualified candidates to an already struggling venture, a vicious cycle of failure and punishment began. As the missionaries consistently failed to meet the goals of the missionary societies, the missionary societies reduced funding, staffing, and support. Meanwhile, they increased these resources to the continuously successful missions of Africa, India, and China. North American missions, with less and less support from the missionary societies, had no option but to continue to fail.[6]

Thus, Protestant missionaries to North America found themselves in competition with missionaries to India, China, and eventually Africa. Whereas missionaries to India listed thousands of converts (though their numbers were often questionable), North American missionaries recorded conversions in the single digits—a clear sign to the missionary societies that they had failed to follow the missionary societies' original plans.

Because the number of converts in North America lagged behind those in the rest of the world, missionary societies encouraged and commended missionaries in this region whenever they achieved the goal of establishing self-sufficient missions. Missionary societies openly praised any native group that attempted to be self-sufficient, in hopes of encouraging more converts to follow their lead. A report of the American Board of Commissioners for Foreign Missions gleefully announced in 1858 that the Dakota "have subscribed some thirty dollars to the treasury of the Board." Additionally, "they have subscribed one hundred and forty dollars for the printing of the Pilgrim's Progress in Dakota, . . . and they have paid more than one-half this sum already."[7] In this rare instance, the Dakota actually fulfilled the plan set forth by the missionary society. They tithed to the sponsoring board—the American Board of Commissioners for Foreign Missions—and financially supported the production of missionary tracts.

In a few other cases, North American natives helped support their own Protestant churches. When the converts possessed money, be it from trade, annuities, or interest payments made by the Canadian and U.S. governments on ceded land, they often subscribed to church funds. Stephen Return Riggs described how Dakota converts helped raise money for a church. When the American Board of Commissioners for Foreign Missions would supply only two hundred out of the seven hundred dollars needed for a church that Riggs had erected, he endeavored to raise the rest of the money. He felt that since the Indians received about thirty to fifty dollars in annuities, they might help with the cost. As he explained, "At the propitious time I made a tea-party, which was attended by our civilized men [Indians] largely, and the result was, that with some assistance from white people, they were able to raise about five hundred dollars."[8] Interestingly, this account appears only in Riggs's autobiography, published in 1880, without a corollary in the American Board of Commissioners for Foreign Missions newsletters or reports. The selective appearance suggests that he used this story in his autobiography to prove that he followed the plans of the Board. He carefully mentions that the attendees of the tea party consisted mainly of the "civilized men" (i.e., church members)—implying that he had a core of supportive converts. He also does not specify how much of the five hundred dollars came from whites.

Bishop William Hobart Hare, who helped found the Indian Rights Association, an organization that supported Indian policy reform and lobbied for Indians, followed Riggs's example and reported on natives who supported mission work. In his 1890 publication *The Indian,* printed by the association, Hare expressed great enthusiasm for Sioux who participated in fund-raising and church activities:

> Nine Sioux Indian nobly working in the Sacred ministry! About forty Sioux Indians helping them as licensed catechists! Forty branches of the Woman's Auxiliary among the Sioux Indian women! Sioux Indians contributing nearly $3,000 annually for religious purposes![9]

Hare proudly reported that forty-nine Sioux had furthered mission work according to plan. He also made sure to point out the forty branches of the Woman's Auxiliary, a group in the Episcopal Church that focused on raising money for missionary work. And by listing the amount that the Sioux raised, he gave more evidence that the missionary societies' plan worked, at least with the Sioux. These few cases of success became extremely important to the missionary societies because they seemed to demonstrate that the plan to convert and civilize the Indians could work for all tribes.

The stories of Riggs and Hare are interesting for three reasons. First, they are examples of the infrequent cases in which the Indians volunteered their money to the church. Second, they reveal the way Canadian and U.S. missionaries portrayed Indians positively only when they acted in the manner expected by the missionaries and the missionary societies. Third, and most importantly, they illustrate the significance and pervasiveness of the missionary societies' goals.

These success stories aside, few native groups wanted to give their annuities to Protestant missionaries, whom they saw as interlopers. As early as 1834, the Chickasaw requested that their annuity be "appropriated according to the request of the Chickasaw chiefs, to another purpose" instead of being used to support mission schools.[10] This resentment continued through the end of the nineteenth century as Bishop John Horden found it difficult to collect promised subscriptions after a failed fur hunt.[11] With few exceptions, native groups in both Canada and the United States declined to support the missions established for them, further frustrating the missionary societies' goal of self-sufficiency.

Missionary societies envisioned missions that called for the short-term investment of white missionaries and the long-term dividends of tithing native converts. They believed that they would financially support the missions for only a few years. By the 1850s, U.S. missionary societies had discovered that the costs of missionary work in North America were quickly escalating while support from converts lagged far behind in most cases. As early as 1820, the American Board of Commissioners for Foreign Missions reported that it cost a total of $21,531 to set up and support just three U.S. missions to the natives.[12] Just twelve years later, the Board announced that the Choctaw mission alone cost $140,000 for construction, educational supplies, and other support.[13] Expenditures on this scale were not unusual, as costs increased similarly for all missionary societies. Even smaller missionary societies faced the high costs of operating missions. The Methodist Episcopal Church, South, which managed only a few U.S. missions, spent a total of $379,275 on Indian missions during the periods 1846–1862 and 1870–1888. Between 1862 and 1870, this missionary society actually lost money as the Civil War forced the abandonment of their missions and the property around them.[14]

The missions in Canada required equally large expenditures. In 1842 alone British missionary societies spent £505,000 for work with the heathens, including those in Canada.[15] The missionary societies quickly became disheartened over these costs. If they were to reach as many of the unconverted as possible, then the North American missions needed to become self-supporting. Otherwise, the missionary societies had to reconcile themselves to a limited number of expensive missions.

After about thirty years of missionary work in North America, self-sufficient missions still eluded the missionary societies. A core of native ministers and congregations that financially and spiritually supported their own Protestant churches failed to appear. The missionary societies expressed doubts about continuing these unproductive North American missions. Bemoaned the American Board of Commissioners for Foreign Missions in 1855, "these missions [to the Ojibwa, Dakota, Seneca, Tuscarora, and Abenaqui] present but little to the worldly eye."[16] Ten years later, the Board wondered openly about its mission to the Ojibwa: "In these circumstances, is it wise to continue a mission that is almost certain to be expensive and quite likely to be unfruitful?"[17] As expenses rose faster than the number of converts, it became increasingly clear that on the North American frontiers, the vision of self-sufficient missions was just that—a vision.[18] Bishop William Hobart Hare aptly commented in his *Annual Report for the Niobrara Mission* in 1883: "The notion that all that is necessary to the conversion of the Indians is that an English speaking, well-meaning white man should, for a year or two, take up his residence among them and preach the Gospel, however often such enterprises may be called missionary work, is, of course, absurd."[19]

For men like Hare, who actually worked on the frontier, it seemed obvious that the grand plan of the missionary societies had been ill-conceived. By the 1850s, most missionaries had experienced the absurdity and futility of the missionary societies' plans. Nothing in the missionaries' backgrounds had prepared them for the radical change in culture they encountered in working with the natives of North America. This lack of preparation, coupled with the disinterest of most of the western native societies toward Christianity and conversion, reduced nearly all mission work to an exercise in frustration.

Missionary societies failed to be sympathetic to the problems of mission work in Canada and the United States. The plan appeared to work everywhere else in the world, so why not North America too? The missionary societies simply wanted results for their investments. Missionary societies decided by the 1850s that their financial resources could be better spent elsewhere in the world. As Martin Marty eloquently states, the "cost per soul had become too high" on the North American frontiers.[20] Or as one church official in Canada rather bluntly put it, "We spend about £1 for every 17,000 heathen in China and about £1 every six heathen in the ecclesiastical province of Rupert's land."[21] The Missionary Society of the Methodist Episcopal Church reported in 1862 that operating just four missions in the Fuchow district in China, which could potentially yield thousands of converts, cost two thousand dollars less than running six missions in the United States, where there were fewer heathens to convert.[22] In 1860, the American Board of Commissioners for Foreign Missions spoke directly to the problem. They weighed "the state and prospects of the work among the Cherokee," a mission that cost "five or six thousand dollars" a year to support, against the "claims of other missions, and of other parts of the unevangelized world."[23] Missionary societies, finding it increasingly difficult to justify the expenses of North American missions when missions in other areas cost less and achieved more, realized that they could not indefinitely support these unproductive missions without help. Thus, Canadian and U.S. missionary societies sought to redefine their relationships with and responsibilities to their missionaries.

By the 1850s and 1860s, the missionary societies began to openly demand that natives lend financial support to the North American missions or else these missions would get less money from the missionary societies. In 1859, the American Board of Commissioners for Foreign Missions announced that native churches needed to be "fully prepared to sustain the institution of religion without further aid."[24] Missionary societies bluntly informed their missionaries that they must produce converts or find other means of financial support. In the same report, the Board dissolved the Choctaw mission for the "embarrassment" of failing to raise enough money for the treasury. Because of this failure, "the donations to the treasury [were] less than they would otherwise [have been], to the manifest injury of our churches, on the one hand, and of our missions, on the other."[25] In the same report, the Board also refused to send replacement missionaries to the Cherokee mission. Despite all this, many missionaries continued to cling to the belief that financial support remained the sole responsibility of the missionary societies. As late as 1872, Reverend George Lee in Michigan wrote to the Methodist Episcopal Church, "For the Indian missions, we must have white men, and support [the missions] until they become self-supporting fields."[26] Even as missionary societies made it clear that change was on the horizon, missionaries fought for the status quo. To ease the transition and cover the funds expected from future converts, missionary societies sought more supplements from their governments. They did this by building stronger economic relationships with the governments, who saw missionaries as low-cost agents on the frontier.[27]

PARTNERSHIP WITH GOVERNMENT

Even before the 1850s, missionary societies had petitioned governments for support in the guise of educational funds, always believing that an educated native converted faster than an uneducated one.[28] From the beginning of missionary work in North America, both the U.S. and the pre-Confederation Canadian governments specified certain funds for the civilization of the Indians.[29] In the nineteenth century, to demand the "taming" of the Indians was a strong platform for any politician.[30] To be known as the president or governor who brought Christianity and civilization to the natives guaranteed political success. As early as 1821, President James Monroe had visited the Brainerd Mission (in what is now Chattanooga, Tennessee) and demanded that a school for girls be started, with "the cost to be defrayed by government."[31] Though in this case little of the promised money materialized, governments in the United States and Canada often provided funds for missionary work. In 1825, a report of the American Board of Commissioners for Foreign Missions commented on the appropriation of $10,000 by the Committee of Congress for the Indians' civilization: "It seems to be taken for granted by intelligent men, who have paid some attention to the subject, that the plan, now passed for the benefit of the Indians, bids fair to rescue them from their present condition, and to raise their aims, their hopes and their characters."[32] In a report from 1856, politicians recognized that missions served as important signposts of progress on the frontier and indications of the advancement of settlement, and that "an English education" would "prepare the coming generations [of natives] to stand on equal terms in every respect with their white neighbors."[33] Or as Edward Dewdney, superintendent of Indian affairs for the Canadian government, declared to Reverend J. A. Mackay in September 1879, "I am glad to be able to tell you that I have found the Indians connected with your missions much more reasonable, talk more sensibly, and are much more civilized, than any others I have met with."[34]

But as costs mounted, missionary societies began to demand more government money. In the nineteenth century, church and state remained closely connected; government support of religious groups and their schools seemed reasonable. Many politicians openly supported the role of missionaries in education, and missionary societies were proud of such endorsements. The American Board of Commissioners for Foreign Missions boasted in 1821 that "the Governor [of Arkansas] expressed to 'Messrs. Finney and Washburn' his cordial approbation of their missions, and his readiness to render them all the aid in his power."[35] The Presbyterian Church smugly repeated an endorsement for mission schools from the Secretary of the Interior in 1856: "Above all should Christian instruction be introduced and sedulously prosecuted by teachers devoted to the cause in the true spirit of their divine mission. Without this, all the subordinate means will be in vain, and the great duty which humanity imposes on us to rescue this unhappy race from entire degradation and speedy extinction will be but a dream of impractical philanthropy."[36] Pleased by such support, Canadian and American missionary societies utilized government connections and finances to further their mission work.

Though U.S. missionary societies were maintaining solid relationships with their government as early as the 1830s, in the 1850s and 1860s missionary societies moved toward closer relations with the U.S. and pre-Confederation Canadian governments and slowly shifted their financial responsibilities to these governments; the missionary societies began to give less money to missionaries as the governments gave more. Even as late as the 1840s, native groups fought government stipulations that sent their money to missionaries and educational groups. Several missionaries ran headlong into this opposition. When Stephen Return Riggs attempted to use government-provided Sioux annuities, he encountered antagonism from them. He recalled that his colleagues "were charged with wanting to get hold of the Indians' money, and . . . the provision for education made by the treaty of 1837 effectually blocked all efforts at teaching among those lower Sioux."[37] The American Board of Commissioners for Foreign Missions supported Riggs by declaring in 1849: "The general Government have always contended that [the treaty annuities from 1837 were] to be expended for the support of the schools." The Board also saw the Sioux as simply "wishing to have the money paid directly into their hands, [and having] steadfastly resisted the establishment of schools, in the hope of ultimately gaining their end by such a course."[38] Riggs, though, quickly discovered that the Sioux had powerful allies as "Indians and traders joined to oppose the use of [funds] for the purpose for which [they were] intended, and finally the government yielded and turned over the accumulated money to be distributed among themselves."[39] Because Riggs places the blame for the lost funds on the traders, he ignores the Sioux's open rejection of the plan. The missionary society saw only monetary greed in the Sioux's rejection.

Because of such resistance by Indians, provisions that authorized Indian funds to be placed at the disposal of missionary societies for education became standard, nonnegotiable parts of every treaty in the United States by the 1850s. Traders and trappers and other groups also clamored for the annuities, but missionaries won out because they were a stabilizing influence on the frontier that could be justified to constituents. Treaties in Kansas and Nebraska in the 1850s "stipulated for the payment of annuities according to population, a portion of which, with consent of the Indians, was set apart for education and the purchase of implements of civilized labor."[40] Isaac McCoy, a missionary in Kansas, reported to Congress that "in addition to these [Kansas Indians], there are 113 Indian youths at the Choctaw Academy in Kentucky, the expenses of whose education are paid from funds set apart by the Indians themselves, and by treaty stipulations for this purpose."[41] Annuities became the primary means by which U.S. missionary societies preserved their missions on reservations and reserves, freeing missionary society funds for other projects.

The pre-Confederation Canadian government also provided funds for the missionary societies, but through a different process. First of all, the treaty process in western Canada did not begin until after Confederation in 1867.[42] Second, in Canada the natives were the ones who demanded that their funds be spent for education, according to J. R. Miller, historian of native residential schools.[43] Miller argues that because the natives of the prairie provinces had not experienced the crushing effects of the traders and the military by the 1870s, as Indians had in the United States, they saw education as an advantage. Additionally, the wave of immigration to the Canadian prairie provinces was just beginning, for the Hudson's Bay Company had only recently reduced its control over the area. But like those in the United States, missionaries and missionary societies in Canada quickly found themselves fighting with the Canadian government to maintain funding of the schools. In 1872, the Methodist Central Missionary Board of Canada expressed concerns "in reference to the Indian Missions, and our possession of property on Indian Reserves, with other subjects affecting our Indian work." They resolved "that a committee should be appointed to take into consideration such matters relating to our Indian Missions as it may be necessary to bring under the notice of the government, and that the committee act as a deputation to the Head of the Government when it may be deemed expedient."[44] Even though the negotiations began later in Canada than in the United States, the issues—missionary societies' possession of permanent property on native lands and the need to insert missionary societies into the political process—were the same.

In the 1850s, missionary societies began to seek more regular financial support in treaties between the governments and native groups. By granting treaty money to the missionaries, the governments passed the problem of Indian pacification and civilization onto them. The annuities and grants given by the governments decreased the financial responsibilities of the missionary societies and were an important source of financial security for their missions. Missionary societies pressured the governments to direct a certain amount of money to mission maintenance from the 1850s until the end of the nineteenth century. However, Canada's treaty process with the Indians did not begin in the western provinces until after Confederation in 1867, while the treaty process in the United States began in the early 1830s and ran roughly parallel to the mission movement.

Missionary societies in both countries also wanted a pledge from their governments that their missions would be maintained with or without the consent of the native groups. Especially after the removal of the Cherokee, Choctaw, and Creek from the American South in the 1830s,[45] missionary societies in Canada and the United States carefully watched how the governments defined treaties with the Indians. They pushed to have funds and land grants included in the text of these treaties. U.S. missionaries had learned their lesson in the early 1830s when the American Board of Commissioners for Foreign Missions Annual Report bemoaned being bypassed: "No provision was made in the treaty [with the Chickasaw] to compensate the Board for [the missions to the Chickasaw], which of course are rendered useless for missionary purposes by the situation in which the treaty places the Indians."[46] No missionary society wanted to lose its foothold to the whims of government. By legitimizing their claims through the treaty process, missionary societies hoped to prevent another loss like that of the American Board of Commissioners for Foreign Missions. To solidify their position on the frontier, U.S. missionary societies requested land grants. When the government settled native groups, missionary societies demanded that a certain amount of land be set aside for a church and school. Initially, the government ignored these requests, but in one case from 1856, the U.S. government guaranteed only that Methodist Episcopal missionaries in Michigan could "follow [the natives] to their new home, and that the Indians will settle around their missions respectively."[47] Slowly though, U.S. missionary societies managed to make their position clear to the government and finally received a response.

Protestant missionaries in Canada faced the same problem. In 1873, James Nisbet wrote the "Honorable Secretary Governor" Alexander Morris to try to protect the Presbyterian missions of Saskatchewan from removal by insuring that the missionary societies or missions had land title.[48] In 1892, J. William Tims wrote to the Indian commissioner to secure Church Missionary Society property on the Blood reservation against removal.[49] And in 1897, Jervois Newnham fought with both the Church Missionary Society and the Canadian government over land. He pleaded, "My request was definite enough, asking for freehold, as gift or sale, of all the grounds & buildings we occupy & I don't see what I can do till I get a definite answer."[50] Permanent land grants to missionary societies enforced a missionary's presence on the reservation or reserve. Without these land grants, the missionaries ran the risk of being dismissed or removed, and having to leave behind anything they might have accomplished.

Even as missionary societies reduced their economic burden by forming ties with the governments, they were reconsidering their role on the western North American frontiers. The cost of missions continued to mount, and closer ties to governments made missionary societies more accountable to them. Canadian and U.S. missionary societies and their missionaries needed to produce results in order to justify and sustain government support for their work. This pressure led the missionary societies to push missionaries harder to either create self-sufficient operations immediately or face the withdrawal of missionary society aid.

In the 1850s, after over thirty years of unquestioned financial support of their missions, missionary societies began to cut funding and staff to those whose costs clearly exceeded their benefits. Though they maintained denominational affiliation with their missions, North American missionary societies curtailed the number of replacements and new missionaries sent to the field. An 1871 pamphlet titled "Appeal for the Native Race, Settlers, and Miners of British Columbia" issued an URGENT CALL for more missionaries. The pamphlet requested "two additional missionaries" for the Fraser and Thompson rivers and four missionaries for the Queen Charlotte Islands. It also warned that "if unheeded now, [these calls] must result in ground being lost and openings neglected never afterwards to be regained."[51] The Church Missionary Society ignored this "urgent call." As late as the 1890s, Jervois Newnham complained in his private journal, "The CMS [Church Missionary Society] can give me no European clergymen at Moose, as Bishop Horden had, and have practically withdrawn 2 others from the Diocese: i.e., Archbishop Winter from York has left, and will not be replaced, and Mr. Peck is withdrawn from E. Main and devoted to the Esquimaux." It was clear to Newnham that the Church Missionary Society was "reducing men and money from Indian work (and say I must get these [men and money] from Canada) and increasing them for Esquimaux work."[52] In the United States, the

Methodist Episcopal Church, South, realized by the 1880s that there was a shortage of men for the Indian missions, as they preferred to send men to other countries.[53] Missionary societies even reduced the amount of publication space dedicated to news of these missions and, in the case of the American Board of Commissioners for Foreign Missions reports, moved discussion of native missions to the "Miscellany" section. Less space for the North American Indians meant less publicity and thus less financial and political support from the general population. Through this process, missionary societies began to shape the literate Christian public's perceptions of what groups of natives were important and how those groups were defined.

At the same time that these new pressures for missionaries were mounting, public interest in both Canada and the United States began to shift away from the western missions. Begged the American Baptist Missionary Union, "While, therefore, the cup of Burmah [*sic*] and of China and of far off Teloogoos [*sic*], awakens properly a response in the bosom of American Christians, your Committee would recommend that the cup of America's own perishing children should not be less heeded and effective."[54] Though the missionary societies were reducing funds to the western missions, they initially tried to keep the public interested in supporting them. But as the white population spread westward and the natives were displaced, the missionary societies as well as the public focused on the missions of India, Africa, and China. Discussion of African missions became so prevalent that even a biographer of Bishop William Carpenter Bompas used imagery from Africa to portray the importance of mission work. In this 1910 biography, H. A. Cody wrote, "The statue erected to David Livingston [*sic*] in Edinburgh represents the great missionary standing on a lofty pedestal with the calm confidence of the conqueror, his eager eyes toward *Africa,* the Bible in one hand, while the other rests on an axe. These are suggestive influences that all missionaries stood for—world's redemption and civilization."[55] Cody must have felt that a comparison to Livingstone would help a reader understand Bompas's work better. As the missionaries slowly introduced the image of the wretched Indian to replace that of the noble savage, the public searched for images of more malleable natives in other countries. As the interests shifted, so did the money.

The period from 1850 to 1880 represented a time of crisis and restructuring for the missionary societies and their missions. After thirty years of work among the Canadian and U.S. natives, missionary societies found that they had few converts to show for the money they had invested in their missions. Perhaps more important, the missions had failed to produce tithing converts or reliable markets for missionary publications. In 1852, Mr. Treat wrote an article titled "The Success of the Indian Missions" for the *Report of the American Board of Commissioners for Foreign Missions.* In it he queried, "But what is there, standing as we now do, at the commencement of efforts of the Board for the Indian race, to strengthen our faith? Almost nothing." Later in the article, he used the missions to the Dakota and Ojibwa as examples of failure and frustration. He cried, "Look, for instance, at our brethren among the Dakotas and Ojibways, far away from Christian fellowship, sowing their seed with weeping, year after year, but finding few sheaves in the day of harvest; having their choicest hopes ever and anon blighted by their own 'pale-faced' kindred and always bearing about in their bosoms, as a heavy burden, the fear that all their toil must be in vain."[56] African, Indian, and Chinese missions began to take precedence as they produced converts, contributors, and consumers for the missionary societies. This crisis, combined with other changes that occurred during the mid-nineteenth century, would dramatically alter how Canadian and American missionaries portrayed the Indians to their audiences.

CANADA AND THE UNITED STATES: 1850 TO 1880

The period from 1850 to 1880 represents one of change for the missionary societies, the image of the Indians, the missionaries, and particularly, the U.S. and Canadian governments. Profound institutional changes within the missionary societies and the governments hastened image changes forward. Throughout these years, the western frontiers and their regulation changed dramatically in both countries.

Beginning in 1850, the pre-Confederation Canadian government attempted to encourage natives to give up their Indian status and become citizens voluntarily. The act of 1850 tried to protect native lands while encouraging natives to become British citizens. Canada was still under British rule at this point and many Indian policies reflected standard colonial attitudes of the time. The act of 1850 shielded native land from non-native trespass, seizure for nonpayment of debts, and taxation. While this act was in line with early policies of creating a stable environment for the natives, it also moved closer to treating them as inferior peoples in need of protection. Though guarding the Indians against taxation illustrates that British policymakers still saw them as autonomous, the push for them to become British citizens shows that there was a strong desire for the natives to voluntarily assimilate and abandon the frontier. This policy of voluntary assimilation fell in line with missionary societies' desires and provided missionaries with an incentive—citizenship—to offer the natives.

The legislation of 1850 was followed in 1857 by "An Act for the Gradual Civilization of the Indian Tribes of Canada." This law stated that any male native who was literate in English, over twenty-one, free of debt, and had "good character" could be enfranchised. The Canadian government appeared to be offering the same rights to natives as they had to other indigenous peoples in their colonies. But the natives of Canada had to give something in exchange for their enfranchisement. If a native gave up his status as an Indian, he also forfeited his *land.* The more natives who chose enfranchisement, the more land available for white settlement. Olive Dickason, a historian of native policy in Canada, describes this law as an act that "confused the goal of civilization by announcing the noble intention to remove all legal distinctions between Indians and other Canadians."[57] While not directly forcing the natives off their land and into assimilation, as happened with the removals in the United States, Canada still pursued a policy of assimilation that was openly supported by the Protestant missionaries.

During this period from 1850 to 1880, the main purpose of the Indian Affairs Office in Canada was to accumulate land for white settlement.[58] The focus of the pre-Confederation Canadian government during much of the 1860s was on confederation of Canada into a federal union with ties to the British commonwealth. These primary factors led to this confederation in 1867: border tensions with and concern about the rapid growth of the United States toward the Pacific Coast; a shortage of arable land in eastern Canada; and the British government's desire to shed the responsibility of defending Canada.[59]

Two crises erupted in the western half of Canada—one just before Confederation and one just after—that transformed Canadian Indian policy into a design more like that of the United States. The first crisis developed in British Columbia. In the 1840s, the British government had given British Columbia to the Hudson's Bay Company after losing Washington and the Oregon Territory to the United States. It remained a desolate trading outpost until gold was discovered on the Frasier River in 1858.[60] Then settlement in the area temporarily exploded, and with a rapidly growing white population, the native population became displaced without the binding protection of treaties or agreements. As the gold rush subsided, some former miners became farmers, pushing inland and disturbing even more native groups. In several ways, British Columbia began to resemble the U.S. frontier as tensions over land possession increased. Whereas white settlement occurred gradually and with some regulation in Manitoba and the North-West Territories, white settlers poured hurriedly into British Columbia, squatting on native lands and taking over native industries.[61] Though less so than in the United States, missionaries in British Columbia found themselves under pressure from the colonial government to Christianize, civilize, and assimilate the natives, all of which would supposedly reduce tension.[62]

Immediately after Confederation, a second crisis emerged farther east, in the Red River Settlement of Manitoba. In the early 1860s, tension had begun to build in this community between the Métis and the new English settlers. The Métis felt that they had been pushed off their land—much of which they owned by custom but not by law, like other natives in the area. At the same time that tension was rising in Red River, the Hudson's Bay Company—the Métis's former economic protector—transferred authority of the land from the territories to the colonial government, leaving the Métis unprotected. With the arrival of surveyors on their territory and the exposure of a scheme in which a government employee illegally was buying native and Métis land, the Métis felt cornered. Despite being the majority in the Red River Settlement of Manitoba, the Métis appeared to be left out of negotiations over the transfer of the territory. Out of desperation and frustration, a group of Métis led by Louis Riel occupied Fort Garry and established a provisional government.[63] This revolt, often called the Riel Rebellion, helped force a compromise with the Canadian government— officially known as the Manitoba Act of 1870—that reserved 1.4 million acres for Métis, half-breeds, and their children, and also respected all existing titles and occupancies. From this point forward, the Canadian government began to deal with mixed bloods in Manitoba and the North-West Territories as a separate group. On the contrary, the U.S. government forced mixed bloods to choose to be Indian or white.

Immediately after Confederation, the newly founded Canadian government began to "settle" the frontiers of Manitoba and the North-West Territories with immigrants by pursuing land cession treaties with native groups.[64] In some cases, Protestant missionaries delivered the treaties for the Canadian government. With the Indian Act of 1868 and the Enfranchisement Act of 1869 (the latter granted natives the same legal and political rights as whites if they surrendered their Indian status), the legal division between "uncivilized Indians" and "civilized whites" solidified. Between 1871 and 1877, the Canadian government signed seven major land cession treaties with native groups over an area that covered the lower halves of present-day Manitoba, Saskatchewan, and Alberta, clearly separating the uncivilized from the civilized.[65] These treaties were the first step in forcing the remaining native groups of the Canadian Plains onto reserves, opening up more land to white settlement. Those natives that chose Canadian rights became Canadian, not native. The settlement of this land increased pressure on the missionaries, who now worked under the aegis of the Canadian government rather than the Hudson's Bay Company, to pacify the frontier. Though less violent, the Canadian frontier began to function like the American one. The Canadian government now moved closer to following the established U.S. policies for forced assimilation and for replacing native cultures with their own. Canadian Indian policies, while still creating safe, isolated environments for the natives, moved toward integrating them into society.

During the period from 1850 to 1880, U.S. Indian policy took a new turn. In the 1840s, the United States had gained vast amounts of territory in the Southwest following the Mexican-American War. Subsequently they had encountered native groups with legal title to land in the new territory. Until the beginning of the Civil War in 1860, U.S. Indian policy had focused mainly on the removal of Indians from the East Coast to the Great Plains. But removal had been based on the idea that no legal title meant no possession of land. The southwestern native groups and their land titles clouded the issue. This complication, combined with the Civil War, led to a redefining of Indian policy in the 1860s.

The Civil War disrupted Indian policy as native groups forced settlers, agents, and missionaries off native lands. The military became the definers of Indian policy as they remained in the West primarily to protect the gold routes for the Union, but also to protect the settlers heading west. Immediately after the Civil War, in 1866 and 1867, the military influence on Indian policy continued. But as costs and casualties rose, the U.S. government began to look for other ways to monitor the Indian Problem (or what would happen to the natives as the frontiers closed). They toyed with new policies that would quiet the constant disapproval voiced by missionary societies and their supporters over military policy toward the natives. In 1872, President Grant initiated an unprecedented policy, known as the Peace Policy, to allow missionary societies the chance to solve problems such as endemic corruption. This plan granted these institutions more say in the implementation of native policy (ironically, the Peace Policy came at a time when many missionary societies were in the process of phasing out their western missions). Missionary societies ran schools and chose Indian agents to represent government interests on the frontier, officially participating in policy making and execution. Grant hoped the policy would end years of disorganization, fraud, and trouble within the Bureau of Indian Affairs as well as portray him as a humane, Christian president. As historian Robert Keller points out, though, "Grant had begun his peace policy because he believed Indian affairs were in a fearful mess; he had not guessed that Christians would come to condemn Indian missions as a lavish waste."[66] In many ways, the Peace Policy backfired, confirming the decline of missionary work among native groups.

The Peace Policy relied on missionary enthusiasm for the tenets of government policy regarding the natives. For once, the United States openly recognized the importance of missionary societies in enforcing policy. The plan would have been successful twenty years earlier, but by the 1870s, U.S. missionary societies were in the process of reducing their expenditures to the missions. Thus, despite the fact that missionary societies suddenly possessed more control over the destiny of the Indians, they could not exercise it because they were at odds with their own missionaries. While missionary societies praised the United States for implementing the Peace Policy, they increased neither funds nor staff to missions under the plan. They showed little or no interest in financially supporting the efforts of their missionaries. Missionary societies instead saw the Peace Policy as a chance to relieve themselves of the financial burden that missions to the natives brought. The various missionary societies spent much of the 1870s squabbling over the distribution of Peace Policy funds, each missionary society wanting the largest share for its missions so as to reduce its own fiscal responsibilities. Nonetheless, missionaries still labored under financial constraints and achieved little success in the years this policy existed. Though the Peace Policy seemed to cement the relationship between the missionary societies and the U.S. government, it only further alienated missionaries from their sponsoring societies. When the government withdrew the Peace Policy in 1882, little progress had been made in settling and assimilating the native populations and cleaning up corruption within the policy system.

CANADIAN AND U.S. FRONTIERS

During the mid-nineteenth century, the Canadian and U.S. frontiers shared some important, if general, similarities. First, rapid westward expansion suddenly introduced both governments to previous colonial interactions with the native populations. For Canada, this expansion meant a clash with the French-Canadian Métis's ideas of land tenure and those of the British Canadians. For the United States, it meant a contrast between the conditions of the land titles that the Spanish had granted to southwestern native groups and American ideals of land tenure. Second, both countries experienced a rapid, if in some cases temporary, increase in white settlement in the West from both the interior and the coast. This growth heightened the need for clear, effective native policy. Rapid settlement also led to tensions between natives and white settlers. Skirmishes over land, customs, and social issues arose in both countries.

Despite these similarities, Canada and the United States differed on fundamental levels during the middle period of the nineteenth century. Perhaps the biggest difference in reference to attitudes and stereotypes about Indians, centered around the rising power and importance of the Métis population in Manitoba and the North-West Territories. As far as policy went, Métis and half-breeds did not exist as separate legal and political categories in the United States. A person was either white—a sign of progress—or Indian—a sign of backwardness. However, Canada legally accepted Métis with the Manitoba Act, granting them land rights and political recognition. Once the Canadian government officially acknowledged this group, future policy concerning native peoples became more complex as the Canadian government was forced to find land for the Métis in addition to the Indians.

Furthermore, though both Canada, with British Columbia and the prairies, and the United States, with California and the prairies, faced a two-front Indian frontier, the importance of the split frontiers differed between the two countries. As the white population grew rapidly in British Columbia, Canada needed a quick solution to land tensions and so had to settle the frontier without treaties. Settlers simply pushed natives off the land with the government's tacit blessing. The Canadian prairie frontier was settled more typically—with treaties, Parliamentary acts, and regulations. But the prairies possessed the bulk of the Métis population, which further complicated settlement as compromises had to be worked out with the Métis. In the United States, problems in California mirrored those in British Columbia only writ large. The explosion of the mining industry in California led to a massive influx of white settlers and demanded a swift solution to land tensions. But the U.S. government's solution—extermination and removal of the Indians—followed the pattern set in the previous twenty years, whereas the situation in British Columbia was atypical. Also in contrast to Canadian policy, the process of removal and extermination continued on the

U.S. prairies. Thus, while the two frontiers in Canada differed geographically and policy-wise, the U.S. frontiers differed only geographically.

Radical power shifts in Canada and the United States in the mid-nineteenth century led to changed Indian policies in both countries—though the shifts themselves were unique to each country. With Confederation, Canada redefined itself as a separate entity but remained politically and ideologically tied to Britain. The United States experienced a rupture in nationhood as the Civil War temporarily split the United States into not just two, but three, political entities. Clearly the Union and the Confederacy had different agendas. Yet, the West became its own political region also. Most missionary observers in the West remained blissfully untouched by the Civil War and Indian policy in this region remained stagnant until after the war.

After Confederation, Canada began to treat the Métis as a separate political group and began active legal settlement of the western prairies. But the government also began a slow, cumbersome shift toward American policy, offering the Indians enfranchisement in return for renunciation of their Indianness. In British Columbia, the government tossed away the idea of treaties altogether and forcibly removed natives out of the way of white settlers. Subtly, the Canadian government began to focus on removal in addition to isolation as a policy with which to protect and subdue the native population.

Immediately after the Civil War, U.S. Indian policy changed as well. The war demonstrated the abilities of the military in the West and so Indian policy fell under the control of the War Department. U.S. policy moved closer and closer toward a declaration of war against everything Indian. Though the Peace Policy appears on the surface to refute this idea, the plan was actually an extension of the idea behind the post–Civil War military campaigns against the Indians: Capitulate, be it life, culture, language, or society.

The implementation of Canadian and U.S. Indian policy in the mid-nineteenth century differed fundamentally as well. Having lost the Hudson's Bay Company as an influence on policy, Canada developed a system of negotiators and agents to carry out laws. The line between government authorities and missionaries remained relatively firm. By contrast, the United States did two things that Canada tried to avoid. The U.S. government sent the military after the Indians and tried to co-opt the missionaries into participating in policy. On both counts, the government failed more than it succeeded. While the Canadian government sent troops to subdue the Riel Rebellion, it assiduously avoided using the military as an enforcer of Indian policy. Similarly, though the Canadian government often required missionaries to deliver treaties or other policy decisions, they never became an official part of the policy process.

In the mid-nineteenth century, Canada and the United States appeared to be experiencing similar patterns of growth and similar tensions on their frontiers. But upon close examination of these patterns, it becomes clear that each country had a unique set of problems with its frontier and unique solutions to those problems. Just as the missionary societies, and eventually their missionaries, began to look to the governments for more financial support, the Canadian and U.S. governments began to undergo radical shifts in power and structure. And though Canadian policy moved closer to that of the United States, it still remained fundamentally different in philosophy and implementation. Yet, as shifts in government and reorganization of the missionary societies swirled around them, North American missionaries clung to similar definitions of the Indian and found highly receptive audiences among the literate Christian public in both countries.

ACCEPTANCE OF THE WRETCHED INDIAN

By the 1850s, most missionaries who had experience with native groups had come to accept the concept of the wretched Indian. They had abandoned any hope of discovering one last tribe that might prove the image of the noble savage correct. Reverend J. Reynard, a missionary on Vancouver Island, declared in 1867 that upon his arrival the previous year, he "made acquaintance with strange and interesting nationalities but the nameless sin, degradation, immodesty, of the lower Indians, are simply repulsive."[67] Reynard clearly disregarded the qualities that supported the noble savage image and instead attached significance to the wretched aspects of the natives. Despite meeting many "interesting nationalities," Reynard found all of them "simply repulsive." Reynard and others began to build their mission work around the image of the wretched Indian.

Soon after missionaries made their first contact with native groups, the image of the wretched Indian overlapped with that of the noble savage. The wretched Indian invoked the picture of an economically struggling, dirty male Indian prone to theft, drunkenness, and wife abuse. This image grew out of two frustrations for Canadian and U.S. missionaries. First, the natives they encountered in no way resembled the noble savages of their preconceptions. Second, missionaries realized that the noble savage image best represented what their white congregations in eastern Canada and the United States believed about Indians. In an attempt to accommodate these conflicting perceptions, the missionaries tried to portray the natives as victims of a poor environment—one full of white traders and trappers. The fall of the Indians became the fault of the traders and trappers, which made white Canadians and Americans feel guilty. The missionaries also employed the wretched Indian image to portray Indians as similar to whites or as "a man and a brother," as Herbert Malchow put it when discussing the changing image of Africans.[68] Missionaries tried to focus on foibles well-known to the Canadian and American public, such as theft, lying, and violence. Using this imagery backfired in many ways, though, instead depicting the Indians as childlike, exotic, and a threat to North American Christian society.

To help acquaint their audiences with the idea of the wretched Indian, missionaries described aspects of native life that they hoped would especially offend the literate Christian public. Missionaries almost gleefully recounted the faults of natives. Theft emerged as a major shortcoming, probably because it illustrated how disrespectfully Indians treated property and set them up as threats without implying that they threatened lives. Mary Riggs called the Sioux of Minnesota "poor creatures, thieves from habit and from a kind of necessity, though one of their own creating."[69] Alfred James Hall declared in 1879 that he "found the Indians in a very wretched condition . . . they are very poor and live by scheming and stealing."[70] Both of these quotes suggest that Indians stole by choice rather than because of some genetic flaw, implying that Christianity and civilization might halt the process, and demonstrating that missionaries embraced the wretched Indian image but did not always embrace the most current racial theories. Missionaries pointed to Indians' "criminal" behavior to prove that the Indians needed salvation.

The wandering habits of the prairie natives also provoked condemnation from the missionaries. Wrote Abraham Cowley of the Church Missionary Society in Manitoba in 1852, "I long to see them all with a home, a farm and a stock of cattle, for while they are so poor and wretched they must wander like a wolf prowling for their prey."[71] Here Cowley employs animal imagery to suggest to the reader a combination of the noble savage and the wretched Indian. In many ways, Cowley's quote illustrates that he longs to see the Indians domesticated. By remaining nomadic, natives avoided conversion. Missionaries saw them only during brief periods when they drifted past the mission. This mobility frustrated missionary efforts at conversion and civilization and evoked harsh criticism from the missionaries at the native habits.

War and violence quickly followed on the list of native faults. Thomas Crosby recalled that "among the Indians there were to be heard awful stories of massacre, of the scalping of men and the enslaving of women and children."[72] It is important to remember that Crosby worked only with Indian groups in British Columbia, yet he employed the general term "Indian" in his report—implying that all North American native groups acted the same way. By repeating these stories, Crosby and others only exaggerated the idea of the violent Indian. Such derogatory reports helped missionaries prove that the natives fell far short of being noble savages.

In both subtle and overt ways, missionaries expressed their acceptance of the fall of the noble savage and the birth of the wretched Indian. The image of the wretched Indian helped missionaries illustrate the sacrifices they made for their work. In describing the death of Mrs. Emmeline Gayland Hall, an American Board of Commissioners for Foreign Missions missionary, an unknown author focused on the hopelessness of missionary work with Indians as well as on the need for missions. While praising laborers among the Indians for the great "self-denial . . . which is devoted to that of the fragmenting tribes," the author condemned missions to the natives as "a dull half-cultivated Indian reservation, with scattered cabins, half-cleared lands and poorly tilled fields."[73] As suggested by the words of this memorial, few romantic ideas about work among the Indians remained by the latter half of the nineteenth century. The job of missionary had become one of self-sacrifice and struggle. As missionary societies cut off financial support to the missions and missionaries then searched for new sponsors, they had to prove their work was needed on the frontier. Stymied due to obstacles set up by the missionary societies and the natives, missionaries attempted to deflect criticism of their lack of progress by depicting the Indians as the problem.

North American missionaries attempted to reconcile their disappointment in their lack of success with the desire to remain active on the frontier.[74] They found themselves deserted financially, politically, and otherwise by their missionary societies who had turned their attention to more lucrative sites in Africa, India, and China. Canadian and U.S. missionaries confronted their failures and looked for means to support themselves and continue with their work. Stephen Return Riggs lamented, "We know the real savage, and know him almost to [*sic*] well." He also felt, though, that "if we have known more discouragements of the work, we also know more of its hopefulness." This hope lay in the conviction that "we know the real savages, but we now know and fully believe in [their] real humanity and salvability by the power of the cross."[75] Many missionaries felt that they had gotten through the worst part of mission work and could continue with a better understanding of native societies. By tagging natives as the problem, North American missionaries could focus on understanding them and could renew their own efforts to help them. They were convinced they could now succeed at conversion and civilization.

The acceptance and regular use of the wretched Indian image in the 1850s over the noble savage image corresponded with the beginning of a financial crisis for missionaries. Missionary societies, disappointed in the lack of converts and the high cost of running North American missions, began to limit funds to their missionaries. The missionaries struggled to keep going, searching out other supporters—like the governments—to help finance their work. They desperately needed to convince the white Christian congregations in Canada and the United States that they were not failures and that work with the Indians was necessary and important. The wretched Indian image aided the missionaries in making this plea. By declaring the natives to be wretched and highlighting their faults and the damage done to them by morally lax whites, missionaries produced an explanation for the slow pace of their work. Just as they had in their initial reports and translations, Canadian and American Protestant missionaries again tried to teach their audiences—which included both the missionary societies and the literate Christian public—about the inaccuracy of the noble savage image. Missionaries and other authors attempted to explain that the Indians with whom they worked lacked the rationality and nobleness of the noble savage. They illustrated how white traders and trappers as well as settlers had degraded the Indians. By being able to blame fellow whites for the Indians' ruin, missionaries seemed able to accept it. The image of the wretched Indian ruined by immoral whites also helped missionaries solicit support from Canadian and American audiences.

From the 1850s to the 1880s, the blame for the condition of the Indians shifted again. Morally lax whites slowly faded as the cause for the wretched Indian and the idea that the Indians might be biologically inferior were incorporated into the concept. Missionaries restructured their own beliefs as well, claiming that the Indians' inferior societies clearly needed the help of superior societies like Canada and the United States. This transition was concurrent with a shift in racial theory. Racial theorists began to reject monogeneticism and started to adopt the idea that different cultures had different origins, that blood determined behavior, and that some actions were genetically predestined. Hence, the Indians' inferior nature transcended their immoral environment. Missionaries modified the wretched Indian image to fit their new thinking and continued using the image to help further their work. They preached that a truly superior society would protect an inferior one, and that part of the responsibility of the United States and Canada was to save the wretched Indians from their inherent wretchedness and possible extinction in the face of progress. Missionaries found that the image of the wretched Indian and its nuances helped gather financial and political support for their missions. It appealed to Christian audiences' belief in their own superiority. And since missionaries during this period used the general term "Indian" to refer to native peoples instead of specific tribal names, their writings firmly established the idea of all native groups as wretches.

Missionaries found the wretched Indian image useful in soliciting funds from a broader audience of Christians. Canadian and U.S. Protestant missionaries manipulated the image of the Indians to support their own work. They attempted to show that without the Christianity and civilization they offered, the natives of North America would simply disappear before the ever-increasing tide of settlers. Missionaries portrayed the natives' future as limited, their lives tottering on the edge of destruction, as they pushed for more financial support, more control, and more publicity.

In the second half of the nineteenth century, more and more Canadian and U.S. citizens expressed concern and had plans for either the assimilation or destruction of the Indians. In a collection of essays on natives, W. H. Withrow acknowledged that "few spectacles are more sad than of the decay of the once numerous and powerful native tribes that inhabited these vast regions." He felt that "the extinction of the race in the not very remote future seems to be its probable destiny."[76] Missionaries expressed this same fear. Many thought they saw their native congregations fading away before the white emigration. Missionaries wielded the images of wretchedness and extinction to try to convince their missionary societies, the governments, and the general public that time was of the essence for both spiritually and physically saving the North American Indians.

Missionaries in both countries found themselves in the center of a maelstrom in the mid-nineteenth century. All of their expectations and relationships changed. The institutions that had shaped them—the missionary societies—underwent dramatic change as they began to redirect their efforts toward the more lucrative fields of India, Africa, and China. Their political and financial support followed this movement, and Canadian and U.S. missionaries found themselves with fewer resources and less support for their missions. The missionary societies also strengthened their relationships with the Canadian and U.S. governments and came to expect these governments to take over more of their financial responsibilities. The missionary societies consequently gave up some control over their missions. By the 1870s, most Protestant missionaries in Canada and the United States found themselves under the control of two masters: the missionary societies and the governments.

This situation alone influenced the missionaries and their relationships with native congregations and white audiences. But, the Canadian and U.S. governments also underwent dramatic changes during the second half of the nineteenth century, which affected their interactions with native populations and missionaries. Canada became an independent confederation with ties to the British Commonwealth, while the United States fought a civil war. The Indian policies in the two nations also changed during this time period. The Canadian government dealt with rampant growth in British Columbia by adopting American-style procedures of removal, and it reshaped native policy by including the Métis in the law-making process. In the United States, the military took control of policy during the 1860s and part of the 1870s. From the rest of the 1870s to the 1890s, the government attempted to formally include missionaries in the policy process. Though Canada and the United States faced different problems, they sought out similar solutions. All of these changes shaped how the citizens of the two countries viewed the native population in the West and how they judged missionary work.

Thus, beginning in the 1850s, Protestant missionaries' financial and political ties began to unravel, forcing them to find new means of support. While the image of the noble savage persisted, missionaries learned how to convince audiences that the wretched Indians needed help. Though the shift to the image of the wretched Indian began before the missionary societies' financial crisis, general acceptance of the image among missionaries coincided with the crisis. The noble savage image romanticized the Indians; the wretched Indian was a swing in the opposite direction. Now the Indians had devolved to a shameful level of thievery and violence, caused in part by uncontrolled contact with disreputable whites. The image of the wretched Indian provided missionaries with a perfect scapegoat for their failure to carry out the missionary societies' grand plan. The goal of self-sufficient missions was based on the missionary societies' image of how missionary work would progress. Missionaries had failed to succeed because they did not understand the Indians. Now those with established missions understood who the Indians really were, that immoral whites had degraded them, and that they struggled because of the environment of evil and decay in which they lived. Protestant missionaries knew both the cause and effect of the wretchedness. Now they needed to re-educate their audiences and sustain the financial and political support to help them "save" the Indians.

CHAPTER FIVE

Courting the Public

As funding from missionary societies evaporated, missionaries began to look to the governments and the general public for financial support. By the 1850s, missionaries needed to find sources of unqualified funds and to prove their own value to the pre-Confederation Canadian and the U.S. governments. To accomplish this goal, they needed to reach a broad audience quickly. Missionaries turned to lecturing and to publishing their works to garner support from the general public.

Missionary lectures and publications helped define and expand on the idea of the wretched Indian. Though missionary writers had begun creating the concept in the 1830s, they had blamed the wretchedness on the influence of traders and trappers. Now missionaries were exasperated over funding and felt underappreciated by the missionary societies and the governments. Unfortunately for the Indians, in their desire to alleviate their frustration, the missionaries employed images built from prevalent racial concepts that attracted attention and titillated audiences. Even as missionaries sought public support for their missions, they slowly replaced the Canadian and U.S. conception of the noble savage with that of the wretched Indian. As missionaries faced financial pressures and political crises, they helped the image of the wretched Indian mutate. Through their publications and lectures, they subtly shifted the blame for the Indians' wretchedness from traders and trappers to the Indians themselves. As the focus of racial theories about the Indians moved from the idea that environment shaped racial differences to the idea that racial traits were inherited, so did the opinions of missionary authors.

MISSIONARIES ON THEIR OWN

As missionary society support of missions declined from the 1850s to the end of the nineteenth century, missionaries followed the missionary societies' example and tried to create stronger ties to the Canadian and U.S. governments.[1] When the missionary societies originally built relationships with the governments, missionaries had little or no input about the nature of the relationships. Now missionaries hoped that by creating their own links with the governments, they would have a voice in policy decisions affecting themselves and the natives with whom they worked.

Initially, missionaries found little monetary aid available. In the 1850s and 1860s, the Presbyterian Church U.S.A. complained about the lack of support from the U.S. government. The treaties signed in the 1850s for Kansas and Nebraska stipulated that annuities be applied to the educational costs of the Indians. Presbyterian missionaries in these states assumed that the annuities would pay their expenses. But they soon found this to be untrue. Writing about the situation in 1893, William Rankin complained, "The heavy expense incurred [of building manual labor boarding schools in Kansas and Nebraska] was met in part by advances from the government from the Indian funds within the contracts, but mainly by the Board, though more of it from ordinary receipts." He added, "Teachers were also engaged, whose salaries and traveling expenses were met not from the Indian annuities, but from funds furnished by the churches, as in the cases of other missionaries."[2] For missionaries in British Columbia, aid to the native population appeared to be low on the new post-Confederation Canadian government's list of priorities as well. In his 1870 *Annual Report of the Columbia Missions,* Archbishop Reece of the Church Missionary Society in British Columbia complained that "there does not exist an Indian hospital in the colony to ameliorate the evils which contact with a too advanced stage of civilization has brought upon its unprepared victims. There may be inseparable obstacles in the way of any definite policy of preservation and development being developed."[3] His phrase about the evils of civilization clearly refers to the idea of the wretched Indian. Reece also sensed that the Canadian government had failed to create a policy for protecting the native population. In 1880, John Booth Good added his voice to the criticism. He articulated his discontent in an article from the Church Missionary Society newsletter. He stated, "The Government of this colony affords us no monetary assistance, nor does it pretend to assist our people to rise in the side of being."[4] The apparent availability of money for government Indian agents, whom Protestant missionaries regarded as useless in civilizing the natives, frustrated those abandoned by their sponsoring missionary societies. These complaints mirrored those made by missionaries in the United States. Just as Canadian policy in British Columbia began to reflect that of the United States, so did the missionary complaints. Missionaries saw government agents becoming more and more prosperous and yet allowing the natives to languish in their heathenish lifestyle instead of aiding in their civilization. Whereas Canadian and American Protestant missionaries deemed their own work a means to the end of the Indian Problem, they realized as they watched the actions of government agents that the governments were failing to reward their efforts.

It makes sense that missionaries in British Columbia would have the same complaints as those in the United States. They encountered many of the same problems on the frontier: increased white settlement, few regulations, the lack of missionary society support, and government policies that appeared to be intent on simply eliminating the native population. But these complaints eventually spread to the Canadian prairie provinces also, where policy had appeared to be constant throughout the nineteenth century. As the missionary societies withdrew support from missions in western Canada and the United States, missionaries made arrangements with their governments for grants to cover the reduction. The Canadian and U.S. governments agreed to them as long as they could maintain control of the money. As long as missionary societies gained some financial freedom, that was fine with them. But missionaries, after observing first-hand the behavior of government agents, wanted to have some say in the process.

Canadian and U.S. missionaries, desperate for government support of their missions, began to do contract work for the governments in return for money and contacts. Stephen Return Riggs worked as a translator and interpreter for the U.S. government in the 1850s and 1860s; Myron Eells conducted censuses for the U.S. government in the 1870s and 1880s; George McDougall, a Methodist missionary in Alberta, and William Duncan acted as treaty negotiators for the Canadian government beginning in the 1860s.[5] Missionaries accepted money not only for their missions but also for school support and for the building of schools, churches, and other facilities. By employing missionaries, the Canadian and U.S. governments gained workers without having to recruit, appoint, or fully pay for their services, and they created the impression of having a benevolent native policy. With missionaries acting as unofficial government agents among the Indians, both governments could claim a civil policy toward native groups.

Protestant missionaries thought that they understood their power as civilizers of the heathens. Missionaries assumed, rightly or wrongly, that their relationship with the governments—based on the exchange of information and expertise for money—allowed the missionaries some input into the policymaking process. Missionaries interpreted the monetary support from the Canadian and U.S. governments to mean that they had more time to convert and civilize the natives. Many initially perceived the governments to be more patient about the slow conversion process than the missionary societies had been. The governments fostered these ideas by including Protestant missionaries in congressional and parliamentary hearings.[6]

Missionaries believed themselves to be the only true authorities on the natives, because they lived and dealt with them on a long-term, day-to-day basis. Or as Reverend J. A. Gilfillan, who worked with the Chippewa in Minnesota, stated in 1899, "I have lived with these Indians for the last twenty-five years; know all of them intimately and personally; speak their language, and so have access directly to their minds."[7] Based on these perceptions, Protestant missionaries wrote letters to government officials expressing their views about the natives and suggesting policy.[8] For many government officials, who had to rely on secondhand information about the Indians and only met natives who visited Ottawa or Washington, missionaries brought expert opinions and ideas. Even the missionary societies recognized that the missionaries' intimate knowledge of Indian life gave them leverage with Canadian and U.S. policymakers. As early as 1842, the superintendent of Indian affairs in Canada, W. F. Richardson, spoke highly of these "devoutly pious individuals" who have "nothing to prompt them to action but a sincere desire to do good to the red men of the forest."[9] The Methodist Episcopal Church, South, proclaimed in 1888, "The gospel is solving the Indian problem. . . . The Government recognizes the fact and cordially accepts the cooperation of the missionaries in their efforts to lift these wards of the nation to the rank of citizenship."[10] Missionaries took this type of praise seriously and assumed that their work played an important part in settling the frontier. Missionaries saw Christianity as the first step in natives becoming citizens. The Canadian and U.S. governments viewed Christianization and citizenship as a possibility but not a necessity or probability. By the last quarter of the nineteenth century, Protestant missionaries wanted to be included in policy decisions concerning the frontier, which affected their missions. After all, they reasoned, the governments treated them as part of Indian policy.

Missionaries communicated with the governments through personal contacts with officials. Through these channels, missionaries suggested policies or actions to the Canadian and U.S. governments. In Canada in 1885, Egerton Ryerson Young offered himself as an advisor to the North-West Territories.[11] In

1860, William Duncan wrote to the governor of British Columbia, John A. MacDonald, and to the superintendent of Indian affairs with his opinion of how native policy should be developed.[12] In the United States, missionaries wrote to governors, senators, and the president, many of whom also subscribed to missionary newsletters. American missionaries Samuel Hinman, Sheldon Jackson, and Alfred Riggs (son of Stephen Return Riggs) testified before Congress specifically about native policy. All of these dealings created a tight group of missionaries and government officials.

As the governments became more responsive and provided more money, missionaries requested the same things the government granted to the missionary societies: staff and support for educational facilities. Yet, the missionaries still expected to maintain total control of the missions and how they were run. Even as late as 1890, Protestant missionaries fought for control of their missions. In that year, J. William Tims asked rather pointedly if "there would be any objection to communicating with the heads of Missions instead of with the teachers direct in all matters relating to the school?"[13] Tims perceived the missionaries, not the teachers, as the leaders of the missions and expected the government to respect his wishes even though they paid for the teachers. Missionaries like Tims expected to be treated as the authorities on Indians and the frontier and wanted to negotiate their own terms. By 1892, Tims had changed his tune, however, humbly asking the Indian Department in Canada to pay "all salaries of teachers in Indian Schools connected with the Church of England in the Diocese of Calgary."[14] In July 1892, Tims wrote the Indian commissioner again to thank him for the generous offer of four hundred dollars for a building that would house a school for girls on the Blood Reserve.[15] Like Tims, many missionaries had to curb their opinions in order to gain financial support. Consequently, tensions erupted between the governments and the missionaries over control of both the coastal and prairie missions. Because missionary societies also received funds from the governments for the missions, missionaries found themselves with two masters: missionary societies and the governments. By building direct ties to the governments, missionaries attempted to reduce that number to one, or at least to gain direct access and input to both.

Also around this time, Protestant missionaries were thrust into local and world competition. Previously, missionary societies had protected North American missionaries from competing with each other, while still expecting their missions to perform like those elsewhere in the world. But the U.S. and Canadian governments created both inter- and intradenominational competition for missionaries. Bishop John Horden faced this problem in 1889. He wrote to Edward Dewdney, superintendent general of Indian affairs, that he "should feel deeply grateful if the Government would extend the same helping hand to the Missions under my charge which they do to the other Dioceses in the North West Territories."[16] Instead of complaining to the missionary societies about funds being redirected to the heathens in other parts of the world, missionaries now complained to the governments about the competition between missionary societies in North America. Once the missionary societies reduced financial and political support, the missionaries on the Canadian and U.S. frontiers found themselves competing for the rewards offered by their governments. For example, Bishops Horden and William Carpenter Bompas of the Church Missionary Society in Canada might fight for funds against John Maclean and Thomas Crosby of the Methodist Missionary Society. In the United States, Stephen Return Riggs of the American Board of Commissioners for Foreign Missions might compete with Myron Eells and hundreds of other missionaries scattered across the West.

This competition weakened the control of denominations over their missions as well as over their missionaries. By the 1870s and 1880s, the Canadian and U.S. governments had begun intervening in the affairs of missions and dictating their role on the frontiers. The government entities that increasingly took the place of denominational sponsoring agencies could shift their loyalties and control who worked where. For example, if an Anglican minister demanded too much money, fought with a local government agent, or pursued interests different from those of the government, he was simply replaced with a Presbyterian, a Methodist, or—worse yet for the Protestant missionary societies—a Catholic. In 1891, Canadian Indian Commissioner Hayter Reed informed Reverend T. Clark of the Methodist Episcopal Church of Canada that the "authorities of the church" expressed dissatisfaction with Clark's management of the school.[17] The fact that the church complained to Reed instead of to Clark illustrates how much the government had become part of missionary society affairs. The government also controlled annuities and to whom they were paid.

In the 1860s and 1870s, Canadian and U.S. government funds seemed to solve the financial crisis facing the missionaries. With government aid, they could continue their work. But during the last few decades of the nineteenth century, government support became the bane of missionaries' existence. Conflicts arose over everything from the governments' demand that a certain enrollment be maintained in schools to differences over what the priority of the missions should be.[18]

Edward Francis Wilson, who ran several schools for the Ojibwa in southern Ontario, received a grant in the 1880s stipulating that he have no less than fifteen girls in the school.[19] Almost ten years later, Jervois Newnham complained to another minister that he obtained a grant of twelve hundred dollars for six Indian schools with very tight regulations. These "said requirements . . . are so impossible for us, that I doubt if we shall be able to hold it [the grant]."[20] In both cases, the Canadian government acted no differently than the missionary societies would have. Just as the missionary societies expected self-sufficient missions and punished those who did not comply, the governments wanted full schools and would punish those who did not succeed. In the United States, as early as 1848, the War Department closed the American Board of Commissioners for Foreign Missions' Pawnee mission because of violence, despite the entreaties of the missionaries *and* the Secretary of the Board.[21] And in Oregon in 1871, the Methodist Episcopal Church announced in its annual report that it had denied any funds to its missionaries, "forasmuch as one of our preachers has been and is now under appointment from the Government as an agent."[22] Thus, as the missionary societies withdrew more and more funds and the missionaries developed stronger financial relationships with the Canadian and U.S. governments, missionaries discovered that the governments also defined success. The governments demonstrated their power by removing funds, reducing the number of missionaries sent to the frontier, and setting goals and requirements for the missionaries. Missionaries no longer had a sympathetic overseer who allowed them to manage the destiny of their own missions.

Most important, the Canadian and U.S. governments intervened in the way missionaries structured their missions. John Maclean explained the situation in his 1890 book, *The Indians:* "False ideas have arisen regarding the relation of the Government to the churches in the Indian work." He neatly summed up the conflict: "The Church says, 'Christianize first and then civilize'; the State replies, 'Teach the Indians first to work and then to pray.' . . . The State does wrong when it interferes with that which is the distinctive *right* of the Church, [derived] from the expenditure of money, long experience and the employment of specially trained talent."[23] With his criticism of the state, Maclean clearly illustrates how he and many missionaries felt about Indian policy and the unique position that missionaries held on the frontier. Though the governments and the missionary societies believed in similar policies, each required different implementation. More important, both Canadian and American Protestant missionaries obviously saw the church and missionary societies as having precedence over the government and missionaries as champions of the Indians. They had survived the disappointments and frustrations of first contact. After that experience, missionaries felt only they really understood the Indians and their problems. Also, missionaries had fought and had survived being marginalized by the missionary societies, which limited the missionaries' access to the public as they withdrew their support. The missionaries' very survival strengthened their commitment to their work and to the belief that only they understood the tensions on the frontier. Protestant missionaries regarded the Canadian and U.S. governments as interlopers who lacked the insight needed to plan the future of the natives. Economics forced the two groups—the governments and the missionaries—to attempt to work together.

As missionary societies withdrew even more funds in the 1860s and 1870s and the governments proceeded to make even greater demands in exchange for money, missionaries began to seek a group of supporters who would respect their opinions about Indians, provide funds, and thus guarantee the future of mission work on the frontier. Missionaries realized that they needed to reach beyond their own white congregations. If they could influence the general public's ideas about Indians, they might in turn influence Parliament and Congress through a groundswell of public support. So, as governmental pressure mounted to produce more "effective" missions, the missionaries focused on a more sympathetic audience.

They pursued two avenues of funding. As previously discussed, they followed the missionary societies' example and attempted to garner financial support from the Canadian and U.S. governments, but found that government money came with as many, if not more, strings attached to it than the money from the missionary societies. In an effort to find money with fewer stipulations, missionaries began to expand their efforts to reach a broader segment of the public, beyond just the congregations within their own denominations.

The shortage of funds forced the missionaries into the spotlight. Each missionary became responsible for raising funds and support for his own mission. Missionaries developed lecture tours and publications aimed at motivating the populace to give money. They formed associations with more and more secular groups and publications, including governments, forcing the missionaries to focus less on conversion and more on the differences between "civilized" and "uncivilized" natives. The partial rejection of the missionaries by the missionary societies combined with the missionaries' new relationships with the governments, weakened the power of the missionary societies, who still attempted to control the North American missions. Thus, they began to secularize their work as they pleaded with a more popular audience for support. Such changes affected how the missionaries viewed Indians and began to "sell" images of them to Canadian and American audiences.[24] By the 1860s and 1870s, missionaries started to use lecture tours and different portrayals of the Indians to raise money directly from the non-churchgoing public.

LECTURE TOURS

Lecture tours by Protestant missionaries returning from the frontier had long been one of the mainstays of Canadian and American religious life. Tales of danger, conversion, and exotic experiences drew money and volunteers and shaped generations of missionary societies and church workers. People like Mary C. Greenleaf, Narcissa Whitman, Egerton Ryerson Young, and Edward Francis Wilson found themselves entranced by the stirring accounts of life on the frontier.

Mary C. Greenleaf provides a typical and well-documented example of the effect of lecture tours. In the 1850s, Greenleaf had been living a quiet life in Boston. Well-educated for her era and gender, she spent her time doing charity work, raising funds for missionary societies, attending Bible study, and helping out at the Presbyterian church. One night she attended a lecture by Cyrus Byington. His tales of heathen life and the miracle of conversion among the Indians captivated and inspired her. She began to collect money from women in Boston to aid his work. A few months later, Henry Blatchford, a missionary to tribes in the southern United States, gave a lecture in which he pleaded for teachers to help educate the Indians. Greenleaf quickly joined him and served among the Chickasaw in Indian Territory. In her biography, she wrote that these lectures, as well as articles in the *Missionary Record,* inspired her to become a missionary.[25]

From the beginning of Protestant missionary work in the 1820s and 1830s, talks by missionaries about their work on the frontier inspired many other men and women, such as Stephen Return Riggs, Egerton Ryerson Young, Edward Francis Wilson, and Narcissa Whitman, to join the movement.[26] *The Great Commission* outlined the importance of missionary lectures: "If only by helping to break up the monotony which prevailed in the religious services and topics of the day, [the lectures] rendered a service to the Church, which those who are accustomed to the variety of the present time can scarcely estimate." It added that the "missionary enterprise enlivened the piety, and increased the happiness of those who first espoused it . . ."[27] From the 1850s through the 1880s, financial constraints transformed the lecture tour primarily into a means by which missionaries raised money and interest for their missions. Missionaries now planned their own tours. Before the 1850s, when the missionary societies had directed the tours, missionaries had visited only their own congregations or other congregations within their denomination, thereby limiting the missionaries' influence on other groups. In other words, a member of the Anglican Church in England or eastern Canada might never have heard about the Cherokee because their missionary society (the Church Missionary Society) had no missions to that group. When missionaries planned the tours, they spoke anywhere and everywhere—including churches of all denominations, meeting halls, and fairs. For example, in the 1870s, when he still relied on the Church Missionary Society for funds, William Duncan spoke almost exclusively at Anglican churches in England. But by the 1880s, he spoke at a variety of locales in Canada and the United States.[28] Additionally, the new lecture tours came to be "carried on in the old campaign style."[29] Missionaries exaggerated their experiences to excite their audiences and attracted illiterate listeners who came for the entertainment value. Because the missionaries were reaching a greater number of people, the influence of their ideas about the Indians and the frontier increased dramatically and the purpose became to entertain and titillate.

In part, Canadian and U.S. missionaries went on lecture tours to try to bolster their reputation. They wanted to establish themselves as valuable authorities who knew the frontier and the Indians better than anyone else. Some succeeded—William Duncan listed Senator John A. MacDonald of Toronto and the wife of Senator Dawes of Washington, D.C., as among his contributors and audience members.[30] And President Grover Cleveland invited Canadian Methodist missionary Egerton Ryerson Young to speak at the White House.[31] By building relationships with such important officials, missionaries sought to become formal government liaisons, therefore protecting their position in the West.

Missionary lecturers influenced their audiences in several ways. First, they informed listeners about the expense of civilizing and converting the Indians. Second, they inspired popular images of missionaries. Finally, and perhaps most importantly, the lectures developed and disseminated an image of the Indians as wretched or as "redeemable savages" at a broader level that would endure for decades afterward. With first contact, missionaries had come to realize that their initial ideas about the Indians were false. They also knew that these preconceptions were the same as those of most of the Canadian and U.S. public. As the missionary societies punished them for failing to convert the Indians, missionaries understood that they needed to reach out to a broader cross-section of society and tell them the truth about the Indians in a framework with which the public would be comfortable. The image of the wretched Indian served this purpose and complemented the new style of lectures.

Of course, the primary goal of missionary lectures had always been to raise money for the missions. Missionaries scheduled their tours to correspond with church fund-raising occasions, acting as a drawing card for those events. Missionary society publications praised missionaries who were successful at raising money.[32] The efforts of Thomas Crosby illustrate the different pressures and issues facing missionaries in the new era of fund-raising. The *Western Methodist Recorder* commended Crosby in 1899 for describing "the incidents of his recent experiences with surprising eloquence and unsurpassed effect." Crosby "travelled 9,000 miles to address missionary meetings, and the income of the society went up $22,000." He also raised an additional four thousand dollars "to start the Simpson Mission, a work he had been implored to undertake by Indians from that place, converted under him in Victoria."[33] The *Western Methodist Recorder* praised Crosby for raising so much money for them (22,000 dollars) as well as the 4,000 dollars specifically for his own mission. Despite the fact that missionary societies no longer controlled the tours, they still benefited from them.

Crosby became a favorite lecturer of the Methodist Church, despite the fact that initially the church had refused to sponsor Crosby because he lacked the education necessary to be a missionary. Crosby had paid no attention and worked his way to the west coast of Canada on a steamer. Upon arriving in Victoria, he did itinerant work for local Methodist churches. These churches eventually convinced the Methodist Missionary Society to ordain Crosby and give him a mission. He then took over the Thompson River mission, where he became quite successful through the use of unconventional methods—he ordained native ministers during revivals and incorporated aspects of native religions into the church. Because his success on the lecture tour allowed him to support his own missions as well as others, the Methodist Church overlooked many of his actions. Crosby, by raising money from outside the Methodist Missionary Society, fulfilled the goal of having a self-sufficient mission—even if the mission did not have tithing natives. The Methodists deemed him a success because he cost them less money and drew attention to their cause. Crowed the *Western Methodist Recorder*, "It is more than 'a remarkable coincidence' that on each of his visits 'home' as he calls it, the general fund has shown a large advance . . . he appealed for an income of $30,000. There was a response of $23,000."[34] Note again that, besides raising money for his own work, Crosby also added to the coffers of the Methodist Church. The tales of missionaries and their pleas for money were highly successful financially, as missionaries were often considered heroes.[35] In Crosby's case, though, the Methodist Church eventually tired of his bravado and independence and dismissed him.[36] He died a broken man, without his beloved mission or any official ties to the Methodist Church.

The case of Thomas Crosby illustrates the problems of missionary funding. The Canadian government granted less money to the Methodists than they did to the Anglicans or the Presbyterians. Consequently, the Methodists supported fewer missions. For one of their missionaries, especially one they initially rejected, to consistently raise large amounts of money meant publicity for the church and the possibility of pressuring the Canadian government for more support.

Like Thomas Crosby's journey of nine thousand miles, missionary lecture tours lasted several months, covered large amounts of territory, raised money, and played to packed houses. To people looking for signs of good acts of Christianity, the work described by missionaries bordered on miracle-making. One Methodist audience member recalled with awe that Crosby helped them see "Port Simpson transformed under the power of the Gospel from a village of semi-savages into a model community." The audience, he said, also "saw the Indian character unfolded in its weaknesses and strengths and [they] caught the flame of the great revival which travelled marvelously with Crosby and his workers from Simpson into the heart of Alaska." Here, Crosby was receiving credit for creating self-spreading missions, in addition to raising funds. In the same lecture, Crosby later declared, much to the delight of the Methodist audience, "that he would rather go back North with the Gospel to 'those dear people' than spend the next year in heaven."[37]

In addition to impressing audiences with their work, missionaries also helped reinforce ideas of racial superiority that flourished during the late nineteenth century. By portraying the Indians as uncivilized and thus inferior, missionaries confirmed the belief that Canadian and American white societies were superior. As missionaries continued to spread civilization and Christianity to Indian groups, their descriptions of these "lesser societies" reaffirmed the vision that white Canadians and Americans had of their own inevitable conquering destiny. White Christian audiences could feel comfortable with such ideas because "authorities" presented them.

Missionary lecture tours played as grand theater to the populace, with tears and natives and singing in foreign tongues. Thomas Crosby, after attending a lecture by fellow Methodist missionary Egerton Ryerson Young, described it with great awe. "The results were most encouraging. The whole Canadian Church became aroused."[38] Young, known for his fictionalized tales of frontier work, inspired Crosby to follow suit.

Lectures signified revival and rebirth for both the congregations and the missionaries. For the audience, these lectures were evidence of the progress of their society. Whatever problems their own society might have, they knew that at least white Canadian and American societies controlled and influenced certain other societies. The lectures also allowed audiences to experience vicariously the joys and frustrations of missionary work and to understand the obstacles the missionaries faced. This grasp of the trials and tribulations of Protestant missionaries helped audiences rethink their understanding of the missionaries and their work.

For the missionaries, the lectures provided an opportunity to explain their supposed failure and to reassert themselves as valuable workers on the frontier. They were able to demonstrate their intimate knowledge of the Indians and gain financial support from it. In their lectures, missionaries in the mid-nineteenth century fought the impression—caused by the missionary societies' desertion of them—that they had failed in their task. Missionary lecturers came back to the East Coast with tales of success and needed to capitalize on this success. Lecture tours also gave missionaries the chance to brag about government connections. Missionary descriptions of government connections left audiences with the impression that the Canadian and U.S. governments actively pursued conversion, making the governments appear charitable. Audiences also got the idea that missionaries somehow influenced native policy, and that there was an important connection between church and state. The 1900 lectures of J. D. Mullins of Mackenzie River in Canada projected the image of the relationship between church and state that the missionaries had hoped to portray. In his lecture, he stated that "the Tribes would have perished long ago had it not been for our Government interfering to protect them and securing them large Reserves in which they might live unmolested."[39] Missionaries wanted to appear to be supportive of and to have a part in government policy so that they could remain active on the frontier. After the harsh cutbacks from the missionary societies, they needed to convince supporters that mission work mattered for the future. If they no longer served a purpose—either spiritually, economically, or politically—for Canadian and American societies, missionaries faced termination from the frontier.

Missionary lecture tours in Canada and the United States reached many more people in the latter half of the nineteenth century than they had before the withdrawal of missionary society support. From the 1820s through the 1850s, when missionary societies primarily sponsored the tours, missionaries spoke mainly to congregations or to their colleagues.[40] These denominationally specific audiences drastically limited the missionaries' influence. When missionaries began scheduling their own tours and controlling their own destiny, they increased their influence by lecturing to any group willing to listen. They not only lectured to large groups but Canadian missionaries switched their geographic focus from eastern Canada and England to the United States, where they found overwhelming support for their work. John Maclean completed at least one tour in Maryland in the 1870s. From 1894 to 1900, Egerton Ryerson Young spoke to both Methodist and mixed audiences in Massachusetts, Virginia, Missouri, Nebraska, Iowa, Pennsylvania, Ohio, Maryland, and New York.[41] William Duncan, prior to his fight with the Anglican church, spoke in England in the 1870s, but to plead his case for remaining in charge of Metlakahtla and to raise money for his move to Alaska, he lectured in Oregon, Washington, and other western states from the 1880s to 1900.[42]

By crossing the border, Canadian missionaries achieved two things. First, they increased their audience and their base of support. Second, and more importantly, they contributed to the changing stereotype of the Indians by combining their own ideas of the Indians with American ones. Canadian missionaries clearly found U.S. audiences who were receptive to their presentations of the Indians or they would not have included the United States in their tours. They helped to meld Canadian and American images of Indians into one slowly evolving image that remained central within these societies for years. And as American missionaries lectured across the United States and Canada, they too added credibility to this evolving image.

Canadian and American Protestant missionaries differed on one significant issue, though, when lecturing to their expanded audiences: the incidence of Indian aggression against whites. In Canada, few native uprisings erupted in the nineteenth century. In the United States, however, many bloody battles broke out between whites and natives—battles started by whites more often than not. Several missionaries found themselves in the middle of these situations. For example, Stephen Return Riggs became involved in the Sioux Uprising of 1862 in Minnesota. Though in his autobiography Riggs carefully and accurately described the insensitivity and irresponsibility of the local government agent as the cause of the uprising, newspapers excerpted only his descriptions of death and torture. Newspapers contributed to conflict-created stereotypes of violent Indians faced by missionaries in both countries. In Canada, missionaries could blame the U.S. government for these conflicts. But U.S. missionaries worked with the government and thus did not pass blame, especially since some of them had been targets of Indian aggression.

U.S. Protestant missionaries found the issue of Indian aggression both helpful and harmful to their cause. The image of the bloodthirsty savage aided them in two ways. First, missionaries could point to it as a demonstration of what happened without Christianity. Second, no matter how few Indians they managed to convert, missionaries believed these converts still provided an antithesis to the violent Indian. Unfortunately, though, the idea of Indians constantly on the warpath and as a threat to American society was a hard image to replace, especially since many missionary authors had invoked this image in attempts to disabuse their congregations of the idea of the noble savage.

With the murder of Marcus and Narcissa Whitman in 1847, American missionaries and their audiences seemed to become both accepting and obsessed with the "savagery" of the Indians. Their murders are an example of how missionaries turned their slain colleagues into martyrs for the sake of drawing crowds to their lectures. The Whitmans worked with the Nez Perce in Oregon Territory. Marcus became deeply involved in the movement to claim this territory for the United States from Britain and spent much of his time traveling between the West Coast and Washington, D.C. In 1847, the Nez Perce attacked the missionaries and settlers, killing all but a few women and children and those who were away at the time. This attack, known as the Whitman Massacre, became standard fare in both history books and collections of missionary stories.[43] The incident, along with the native/white conflicts that followed in the U.S. West, spurred a morbid interest in the Whitmans. The massacre so captured American fears about the supposed violence of Indians that, in the 1850s and again in the 1870s, Congress debated how Marcus Whitman should be remembered and honored officially.[44]

Subsequently, at least one American missionary who embarked on lecture tours compared himself and his work to this incident. Henry Harmon Spalding, a survivor of the Whitman Massacre, became one of the most prolific lecturers on the subject of natives and the Indian Problem. Spalding survived only because he was headed east to demand his job back after the American Board of Commissioners for Foreign Missions recalled him. He spoke continually about the savagery of the Indian population of the western United States. As late as 1870 he lectured about the massacre and its consequences in Elmira, New York, where the local paper stated, "The history of his escape is a recital of fearful interest."[45] By any standard, Spalding was an unreliable witness to the massacre. He feared the Indians even before he got into mission work.[46] In the time leading up to the massacre, the American Board of Commissioners for Foreign Missions censured him because of his actions against natives. He fought continually with the other missionaries in Oregon and constantly made derogatory comments about the people—white and native—with whom he worked. Asa Bowen Smith, another missionary in Oregon Territory, complained to his colleague Elkanah Walker in 1839 that he felt he could not join the northernmost Oregon mission where Spalding worked because "Mr. Spalding I suppose will not be willing to have me there."[47] In 1840, Smith accused Spalding of "taking a gun to shoot an Indian" and "keeping his gun loaded for fear of injury from the natives."[48] In all the Canadian and U.S. missionary papers and accounts, Smith's accusations about Spalding stand out. Many missionaries in nineteenth-century North America exhibited odd behavior at times, but only Spalding actively and openly feared the very people with whom he worked.[49] Thus, Spalding's reminiscences presented a point of view completely different from that of the average missionary lecturer. But Spalding also played into fears about the inherent violence of the Indians, thus supporting American congregations' preconceived ideas.

Canadian and U.S. missionary lectures "canonized" missionaries and romanticized missionary life and the natives with whom they worked. As John Hines recollected in *Red Indians of the Plains,* "A missionary sermon was always a great event in a country parish in those days, especially so if we were led to expect a real 'live missionary' to address us, and it goes without saying that the darker his complexion, the more interesting he was sure to be." The lectures perpetuated the image of the good missionary toiling among the savage heathens. Hines further described how "in those early days, all heathens were looked upon by the uninitiated as black people, and some even thought that a white missionary after spending a number of years among the blacks would become dark, if not actually black, himself."[50] This last idea is just one in a wide range of racial theories accepted by congregations and audiences in the nineteenth century. The assumption that all heathens were black people, a belief based on the imagery of light and dark in the Bible, shows the way that many church members conceived of non-Christians. The reference to a white missionary becoming dark suggests how easily people expected missionaries and their subjects to change skin color and shift from civilized to uncivilized and vice versa. These uninitiated audiences were fertile ground for the opinions of missionaries. With images of the contagiousness of one's skin color already in place, terms like "red men" and "devil worship" easily entered the vocabulary of secular audiences, shifting conversation away from the noble savage image. The re-education of the public appeared to be working in the mid-nineteenth century.

Canadian and American congregations and secular audiences came to regard missionaries as authorities on Indian life. Reverend Jason Lee, one of the first white missionaries in Oregon Territory, often returned to the eastern United States to enthrall audiences with tales about the Nez Perce. One listener described a lecture in Pittsburgh where he "addressed the audience with great effect for more than an hour." Reverend Lee "spoke of the American Indians, of their condition before the European had visited them, and their present state of darkness and degradation." Lee also discussed the "Flathead Indians," with whom he actually worked, "and gave such information as he was able to gather respecting the tribe and others beyond the Rocky Mountains, and of his determination to visit them or fall in the attempt."[51] This account of Lee's speech bears particular significance; it appeared in *Extracts from the New York Christian Advocate and Journal,* and a clipping of it was included in the Clarence Booth Bayley Papers in British Columbia. Obviously, American missionary activities interested Canadians, particularly British Columbians.

It is particularly notable how often the terms "darkness" and "blackness" appear in lectures and works by missionaries in both countries. Traditionally, converts to Christianity were exposed to the light of the gospel, while the unconverted remained in darkness. But in missionary writings and lectures, the lines between "darkness" (meaning "unconverted") and "blackness" (used as a racial term) blurred, which led to a static image of the Indians as racially inferior. Reverend John Smithurst of Canada illustrates this blurring in writing about the Indians with whom he worked. "[T]hey have been industrious, anxious to be well clothed, appear at Church tolerably clean and are ready to listen to any advice I give them, generally following my suggestions, so that I feel myself quite at home, finding it far less difficult to manage my *blacks* than I should if I had so many Europeans."[52] It is unclear whether the Indians are "black" because of their skin color or because they had not converted. It is also unclear whether they are easier for Smithurst to handle because they listen to everything he says, whereas European congregations might be more likely to question his interpretations. Missionaries often considered natives with light complexions more intelligent and more civilized than those with dark skin—a belief that fit Canadian and American societies' preconceived ideas, as well as their own. The rhetoric of light and dark became endemic in the culture of imperialism and colonialism, partly because of its use in missionary writings and lectures. This discourse supported the growing belief that race determined destiny.[53]

To further blur racial lines, many missionaries on lecture tours brought along proof of their good work—converted natives. From the beginning of European contact, explorers had brought natives back to Canadian and American societies as examples of the culture of the "New World."[54] Nineteenth-century missionaries carefully chose the "samples" they took back to their Canadian and American audiences. In some cases, they picked converted chiefs or their progeny, perhaps to illustrate missionaries' power and influence in native society. As they felt more and more powerless against both the missionary societies and the governments, missionaries sought to prove their importance to the public. Converted chiefs, even if self-appointed, had power over someone, and thus made the missionaries look more important by association. Other times, they simply brought along converts—the more assimilated the better—to convince audiences of the effect of their work. These converts were proof that the missionaries had achieved some success in following the grand plan of the missionary societies. Missionaries were salesmen and converted, assimilated natives represented how well their product—conversion and civilization—would help support Protestant churches in the future.

The converted Indians on the lecture tours were reminders that salvation of the natives was possible. As early as 1839, Mr. Dunbar of the Pawnee mission took a delegation of Indian chiefs to Washington.[55] Edward Francis Wilson, missionary to the Ojibwa of southern Ontario, also recognized the value of taking natives on tour. He took Chief Buhkwijjemene to London on a speaking tour, where the native narrated the Ojibwa story of the flood as part of the creation of the world. His recounting of the tale alluded to the popular idea that Indians were the lost tribes of Israel, making their salvation and conversion seem much more likely.[56] He then gave a brief biographical sketch stating that as a child, he "was very badly off. My mother was dead, and my father loved firewater." The chief often went "cold and hungry, and at night would sometimes crawl into the wigwam and lie down beside [his] drunken father."[57] His account echoed the common nineteenth-century story of rising from the depths of society. Though the idea that race determined destiny was beginning to emerge, many people still believed in the innate ability of mankind to improve.[58] Chief

Buhkwijjemene illustrated how a changed environment had produced an improved man; he had overcome degrading, vulgar beginnings to become chief and, more importantly, a Protestant Christian. The concept of being one of the chosen few—a spiritual, existential example of Calvinism and Darwinism—appeared in missionary lectures, religious pamphlets and doctrine, and novels of the time. Natives who espoused the concept of being selected for salvation helped missionaries tap into common images of Indians as degraded while supporting the idea that at least some were worth saving. Missionaries who brought native converts with them on lecture tours used pre-existing ideas to their full advantage to encourage financial support from audiences in Canada and the United States.

The effect of Protestant missionary lectures lay in the content as well as the style. Even those missionaries sympathetic to the natives' desire to remain an individual society lectured on the "savageness" of these same people, in hopes of attracting and maintaining a large base of financial support. William Duncan played to his audiences in Canada and the United States from the 1870s to the 1890s. When measured against other missionaries, he achieved notable success in building a small-scale version of English society—though he did allow the Tshimshian an unusual amount of control and input into the mission. Despite this success, he still fell back on the ideas of savage and heathen Indians in his lectures to white audiences. Many of his speeches focused on the most bizarre and shocking aspects of native society. One lecture titled "People How Found" [*sic*] discussed the physical appearance of the natives as well as how they were savages, ate slaves, beat their children, fought wars, and encouraged cannibalism.[59] Another lecture, simply called "Blood," recounted that the week Duncan had arrived in Victoria, a man had been murdered and another man and a woman had been eaten, adding fuel to the myth that Tshimshian were cannibals.[60] All of these images reinforced the burgeoning idea of the wretched Indian. Describing cannibalism and other violent, uncontrolled acts allowed missionaries to openly attack the noble savage image. These shocking, bizarre behaviors displayed how wretched and depraved native societies were and how they needed a better influence in order to be saved.

When he toured Washington State, Duncan focused his lectures on two things: the condition of the natives, and their pride. In the first segment of his speech, he gave descriptions of a murder, the death of a slave woman, the work of a medicine man, and the ritual of dog-eating. The second segment discussed the idea of paying for shame to restore one's pride and burning out disgrace.[61] In all of these lectures, Duncan referred not to the Tshimshian and the Haida but to the "Indian," helping to create the image of one race and one culture (i.e., Indian culture). He played upon the idea of the violent Indian by describing an exotic and cruel being who followed what the white audiences considered ruinous and disgusting rituals. By focusing on negative aspects of native life, Duncan presented Indians as horrific caricatures of white fears about the uncivilized. He played upon these fears in an effort to gain support for his cause.[62]

Another Canadian missionary, Egerton Ryerson Young of the Methodist Church, focused his lectures on the adventure in mission work and also on Canadian and American societies' fear of the natives. After he retired from mission work, Young began his lecture career in an effort to support himself and to maintain ties with the Wesleyan Methodist Missionary Society. He offered a series of lectures for audiences in Canada, the United States, and Britain. Titles ranged from "Romantic Life in the Lull of the Auroras" (referring to mission work in the Arctic area) to "In Perils Oft" (implying the natives' threat on the lives of the missionaries). The images in these speeches were in keeping with audiences' assumptions about the Indians. Young's lectures also centered on the transformation of native society as evidenced by lectures titled "(For Women's Conventions.) The Indian Woman as She *Was* and *Is*" and "In the Land of the Red Man, as They Were and Are, with Glimpses of Prairies, Mountains, Lakes, and Glorious Auroras."[63] His speeches attempted to justify the continued presence of missionaries in the Northwest by illustrating how effective their work had been. By relating how missionaries had transformed the natives, Young hoped to inspire both spiritual and financial support for the missions. His discussions of the Indians' transformation illustrated how he had succeeded in fulfilling the missionary societies' goals. His romanticization of the perils and adventures of missionaries played on Canadians' and Americans' fear of Indians and attracted supporters to the cause of taming the Indians.

As much as missionary lectures preyed on the fear of the uncivilized Indians, they also dwelt on the pity that should be extended to the unconverted natives. Jervois Newnham began a lecture series with the questions "Who lives in such a country [as northern Ontario]?" and "Why do you live there?" He answered that "some ten thousand Indians live there. Indians have souls, and the Divine command to evangelize the world includes these poor, much-to-be-pitied Indians; and I and my fellow missionaries live there in obedience to that command."[64] Such attitudes of pity and selflessness allowed the missionaries, and in some cases the government, to look like the natives' saviors. Newnham also described with disdain how the natives of Moosonee survived—that "they live[d] by the chase, I mean, first, trapping furs for the company; and secondly, procuring 'country food,' i.e., rabbits, fish, birds, and a few deer, for their own food and for barter with white men." To Newnham, "they are and must be a poor people, living in poverty, hardship, and frequent starvation as long as they remain in the country."[65] Missionaries like Newnham regarded Indians in a paternalistic manner, embracing the wretched Indian as a controllable one.

Natives came to be viewed like the urban poor of the nineteenth century: childlike, simple, and incapable of taking care of themselves without a paternalistic figure to provide for them. Whereas many urban missionaries pleaded with wealthy factory owners to take care of their workers, the missionaries to the Indians had to elicit support from governments and the Protestant Christian public. And North American missionaries competed with missionaries in other parts of the world. Missionaries portrayed both natives and the urban poor as exotic and dangerous, lacking the moral standards of the day. At a time when poor factory workers seemed like another race in both Britain and the United States, the idea of a transformation of one group of people into a near-perfect reproduction of Canadian and American societies gave hope to reformers everywhere.

Though Canadian and U.S. missionary societies originally designed lecture tours to gain volunteers and inspire white piety, these tours became lucrative ventures for missions. Once missionary societies removed the bulk of their financial support from the missions, missionaries used lecture tours to raise money and interest in their cause. Missionary lecturers inadvertently spread ideas about native groups and influenced a wide variety of the white populace. The authority of missionaries grew accordingly, opening new doors with the governments, educational institutions, and other secular organizations. These lectures and missionary writings left an indelible impression, on a larger segment of the public than had ever been exposed to such ideas, about life among the wretched Indians of North America, and erected new ideas on the foundations of old racial concepts.

THE ANIMALISTIC, EXOTIC INDIAN

Protestant missionaries did not rely solely on lecture tours to secure support and expand their reputations. They also wrote extensively, creating reference material for each other and anyone else interested in Indians. The decades from the 1850s to the 1880s saw a burst in publishing activity beyond dictionaries and lexicographies to include newsletters, pamphlets, and novels.[66] These publications not only institutionalized newly developed images such as that of the wretched Indian, but also meant that mass reproduction of them was possible outside the traditional missionary society structure. Missionaries published with religious and secular presses, and beyond the control of missionary societies.

The idea of the animalistic, exotic Indian is one of the best examples of a new idea that publishing institutionalized. Missionaries often employed comparisons to animals to explain what they considered to be exotic or bizarre actions by natives. The Indians howled like "wild beasts," pranced like "horses," and hunted like "lions." Even the language of conversion was in keeping with these animalistic images—non-Christian natives became "sheep" to be led by the missionaries. Comparing the Indians to animals allowed missionaries to dismiss their unexplainable actions as inhuman and to issue a call for salvation of native groups, moving that much closer to the idea of multiple beginnings for mankind.

William Duncan observed just such an unexplainable incident in 1858, barely one year after arriving at his British Columbia mission. He recalled that "a few days ago we were called upon to witness a horrible scene in this land."[67] A chief had ordered that a slave be killed and thrown into the ocean. When a body appeared close to shore, Duncan assumed that the tribe had obeyed the order, but admitted that he "did not see the murder." As the corpse floated in the surf, a band of "furious wretches in a state of nudity" ran toward it, "stepping like a proud horse." Duncan described the scene: "The instant they came to where it was they commenced screaming and rushing around it like so many angry wolves."[68] The group dragged the body from the water, "where the naked men commenced tearing at it with their teeth." At this point, Duncan's view was blocked, but eventually "each of the naked cannibals appeared with half the body in his hand. Separating a few yards, they commenced their horrid feast."[69] Thus Duncan witnessed what he perceived to be cannibalism.

Duncan quickly reported the "cannibalism" incident to his sponsoring agency, the Church Missionary Society. The account of the "naked cannibals" who "stepped like proud horses" spread to missionary societies across the border and appeared in *The Foreign Missionary,* a newspaper of the Presbyterian Church in the United States. Since the work of the Church Missionary Society was largely similar to that of the Presbyterians, the editors felt that the story would draw attention to the plight of the Indians at their missions also. This version, which was not published until 1864, expanded on the original description. In the later account, however, Duncan actually saw the cannibalism and the native leaders "stepped like *two* proud horses." And again, the Indians rushed like "so many angry wolves."[70] Though the newspaper edited this version, the animal imagery remained intact. The fact that the editors of *The Foreign Missionary* picked this story over others suggests that they believed it would help gain support for the goals of the Presbyterian Church. Given that the circulation of *The Foreign Missionary* was about 16,000 copies a month, the story of the Indian cannibals and their animal-like behavior spread quickly in the United States. Duncan's tale helped missionary societies in both countries establish the Indians as a primitive race in need of civilizing, which helped justify their work.

In 1873, Reverend J. J. Halcombe, whose chief activity seemed to be assembling books of strange facts, published *Stranger than Fiction*. In this volume, he repeats Duncan's story of cannibalism, even credits it to him. Halcombe possessed a flair for the dramatic. In his version of the tale, the cannibals rush the corpse "as if in a mockery of the peaceful sound of the waves of the Pacific breaking gently on the shore."[71] The two Indian leaders are "stepping like high-nettled horses" and begin to "sniff like hounds for a trail." Once they find the corpse they "swarm round and rushing like a pack of hungry wolves, they rend it asunder and [each] bear[s] away his portion in triumph."[72] This account of the story heightens the savagery of the actions and includes details that Halcombe may have been inventing. His rendering illustrates the extreme of sensationalist writings among the missionaries that relied on animal imagery and horrifying facts to portray the Indians. As missionaries sought more aid outside of the missionary societies, they tried to engage their audiences in any way possible.

The image of Indians as cannibalistic animals maintained popularity well into the later period (from the 1870s to 1900) of scholarly writing. In 1881, a year when the Church Missionary Society preferred not to discuss Duncan's actions because of his struggle for control of his mission with the church, they published the second edition of *Metlakahtla and the North Pacific Mission*. Basically a reprint of Duncan's journal, it focused upon the cultural aspects of his work with the Indians of British Columbia. It is unclear whether Duncan edited the work or the author, Eugene Stock, simply lifted accounts from the Church Missionary Record. A copy of the second edition appeared in Duncan's papers, suggesting that he at least knew it existed. This new version was published just as Duncan's battle began with the Church Missionary Society and the provincial government for control of his mission. This edition of the tale has many of the same elements as other accounts, but it also appears to be more authoritative.

Though Duncan worked with the Tshimshian, throughout *Metlakahtla* he (or

Stock) continually referred to them as just "Indians." The cannibalism story appeared again in this new edition, gaining detail and depth with its retelling. Now hundreds of Tshimshian watched as the cannibals searched for the corpse and tore it apart. This time, either Duncan or the editor explained the ritual as part of the medicine man tradition and the corpse as an offering by the rest of the tribe to prevent the cannibals from devouring live victims.[73] This version of the story was followed in 1890 by a short reprint in *The Canadian Indian,* a publication put out by Edward Francis Wilson.[74] Despite attempts in this article to justify the Indians' actions, the concept of cannibalism, and of "tearing apart the body," still held elements of shock and fear for the reader, and still suggested a wretched Indian in need of civilization.

Duncan's account of cannibalism and its variations brings to light several tensions in Canadian and American societies. First, the account took on a more definitive tone as the century progressed. The more the Church Missionary Society attempted to isolate and financially punish Duncan, the more he relied on the horrific images of cannibalism to get publicity and raise money for his mission. This reliance suggests that Duncan realized that the revulsion of cannibalism would draw support. Second, as the tales moved from the private to the public realm, they became more repulsive as the action became more ritualized. This ritualization shows how the idea of the wretched Indian was changing. Instead of blaming morally lax whites for cannibalism, the writers portrayed it as an inherent part of Indian culture. Such an idea fit in with the theory that genetics shaped culture. Finally, the wide reach of the tale is evidence of both the legitimization of missionaries as authorities and the effectiveness of the image. By the early twentieth century, this story was regarded as true, supporting the assumption of the time that cannibalism represented the "primitive origins of mankind and the dark urges within us all."[75] Cannibalism merged the wretched Indian concept with white audiences' fears about savagery on the frontier, creating an image that resonated with the public in both countries.

Many Protestant missionaries attempted to break from sensational writing and attain distinction as scholars, but fought against their past in doing so. As the cannibalism story illustrates, Canadian and American missionaries read and contemplated each others' accounts of life on the frontier. This story also shows how missionary writers sent conflicting messages as they attempted to defend aspects of native culture. Duncan, who simply recorded his experiences, set off a storm of public interest in the savagery of native groups. By reprinting the story six years after it happened, *The Foreign Missionary* fueled the fire by exposing even more people to the tale. When the Church Missionary Society chose to reprint it seventeen years later in 1881, they shifted the focus from pure shock to explanation. Yet, they still included the fantastic elements (such as "tearing the body apart") that distracted the reader and dulled empathy for native groups. Despite intentions to absolve the Indians, Duncan's use of animal imagery and horrifying details reinforced the sensationalist ideas propagated for sixty years by missionary writers and racial theorists.

Missionaries grappled not only with the appalling images popularized by past writers but also with Christian images. Converts became "lambs" or "sheep"; a congregation turned into a "flock." Using such constructs, missionaries and their audiences easily saw the wild Indian as an animal. In his poem "A Plea for the Wild Sheep of the Rocky Mountains," Bishop William Carpenter Bompas mixed Christian imagery with animal imagery to elicit support for his mission. Bompas, who served close to the Arctic Circle in Canada, bordered on the eccentric. He avoided contact with Canadian and American societies as much as possible, even skipping his own ordination in Winnipeg, yet remained relatively unsympathetic to his native congregations. An extremely pious man, who wrestled with his own "private sin" for the last twenty years of his life, he focused on conversion much more than civilization at his mission, as illustrated by his poem:

These sheep, so wayward, sinning,
    On hill tops bleak and wild,
Are wild from the beginning,
    Not wanderers from the fold.
They need a change of nature,
    Through plenitude and grace,
To alter every feature
    Inherited by race.[76]

In just this one verse, numerous traditional attitudes of missionaries appear. The idea that natives existed as wild creatures whose inherited traits needed to be altered by Christianity pulses through this poem as it did through the minds of Canadian and U.S. Protestant Christians. Such beliefs made it difficult for those who sought to prove that Indians were human, with different yet legitimate forms of culture. After over forty years of trying to portray native groups as noble and wild, attempts to redefine these images required strength, determination, and the will to break tradition. An alteration of the elements of the noble savage resulted in the idea of the wretched Indian. The natural aspects of the noble savage developed into the equation of Indians with animals.

Animal imagery placed native groups firmly in the natural world, and helped Canadian and U.S. audiences envision themselves saving the Indians. It was their Christian duty to dominate nature as well as to spread the gospel. By imagining the Indians as at least partly animalistic, missionaries and their supporters were able to fulfill both of these roles. As Bompas pleads in the fourth verse of his "Plea":

> Come, Christian brethren, sated
> > With your rich Gospel feast,
> Pity the tribes belated
> > In the dark and lonesome West.
> Relax the purse strings rigid,
> > Pour out the burnished gold,
> Till in the climate frigid
> > The Gospel Truth is told.[77]

Bompas quickly moved from discussing the sheep of the Rocky Mountains to the "tribes belated," again equating natives with animals. The call for money, blatant as it may seem, was probably effective, as Bompas maintained his mission in the Arctic well after the Church Missionary Society deemed it unproductive. And by placing his appeal early in the poem, in the fourth of twenty-four verses, Bompas makes his point effectively: money ensures successful conversions and civilization.

Missionary societies recognized the effectiveness of animal imagery and employed it often in their publications. "A Plea for the Wild Sheep of the Rocky Mountains" appeared alongside a lithograph of a big-horn sheep, rather than a group of praying natives. Equating native groups with animals brought money and support. Working animal imagery into the concept of the wretched Indian allowed missionaries to convey the violence of native societies while implying that Christianity would eliminate it. Using this imagery also neatly combined both genetic and environmental theories of race.

Sheep, horses, and wolves were not the only animals employed to illustrate native life and culture. Dogs figured prominently in writings as well, perhaps as an example of an animal that man had domesticated and integrated into his life. In this context, wolves represented the pure, wild animal while dogs illustrated the domesticated yet degraded animal, much like the pure noble savage and the degraded wretched Indian. Canadian and American missionary writers and other authors in the late nineteenth century adopted these images in their work. In an 1883 plea for justice for native groups, Myron Eells emphasized the importance of animalistic Indians. He wrote that it was crucial "to treat them justly, to keep our promises to them even if we consider them dogs."[78] Eells acknowledged the common assumption that natives resembled dogs in their half-domesticated, degraded manner.

Animal imagery was only one aspect of the sensational writing that helped define Indians in the nineteenth century. But unlike other aspects that faded in and out of missionary works throughout the nineteenth century (such as rejection of the noble savage) animal imagery remained constant. Canadian and U.S. Protestant missionaries used animal imagery to bolster the idea of the noble savage as part of nature and to enhance the concept of the wretched Indian as in need of civilized society's help. Even as Duncan, Eells, Wilson, and others began to strive to preserve and study native culture, they too often used the terms most familiar to them. As they fought to prove that native groups had some aspects of civilized nations, they grappled with their choice of words, a factor they knew affected how others viewed the Indians.

Protestant missionaries in both countries responded as best they could to the dramatic changes facing them in the mid-nineteenth century. They followed the example of the missionary societies and tried to build close relationships with the Canadian and U.S. governments, in hopes of having more input in the development of policies that affected them. Eventually it became clear to the missionaries that whoever had the money defined the policy. Realizing that the missionary societies had abandoned them and that their governments wanted to attach stipulations to their grants, missionaries embarked on lecture tours and publishing blitzes. Due to the institutional pressures placed on them, they found themselves shaping their views of the Indians in order to attract public interest. Financial need forced missionaries to play to expanded audiences. They hoped these efforts would raise public awareness and money to support their work.

Despite radical political and structural changes that affected Canada and the United States in the mid-nineteenth century, Protestant missionaries in both countries reacted the same way to these changes. It was the change itself, not the nature of the change, that most affected them. Also paramount in their lives was the decrease of missionary society support. Missionaries in both countries suffered from these cutbacks and drew on the same systems of support to survive them.

By the end of the 1880s, the images of Indians that missionaries presented to the public appeared to be interchangeable between Canada and the United States. In search of financial support, missionaries and their publications crossed the border and played to international audiences. These border crossings led to a melding of Canadian and American images of the Indian. Just as Canadian and U.S. policy became more similar, so did the imagery used to describe the Indians. But, though policy in the two countries did remain fundamentally different in how it was implemented, Canadian and American missionaries' ideas about the wretched Indian became almost indistinguishable.

From the 1850s through the 1880s, the groundwork was laid for the final structural changes that would affect the missionaries, their missionary societies, and both groups' relationships with the governments. Policy changes and growing settlements in the West during this period would lead to more policy changes and settlement in the last twenty years of the century. These developments placed more and more pressure on missionaries to find new sponsors and to influence the future of the Indians, which would, in turn, shape the way they portrayed the Indians.

CHAPTER SIX

Let No Man Rend Asunder

B Y THE 1880s, the relationships between missionary societies, their missionaries, and the governments had shifted again. Aside from appointing missionaries, publishing their reports, and supplying minimal funds and publications, the
missionary societies held little power over the missionaries in the last twenty years
of the nineteenth century. Yet, the missionaries possessed no more freedom than
they had in earlier decades. Missionaries now found themselves under the political and financial control of the Canadian and U.S. governments. The future of most
mission work appeared to rest on engaging the sympathy and interest of more
secular North American audiences. If they succeeded, the missionaries would regain respect and authority and also expand their influence. Greater influence
would allow them to pressure the governments to keep supporting mission work.

As the nineteenth century drew to a close, missionaries faced challenges on
all sides. The missionary societies continued to reduce support to missionaries as
conversion rates remained static. Both the Canadian and U.S. governments, focusing on settlement and pacification of the frontiers, expected Protestant missionaries either to aid these processes or get out of the way. The missionaries now
relied quite heavily on direct support from an increasingly secular audience that
either had become bored by the Indian Problem or clung to the more shocking
and degrading descriptions of Indians that the missionaries had presented to
them. These circumstances together produced a transnational vision of the Indians and Indian policy that flowed across the border between Canada and the
United States.

IMMIGRATION AND THE CLOSING OF THE FRONTIER

Beginning in the 1850s, as more whites sought land on the western frontiers of
North America, the pressure to pacify the Indians increased on both the gov-

ernments and the missionaries. While the Canadian and U.S. governments encouraged settlers, Protestant missionaries had conflicting views concerning frontier settlement. Many hoped that more God-fearing, hard-working whites—or
as James Nisbet, a missionary to the Red River region, described them in 1868, a
"good class of settlers"—would help inspire conversion among the natives.[1] Yet
missionaries wanted time to prepare the natives and get them established as
farmers before white settlers overwhelmed them. Nisbet felt that "as the white
man encroached on [the natives'] country, their means of living became less, and
the white men must teach them how to live."[2] Nisbet's realization was not a new
one for the missionaries. As early as the 1840s, missionaries had understood that
eventually natives would be overwhelmed by whites. Mary C. Greenleaf had expressed this thought when she heard that "in twenty years [Indian Territory] will
be part of the United States." Thus, she pleaded, "it is very important, we *now*
do all we can for their education and Christianization."[3] Just as missionaries and
missionary societies had disagreed about the amount of time conversion would
take, as the nineteenth century closed they were in conflict over the pace of white
settlement. Missionaries in both countries welcomed good Protestant settlers
who might help influence the Indians to become civilized Christians. But they
wanted to do it on their own schedule. Neither government supported this idea,
increasing tension between the missionaries and the governments.

Canadian and U.S. Protestant missionaries were their own worst enemy during the process of white settlement. They provided valuable information about
the western frontiers in their constant correspondence with the governments.
Because they lived on the frontier year-round, missionaries furnished more in-
depth information about the land and its resources than geological surveyors
and other explorers. They knew rainfall levels, lengths of the seasons, and other
information that helped the governments determine land value and settlement
viability.

By writing informative letters to the governments and publishing descriptions
in missionary newsletters and the secular press, missionaries consistently helped
fuel immigration to the Canadian and American West. In 1873, Nisbet, by then
working in the North-West Territories, provided Secretary Governor Alexander
Morris with a clear description of the resources of Manitoba and present-day
Saskatchewan. Nisbet felt "the land at the base of the Ridway [*sic*] Mountains
seems very well adapted to farming purposes" while other areas "might consti-
tute extensive sheep runs or be employed for the raising of cattle."[4] Nisbet hoped
these statements would encourage the Canadian government to allow natives to

settle and farm this area, and also that they would demonstrate the suitability of the land for this purpose. But he soon discovered that his descriptions had an unintended effect. While defending the Presbyterian church for not encouraging anyone but Indians to settle the area, he wailed that "others have been attracted to the spot, by the fertility of the soil, the facilities for settlement, the beauty of the locality and the success that has attended farming operation."[5] Like other missionaries, Nisbet had hoped to control immigration so that he could prepare the natives for its effects.

Canadian and U.S. Protestant missionaries also shared their information with the secular public in newsletters and autobiographies in hopes of encouraging a slow but steady influx of white Christian settlers. Charlotte Bompas recounted the mineral properties of the Yukon, which "certainly [has] an extensive deposit of coal beneath the banks of the river." She noted that "some gold is also to be found here with exquisite crystals and innumerable forests."[6] And in the United States in 1885, a few years before the opening of Oklahoma to white settlement, a report of the Methodist Episcopal Church, South, described Indian Territory in highly encouraging terms:

> The lands are rich and productive, and the climate is adapted to the most diversified agricultural industry. Rich mines of copper, zinc, salt, petroleum and coal abound. Near Cottonwood Grove, on Quachita River, rich traces of gold have been discovered.[7]

Such descriptions encouraged interest in these regions and often spurred the governments to allow movement into them. Missionaries, whether knowingly or not, sanctioned settlement by carefully describing the resources available, often before they felt the natives were ready to interact with white settlers.

Protestant missionaries may have written these descriptions for two reasons. First, detailing the resources showed that these means would help natives survive in the future. In both Canada and the United States, missionary societies still aimed for the goal of self-supporting missions, which required the natives to earn capital and encouraged missionaries to support them in this pursuit. Second, missionaries may have hoped to lure a more stable and religious class of settler to the frontier. Their disgust with the traders and trappers was well known. Unfortunately for missionaries and the Indians with whom they worked, their depictions attracted every type of settler, particularly those that coveted native land.

Some missionaries recognized the dangers of whites taking over these fertile lands and rich mineral sites. Sherman Hall had foreseen future tensions between whites and Indians as early as 1847. "The tide of immigration . . . is rapidly rolling upon [the natives]."[8] He observed that "the pine lumber of the tributaries of the Mississippi" attracted settlers and lumbermen to Ojibwa country and that "the mines are attracting still more to the region bordering on Lake Superior."[9] This scenario continued over the next fifty years in both Canada and the United States. More than forty years after Hall's observation, Bishop John Horden lamented that "railroads being projected through the Diocese [of Moosonee] and Minerals having been discovered will bring in a large white population: crime will increase."[10] Clearly, Horden held a low opinion of the quality of immigrants attracted by these resources. Despite this understanding, Protestant missionaries in both countries continued to describe and endorse the resources of the West. Some simply felt they were portraying the means by which the natives could survive, assimilate, and become productive citizens. Unfortunately, missionaries' descriptions encouraged too-rapid government and settler interest in native territories, exposing the difference between the missionaries' goals and those of the Canadian and U.S. governments.

Attitudes toward frontier settlement differed in one aspect between Canadian and U.S. missionaries. In some cases, U.S. missionaries joined in the settlement of the frontier, squatting on native land and severing their ties with the missionary societies. These U.S. missionaries displayed a propensity for staking claims to property while doing mission work on the frontier. Canadian missionaries did not share this tendency. Because many of them worked within the bounds of the Hudson's Bay Company, which frowned upon and punished squatting, fewer of them defected to this lifestyle. Missionaries who quit mission work in Canada went back east to work with churches. But in the United States neither the missionary societies nor the governments punished such squatters. After all, the first famous U.S. missionary to the West, Marcus Whitman, spent much of his time settling the Oregon Territory with whites and was deemed the "savior" of the territory by the U.S. Congress.[11] Still, many U.S. missionaries felt conflicted about this issue. Stephen Return Riggs remembered less than fondly that "Mr. and Mrs. Pettijohn had taken the pre-emption fever, and had left the mission and gone to the Traverse [des Sioux] and made a claim."[12] Riggs and other U.S. missionaries had to explain the hypocrisy of missionary squatters to their native congregations, whereas Canadian missionaries generally avoided this problem.

Though some missionaries dreaded the quick pace of westward expansion and others unintentionally encouraged and participated in it, all took credit for the opportunity. Canadian and U.S. missionaries alike bragged about how humanely they had settled the West and enabled its increasing development. John McDougall, who worked as a missionary in Manitoba and the North-West Territories, proudly announced in 1875 that two forces had allowed for the settlement of the Canadian West: the Hudson's Bay Company and the missionaries. He crowed, "The latter [group] was spasmodic and because of the few laborers, very scattered over this tremendous territory, but was nevertheless remarkably fruitful."[13] Clearly aware of the obstacles they had encountered on the frontier, missionaries deemed themselves a success, unlike the missionary societies and the governments who had judged otherwise. Myron Eells proclaimed in an 1884 article: "Who will estimate the wealth accruing to the country from the possession of these Northwestern settlements which were thus saved to the country by missionary influence!"[14] Missionaries perceived themselves as active agents in native settlement of the western frontiers, and as having opened them to Canadian and U.S. settlement. Where they saw success, however, many in the governments and the missionary societies saw failure.

By the 1880s, settlers increasingly began to draw the attention and support of the government away from the missionaries. With the withdrawal of the Hudson's Bay Company from the Canadian West and the end of the Civil War in the United States, the frontiers opened up for a great flood of immigrants from the eastern parts of these countries. Though missionaries had helped broadcast the idea of the fertile West, the mass immigrations horrified them. After two hundred years of involvement in a gradual and relatively unsuccessful assimilation process, the missionaries' time was up. The Canadian and American governments settled the frontiers, shattering their relationships with Protestant missionaries.

CANADIAN AND U.S. POLICY

The last twenty years of the nineteenth century witnessed a denouement in terms of Indian policy in Canada and the United States. Both countries appeared to be placing the finishing touches on their final solution to the Indian Problem. And as the century drew to a close, the two countries seemed to be growing more alike in their methods of dealing with the Indians, just as missionary attitudes had done by the mid-nineteenth century.

As previously discussed, Canadian and U.S. Indian policies seemed to be two sides of the same coin from the 1830s to the 1850s. Canadian policy attempted to change the environment around the native populations in an effort to civilize them as well as to protect them from white intruders. U.S. policy initially sought to remove the natives from the "path of civilization." In the period from the 1850s to the 1880s, Canada had a dichotomous Indian policy. On one hand, it began active settlement of the western prairies through treaties and granted the Métis population legal recognition, all in keeping with past policies. On the other hand, the nation began to shift toward a more American-style policy by offering enfranchisement in return for the abandonment of one's Indian status. In British Columbia, Canada tossed out the treaty process altogether in the late 1850s, letting settlers displace the native population as was done in the United States. U.S. policy moved toward the destruction of all aspects of Indian life, be they social, cultural, or political. By the 1880s, Canadian and U.S. Indian policies reflected the transnational views of Protestant missionaries as they became basic replicas of each other.

In 1880, many of the natives on the Canadian prairies faced a major crisis: the decline of the buffalo population. Even as most of the prairie native groups acquiesced and moved onto reserves, they still subsisted mainly by hunting. With the herds dwindling and their freedom restricted, the natives encountered famine and frustration. They were not alone. The Métis population also suffered with the decline of the buffalo. To make ends meet, many native groups pursued farming, and also continued to rely on the lucrative buffalo robe and pemmican trades. The declining number of buffalo and the Canadian government's reluctance to address this problem, along with other frustrations, led to the Second North-West Rebellion.

Since the First North-West, or Riel, Rebellion in 1869 and 1870, many things had changed on the western Canadian prairies. First, the Canadian government had established the North-West Mounted Police to preserve peace on the frontier. Many historians, like Seymour Martin Lipset and Paul Sharp, point to this organization—an all-white force comprised mainly of immigrants—as evidence of the vast differences between the Canadian and U.S. frontiers.[15] Unlike the U.S. military, the North-West Mounted Police was supposed to be an impartial force meant to implement all laws, not just those that favored the white population.[16] As historian Olive Dickason describes, "The main tasks of the Mounties were the suppression of the liquor trade and the establishment of good relations" with the natives.[17] Still, they acted as an occupying force in many ways.

Second, white settlement had dramatically altered the frontier. By the early 1880s, whites outnumbered both the native and Métis populations. The latter groups had shifted from being the majority, with support from the strong Hudson's Bay Company, to being a minority with little institutional support. Finally, as the Second North-West Rebellion erupted, workers completed the Canadian Pacific Railroad. This development opened the West—particularly British Columbia—to even more extensive settlement and regulation.[18]

In 1884, Louis Riel returned to the North-West Territories from the United States, bristling with ideas. Riel tried to unite the residents of the territories by claiming that the Canadian government overcharged white settlers for their land. He also demanded that the territories become self-governing and that the government treat the native and Métis populations better. Suffering from famine and over-regulation, the native and Métis populations in the region jumped to Riel's support. The white settlers, however, feared Riel's close relationship with the natives. In any case, Riel set up a provisional government and submitted a petition. The Canadian government in Ottawa simply shrugged at the petition and offered only to set up a committee to look into Métis claims of land fraud. Riel responded by demanding the same concessions for the Métis in the North-West Territories that they had in Manitoba: an official patent, the establishment of a province, and the election of legislatures.[19] Riel's forces repelled a militia led by the local Indian agent. With news of this success, natives flooded into the provisional government headquarters to support the cause. The arrival of the native population scared the white settlers, who promptly fled the territory. Several skirmishes ensued and eventually a large Canadian force defeated Riel. The Canadian government arrested 202 Métis and natives and charged them with treason. One Métis and eight natives were hanged, and forty-four natives were sentenced to jail, often by proceedings conducted only in English. Most died in jail or almost immediately after being released.

The outcome of the Second North-West Rebellion shaped native policy on the prairies of Canada until the end of the nineteenth century. The natives' participation in the rebellion shocked many Canadians. As Dickason eloquently comments, "Much as Amerindians might have been appreciated on their own merits in philosophical or artistic circles, in the political arena they were expected to conform to the prevailing ethos as exemplified by the dominant power."[20] As a consequence of the rebellion, the government introduced a pass system, requiring natives to have a pass to be able to leave their reserves. The Canadian government began to dismantle various tribal governments, believing that these institutions had led to the rebellion.[21] By the turn of the century, the Canadian government was attempting to outlaw native religious practices and culture as well.[22] Using legislation, the Canadian government attempted to force Indian assimilation, losing patience with the gradual, voluntary process that missionaries had undertaken. The Second North-West Rebellion firmly established the natives as a threat to the status quo in Canada.

As the Second North-West Rebellion altered life on the prairies, change also came to British Columbia. The completion of the railroad brought a settlement boom to this region, flooding native lands with white settlers.[23] Tensions increased between the natives and a growing white population that coveted their land. The Canadian government tried to regulate assimilation of the British Columbian natives by extending laws that affected the prairie natives to govern cultural institutions, such as the potlatch. This action combined with the lack of treaties protecting native rights in British Columbia caused growing discord.[24] By the end of the 1880s, Canada had lost all patience with its Indian Problem.

During this period, the United States also pursued a policy of legislated assimilation. The U.S. government sought to clear as much land as possible for white settlement, and throughout the 1880s, it focused on herding the natives onto reservations. Its reliance on the military to achieve this goal led to many bloody skirmishes and massacres. But unlike Canada, most terms of the treaties that established reservations failed to be enforced. White settlers squatted on reservation land, took over native farms, and violated agreements. U.S. legislators reasoned that if only the natives would farm, more land would be made available for settlement.

The Dawes Act, or Indian Allotment Act, was passed in the United States in 1887. This act divided the reservations into individual plots in order to accelerate the Indians' transformation into property-owning citizens.[25] The Indian Rights Association, a lobbying group led by Bishop Whipple of the Dakota Territory, felt that the passage of this law reaffirmed their "general policy of gradually making the Indian in all respects as the white man."[26] By this time, the U.S. government was actively legislating agrarian and assimilation policies, no longer waiting for missionaries to achieve these goals. The government reassigned missions to the missionary societies, recalled missionaries, cut funding, and appointed its own agents, quickly reestablishing itself after the failure of the Peace Policy.

By 1890, the majority of natives in the continental United States resided on reservations under deplorable conditions. Instead of turning Indians into property owners, the Dawes Act had effectively chopped up reservations, with the most arable lands having been sold off to settlers. Some natives struggled to farm, while many relied on government rations and annuities, none of which were enough. In 1892, the Ghost Dance emerged. Led by Wovoka, a Paiute prophet who preached that the new millennium would restore the buffalo and that Christ had died for the Indians and not the whites, the Ghost Dance upset the U.S. government as well as many missionaries. Though an impressive blending of Christian and native beliefs, the fact that it drew large crowds of natives and seemed to be building a groundswell of support made it threatening to the U.S. government. With the massacre at Wounded Knee, many Americans considered the natives pacified and the Indian Problem solved. But to make sure, Congress passed several laws and the Bureau of Indian Affairs adopted policies that outlawed many aspects of native cultures, languages, and religions.

Canada and the United States still had some fundamental differences in their Indian situation, even as their policies on natives moved closer in theory and implementation. Canada continued to deal with a Métis population in Manitoba and the North-West Territories that sought legal recognition and political power. The United States, which lacked a large Métis or half-breed population that could force the issue of recognition, staunchly ignored this group. Another difference was that Canada succeeded in placing the native population on reserves with fewer skirmishes and in a shorter amount of time than the United States. Finally, Canada enforced the terms of its treaties with the native population, whereas the United States not only failed to enforce the terms of most treaties, but continually changed the terms of these agreements through new legislation. These conflicting legislative acts meant that reservation boundaries and Indian rights were constantly shifting. The difference in the way the two countries enforced their Indian laws has led many historians and commentators to conclude that Canada had a more orderly frontier.

To many historians, the biggest difference between Indian/white relations in Canada and in the United States was the level of violence. Canada's North-West rebellions and other small battles seem to pale in comparison to the large-scale Indian wars and massacres that took place in the United States. Ostensibly, if Canadians viewed the native population in a fundamentally different manner than those in the United States, then this would explain the lower level of violence. But as previously discussed, the image of the violent Indian existed

in both countries. Canadian policy after the Second North-West Rebellion reflects the fear that this image evoked. The pass system and the dismantling
of tribal governments suggest that Canadian officials viewed the natives as a
threat to the security of the frontier after the relatively tame Second North-West
Rebellion.

Overall, though, the number of similarities between Canadian and U.S. policy was growing. This suggests that images reflected attitudes toward the natives
better than government or legislative action. The establishment of the North-
West Mounted Police moved the country's native policy implementation closer
to that of the United States. Though not as violent as the U.S. Army and cav-
alry, the Mounted Police still acted as an occupying power that enforced policies.
It arrested more native leaders than it killed, but many of those arrested died in
jail after being tried by a system they neither understood nor could participate in
due to language differences. The North-West Mounted Police acted to quell
what the Canadian government perceived to be growing tension on the frontier.
When compared with that of the United States, the frontier north of the border
seemed relatively tame, but the Canadian government called for a security force
nonetheless.

Both Canada and the United States attempted to regulate assimilation at the
end of the nineteenth century. Both governments passed legislation outlawing
tribal governments as well as the cultural and religious practices of the natives.
Clearly, the two countries felt that native governments and cultures posed some
threat to their own. The theory that Canada possessed a kinder, gentler frontier
applies only, if at all, to government actions prior to the 1880s. During the last
twenty years of the nineteenth century, the Canadian government acted in ways
that suggested it perceived the Indian population as a threat to the frontier.

Even though Canadian and U.S. missionary attitudes toward Indians mirrored each other throughout the nineteenth century, the two countries' policies
seemed to lie on different sides of the same issues from the 1830s until the 1880s.
Canada focused on surrounding the Indians with a peaceful and orderly environment that would help mold them into citizens, while the United States
sought to isolate natives. At the beginning of the 1880s, though, both governments attempted to speed up assimilation of the native population and so free up
the frontiers for white settlement. This sudden shift in strategy isolated and
alienated the missionaries who still were trying to follow the original policy of
gradual conversion and civilization. The conflicting goals of the governments
and the missionaries drove them apart at the close of the nineteenth century.

DIVORCE OF CHURCH AND STATE

From the 1830s to the 1880s, missionary societies and their missionaries worked closely with the Canadian and U.S. governments. Originally, the governments worked directly with the missionary societies, granting them permission to enter certain territory and appropriating funds for the education and civilization of the Indians. In the 1850s, as the expenses of North American missions escalated, missionary societies began to rely more heavily on financial and other kinds of assistance from the governments. Eventually costs became too high and the missionary societies withdrew financial support from their missions. Missionaries responded by asking the governments for money and assistance. Both the Canadian and U.S. governments gave aid directly to the missionaries, implicitly allowing them to act as informal government agents.

Starting in the 1850s, missionaries saw themselves as an integral part of the solution to the Indian Problem. They felt that only with their Christian influence could natives assimilate into Canadian and American societies. Protestant missionaries openly embraced the belief that the Indians would soon be extinct without assimilation and agrarianism; they often espoused this conviction with a vigor unmatched by the governments.

By the 1880s, both governments needed to accelerate the pacification of the frontiers. From this time on, relations soured between missionaries and the governments. The governments demanded fewer conflicts between whites and natives, more farms, and a settled frontier. Missionaries found themselves reliving the experience they had had with the missionary societies in the 1850s. Once again a sponsoring institution was criticizing the pace of conversion and questioning the missionaries' level of success. The missionaries felt deserted by the missionary societies, resented being pressured, and took a skeptical view of the influx of white settlers into native territory. The conflict began when the Canadian and U.S. governments took over the implementation of native policy, replacing missionaries with their own agents.

In this struggle, the governments had an advantage over the missionaries. They held the deeds and purse strings for many of the missions. As the western frontiers became settled, they quickly made their power known. In 1846, the U.S. government exercised its control over missionaries by closing a mission to the Spokane and removing the missionary.[27] Later, in the 1850s, the government forced the missionaries to the Dakotas to relinquish all their claims.[28] During the same period in Canada, missionaries were excluded from treaty negotiations and other meetings between natives and government officials. In 1878, Robert Clyde Scott, a missionary in British Columbia, participated in meetings with the Indian reserve commissioners. But in 1887, government officials barred Scott from just such a meeting. Scott fumed, "This is the kind of treatment Missionaries generally receive at the hands of Government Officials, who draw large salaries for reporting *annually* the satisfactory conditions of the Indians." The snub particularly angered Scott because most missionaries provided information about the Indians constantly in weekly and monthly reports. Scott clearly perceived himself as an authority on the Indians. He continued, saying that this "satisfactory condition [was] brought about not by any effort of theirs; but by the self-denying labors of the Missionaries."[29] Suddenly, or so it seemed to missionaries like Scott, they found themselves without a voice in government decisions. Though forced to rely on the governments for financial and political support, the missionaries quickly began to feel as though they had made a pact with the devil.

The Canadian government and the missionaries each struggled for control of the missions as settlement advanced on the British Columbian and prairie frontiers. The government never officially recognized the missionaries as partners in native policy as the United States had done with the Peace Policy.[30] But the Canadian government provided funds, used missionaries as interpreters and negotiators, and demanded results from their investment. The financial support of the government had allowed the missionaries to break away from the missionary societies' control. Still, the government and the missionaries disagreed on how to treat the Indians. In his book, *The Indians: Their Manners and Customs,* John Maclean wrote that the Canadian government wanted the missionaries to "teach the Indians first to work and then to pray" while the missionaries saw fit to "christianize first and then civilize."[31] Just as they had with the missionary societies, missionaries clashed with the governments over the way their goals should be achieved. Adding to the frustration of Canadian missionaries was the fact that government agents were generally appointed with little or no input from the missionary societies. Tensions erupted repeatedly between missionaries and the governments. In Canada in 1888, Reverend A. Sutherland complained that an Indian agent controlled his mission. Sutherland wrote in a letter that "[the Indian agent] claims that the church does not belong to the Methodist Conference, but to the Indians, and consequently under his control."[32] Sutherland and the agent argued about who had authority over the Indians. Missionaries chafed at this type of challenge to their control and wrote letters of protest to higher-up government officials. Sutherland, for example, wrote to the superintendent of

Indian affairs in Canada to rectify his situation with the Indian agent.[33] Prior to Confederation, missionaries in Canada maintained a large degree of autonomy. The increased government regulation in the 1880s infuriated them.

For their part, Canadian government officials began to tire of missionaries who acted on their own. Deputy Superintendent Vankoughnet reminded J. William Tims in 1889 that he was to pursue mission work, not self-interest enterprise such as trade.[34] Missionaries also often expected the government to grant special privileges in return for their work. In 1892, Jervois Newnham wrote to the Minister of Interior to demand custom charges be reduced or eliminated for his diocese. Otherwise, he proposed that the proceeds go to roads, mails, or police, and that a certain amount be spent on schools in his area.[35] These suggestions fell on deaf ears; missionary societies in the early period of missionary work applied most funds to improving the condition of the Indians. But as white settlers increased on the frontier, the Canadian government appropriated more money to benefit that population.

Unlike in the United States, where settlers quickly followed missions onto the frontier, the Hudson's Bay Company controlled emigration onto the prairies of Canada until the time of Confederation. Likewise, settlement was limited in British Columbia until the completion of the railroad. Consequently, missionaries were often the only whites on the frontier, allowing them to make demands on and act—sometimes unofficially—for the government. Until the 1880s, the pre-Confederation Canadian government responded when the missionaries and the missionary societies raised issues about the frontier. The post-Confederation Canadian government became less accommodating as it focused more on settlement than on trade. Indian agents took control of education, farming, and other issues, restricting the power of the missionaries. White settlers demanded more regulation of the frontier, and though the missionaries resisted, the government stepped in where the Hudson's Bay Company and the missionaries had once ruled.

Some historians of Canada suggest that the tension between missionaries and the government arose from the missionaries being *too* successful in settling, assimilating, and representing the interests of the natives. Margaret Whitehead, speaking about British Columbia, contends that "the settlers were far from happy when ministers and priests, interested in the economic welfare of their converts, taught the Indians the due process of law by which they might appeal unsatisfactory government decisions regarding their land."[36] A prime example of economic competition between whites and natives can be found in the native groups under William Duncan in British Columbia that successfully ran a cannery and challenged government control of their council.

British Columbia appears to be the exception to the rule, as Whitehead's statement holds true for neither the rest of western Canada nor the United States during the late nineteenth century. Probably only a few missionaries achieved the economic success of Duncan, and the Canadian and U.S. governments simply felt the need to settle the frontiers. After fifty years, missionaries had made only small—and to the missionary societies and governments, insignificant—gains. Large groups of natives still roamed the prairies. Converts refused to assimilate fully, continuing to uphold native traditions, refusing to farm exactly like the Canadians and Americans, and declining to "become" white. And the costs of mission work continued to spiral upward. In Canada, the government reduced the role and influence of the missionary societies, controlling expenses as well as introducing the North-West Mounted Police to help settle the frontier. The government employed such new methods to pacify the frontier faster.

In the United States, the Peace Policy hastened the split between missionaries and the missionary societies, breaking the hold of the missionary societies over missionaries' goals, but also leaving them without a powerful ally in their fight for survival. In 1879, the Methodist Episcopal Church complained that "the policy of the present administration of the Interior Department has taken from our agents all sense of dependence upon us or responsibility to us," which meant the missionary society had no control over the "educational, civilizing and Christianizing influences."[37] As the Peace Policy dissolved under President Arthur, the missionary societies lost control of many missions. An 1883 essay in the annual report of the Methodist Episcopal Church railed that "the 'Peace Policy' has been entirely sundered, and no official relation is now sustained by us to various Indian Agencies."[38] The Methodist Episcopal Church watched angrily as the U.S. government reduced their influence over their own missionaries. By forcing missionary societies out, the government isolated missionaries from their support system, but also freed them to shop their expertise around to whoever could benefit from it.

With the dissolution of the Peace Policy, the U.S. government wrested control of education out of the hands of missionaries and missionary societies. In most native schools, the government hired teachers, supplied certain books, and dictated the curriculum—all with some help from the missionaries. The missionaries and the government fought constantly about the direction education would take. Stephen Return Riggs echoed John Maclean's goals for mission work in *Tahkoo Wah-kan; or the Gospel among the Dakotas.* Riggs also wanted to Christianize first and civilize second, as "*the Bible is the great civilizer of the nations.*"[39] Like the

Canadian government, the U.S. government preferred the reverse order. If schools existed at all, Indian agents and missionaries argued over how they should be run.[40] Agents tried to convince native parents that the schools were an extravagant expense. In some cases, agents told parents that "their annuities were all needed for corn and blankets and ponies, and that education could do them no good."[41] This point was broadcast widely by Indian agents and traders, and drove natives and their financial contributions away from missionaries' schools. This lack of support allowed agents to argue that missionaries were no longer needed and also opened the door for the government and its agents to claim that missionaries had failed to reach their goals. By the 1880s, such power plays were common.

As the governments withdrew support, missionaries fought their loss of power alone. Missionary societies removed themselves from the fray, focusing on other areas of the world. Missionaries reacted to their loss of influence in two ways. Some became more critical of government laws, attempting to expose flaws in new policies and get themselves reinstated as informal advisors. Others became scholars, trying to educate the public and the governments about the real needs of the Indians. All missionaries attacked Canadian and U.S. native policy with a vengeance in order to sustain a need for their work.

LET NO MAN REND ASUNDER

On the whole, Canada and the United States implemented their Indian policies differently throughout the first three-quarters of the nineteenth century. But as the century came to a close, their policies were becoming more alike. Despite this, many Canadian missionaries continued to believe their government's policy to be superior to that of the United States. John Maclean declared that "our Canadian people ever favoured a policy of peace. Far rather would we feed the Indians than fight them."[42] He neatly sums up the biggest perceived difference between Canadian and U.S. Indian policy: Canada treated Indians gently and charitably while the United States abused them. Even some U.S. missionaries felt that Canadian policy was more successful. In his 1883 treatise, *Justice to the Indian,* Myron Eells commented that because of the Hudson's Bay Company, the honesty of the British government, and the lack of wars between natives and whites, native policy in Canada was more successful.[43] Eells's views agree with those of many historians today who see the Hudson's Bay Company and the British government as major reasons why the Canadian frontier was supposedly more peaceful. In 1891, Edward Francis Wilson of Ontario eloquently explained the perceived differences between the two countries' Indian policies: "In its essentials and on paper the Canadian system does not differ widely from that of the United States." But, "if anyone wishes to appreciate the vital differences between the Canadian and the United States policy," then "let him compare the peaceful development of the Canadian North-west with the bloody series of conflicts which have marked the western march of the white man in the Western States."[44] Apparently, Wilson did not consider the Second North-West Rebellion to have been bloody.

Many people in the nineteenth century saw Canada as a success because they considered the development of the frontier to have been peaceful (and many people today still feel this way). With apparently few casualties and bloody battles, Canada seems to have had a relatively calm conquest. The statements of Maclean, Eells, and Wilson imply then, that stereotypes and images of Canadian Indians would have been fundamentally different from those of Indians in the United States, where tensions clearly existed between the native and white populations. One would expect that Canadian stereotypes of Indians would have been more akin to those held of some immigrant groups: harsh with the immigrants' arrival but slowly lessening as the immigrants became part of the larger society. But, as discussions of the noble savage and the wretched Indian images have demonstrated, the stereotypes invoked by Protestant missionaries persisted in both countries. Yet, Canadians and Americans continued to believe that Canada enjoyed a special relationship with the Indians.

Myron Eells had not only believed in the superiority of Canadian policy but felt so strongly that in 1883, he composed a moving critique of U.S. Indian policy. Entitled *Justice to the Indian,* he began by declaring that "the Indian is not a saint—that his heart is naturally at enmity against God and right." "But," he pointed out, "on the other hand in comparison with the whites, he has very little power and he knows it."[45] Despite this beginning, which acknowledged the perceived flaws of the Indians, Eells's motive was not to criticize the natives but rather the whites. He continued, "But time would fail me to mention all the acts of injustice done by [the U.S.] government to the Indians" as they affect "nearly every tribe in the United States." He asserted these "acts of injustice . . . are a very great obstacle to missions among the Indians because they connect the Christian religion with the whites and with our government."[46] After the failure of the Peace Policy, Eells's statements constituted the first salvo of criticism by missionaries as their relationships with the U.S. and Canadian governments shattered irreparably. He firmly places the blame for missionaries' low conversion rates on the U.S. government and its policies. Yet Canadian missionaries, with their superior government and policies, suffered the same failure.

Eells was particularly well equipped to critique native policy in the American West. The son of Edwin Eells, who was considered the father of missionary work in Oregon and Washington, Myron had spent his entire life as a missionary with the Twana and other coastal native groups. Once the missionary societies reduced funds to the missionaries, Myron survived by doing ethnographic studies for the Smithsonian. Within his lifetime, he witnessed all the radical changes that affected North American native groups: the white invasion, death by disease, the arrival of the military, and the herding of natives onto reservations.

Despite having different relationships with their governments, both U.S. and Canadian missionaries found Indian policy faulty in similar ways. They felt that a dangerous shift toward immediate assimilation appeared in native policy following Confederation in Canada and the end of the Peace Policy in the United States. Thomas Crosby expressed his dissatisfaction after Confederation with government policy that "had been far from what was right and just."[47] In a letter to John A. MacDonald, the superintendent general of Indian affairs, he complained directly to the government. Of course, the major change in policy that missionaries found far from right and just was the reduction of missionary input that the governments sought or accepted. Like Eells and Crosby, Edward Francis Wilson questioned the integrity of the Canadian government's intentions. Even though he felt Canadian policy was superior to that of the United States, he did not see it as flawless. In 1891, he printed a series of attacks in his newsletter, *The Canadian Indian*, on Canadian government policy. He pronounced that "all the actions of our Government, of our Indian Department, of our educational institutions, even the organizations and carrying on of our Christian missions, are from the white man's standpoint."[48] Wilson and others began to express concern that the governments thought it possible for only white civilization to survive. John McDougall angrily wrote about the Canadian government that "we could not find, nor did we try to find, any excuse for the promises made but not fulfilled by the cut-throat policy often exhibited and sometimes enforced by officials of the Indian Department."[49] Missionaries like Wilson and McDougall resented the sudden shift in policy, as it made their work unnecessary. They watched in horror and frustration as government agents and politicians took credit for the few successes they had achieved in fifty years.

Despite the governments' superior attitudes, missionaries still knew more about native issues than almost anyone else. Missionaries still worked on the frontier, where most policymakers and racial theorists feared to tread.[50] They saw first-hand the effects of policy decisions. And by the end of the nineteenth century, many missionaries were spreading their knowledge through articles in scholarly journals, firmly establishing their reputations with the public as experts on the Indians. And even though they received tepid responses from the governments, some missionaries continued to offer suggestions about native policy.

For Canadian and U.S. missionaries, the break with the governments offered them the freedom to point out the hypocrisy of government actions. Kate McBeth, who spent her life working with the Nez Perce in Washington State, accused the U.S. government of such actions when it "talks of civilizing Indians, but wants them to appear at great fairs in their old heathen toggery and go through heathen performances, which is not very consistent."[51] William Duncan blasted the Canadian government for undermining decisions made by native councils in British Columbia. "The maligned Council," he wrote sarcastically, "has unfortunately learned its business too soon and without the aid of the Indian Agent or the Indian Act." Duncan continued, "Had the Indians but remained 25 years longer in barbarism to suit the convenience of the Indian Department, they would now . . . be blessed with a legitimate council."[52] Duncan accused the Canadian government of discounting and even disavowing the work done by missionaries. McBeth, Duncan, and others charged the two governments with demanding natives who behaved like whites, yet still expecting natives to conform to the stereotypes in which they had been cast. Even as they complained about this hypocritical stance, though, many missionaries used their writings to exploit it.

Missionaries in both countries also complained bitterly about the misuse of funds originally intended for the civilization of the Indians. A good example of one of these complaints is found in the case of Thomas Crosby. Despite a tense relationship with a hostile missionary board, he became one of the best fundraisers in the Methodist Church, bringing in tens of thousands of dollars. By 1882, when he wrote a letter of protest to John A. MacDonald, he had proved himself to the missionary board as an able missionary and exemplary fund-raiser. His complaint pointed out that much of the government money earmarked for his region was being misused:

> I beg, also, to call your attention to the management of the Indian agencies, and the distribution of the very liberal grant made by the Dominion Government for the benefit of the Indians. Out of $40,000 given for the instruction and civilization of these tribes, only a very small portion is so applied. Absolutely nothing has been done by the agencies to break up the

cruel, heathen practices and wild, demonic orgies of the people. In fact, the agencies seem rather to encourage than restrain them in these things.[53]

In his complaint, Crosby demonstrates two important techniques that missionaries used in lobbying for their missions. First, he has quite a bit of information at his fingertips. He knows, for example, the amount of the government grant. Second, he criticizes the Canadian government for not civilizing the natives. He implies that the grant might have been more successful if it had been given to the missionary society. The Methodist Missionary Society found this letter to be so significant that they sent it to the superintendent of Indian affairs. They also circulated the letter to the Methodist public, hoping to influence their opinion and encourage them to put pressure on the government.

Missionaries resented hypocritical government policies that destroyed what little trust natives had in whites. Since missionaries were de facto representatives of the white Canadian and American public, they suffered the most from the lack of trust. As Canadian and U.S. lawmakers created restrictive and contradictory policies, the missionaries found themselves caught in the same trap they had been in with the missionary societies. That is, the governments held the missionaries to a certain standard of success but also hindered the missionaries' ability to succeed by alienating the natives. Frustrated by their lack of control, missionaries engaged in a war of criticism with the governments in an attempt to ignite public sympathy.

Missionaries in both countries employed any means available to change the policies that affected their livelihood. The American Presbyterian newspaper, *The Foreign Missionary,* ran prayers to induce Congress to act in favor of missionaries, an unusual step considering that *The Foreign Missionary* virtually ignored the North American missions in most of their late-nineteenth-century publications. In July 1882, the newspaper printed this appeal:

> PRAYER, that all those low estimates which scarcely accord to the Indians a human soul, and only look upon them as wild beasts to be exterminated, may be rebuked by a lofty and widespread public sentiment which acknowledges their claims and recognizes their part in the redemption of a common Saviour.[54]

Notice how this prayer plays upon the image of the wretched Indian by using the words "wild beasts." It also implicitly criticized the U.S. government, which many missionaries felt pursued a policy of extermination. This prospect worried the missionaries, because without the Indians, they would have no missions. The prayer also urged the public to treat the natives as Christians, reinforcing the idea that conversion had been somewhat successful.

Canadian missionaries worried about extermination as well. By 1895, authors of secondary texts were discussing it quite openly, as if it were an established part of government policy. One of these authors, W. H. Withrow, declared that "the extinction of the [Indian] race in the not very remote future seems to be its probable destiny."[55] As the western frontier closed, whites discussed drastic measures to settle it. The possibility of the Indians' extermination was implied in many of the discussions.

After achieving some success in convincing Indians to adopt an agrarian lifestyle, missionaries watched in horror as the governments removed native groups from their farms. Hence, a second prayer appeared in the same issue of *The Foreign Missionary,* exalting the idea of natives as private land owners.

> PRAYER, that better measures may be adopted to secure [Indians] against the aggressions of unscrupulous speculators and adventurers; and that wherever it is possible they may receive well-established titles to their lands in severalty and be shielded by our laws.[56]

To pursue their agricultural plans for native groups, missionaries needed them to own their land. They were delighted to see Indians finally plant crops, only to be dismayed when whites usurped the property. Missionaries resented the lack of support from the governments, which allowed whites to seize native land. In British Columbia, Thomas Crosby complained that "where the Indians have cleared potato-patches, white men have been allowed to come in and pre-empt these patches, and secure government titles for them." The Indians were then "driven off—driven from the very lands they had themselves cleared and cultivated."[57] The agriculture-based native communities that missionaries had helped create disappeared as the Canadian and U.S. governments bowed to the tide of white immigration and settlement.

As will be discussed in more detail in the next chapter, Protestant missionaries shifted the focus of their writing at the end of the nineteenth century from discussion of the wretched Indians to criticism of government policies and expansion of their role as scholars. Their criticism of the governments grew directly out of their crumbling relationship with elected officials. Between 1880 and 1900, the close ties between the missionaries and the governments unraveled. Many missionaries chastised the governments for introducing new policies that hampered their work and limited their success. The governments responded by promptly curtailing funds to missions and in some cases, even closing them. Others complained about their reduced role in creating policy on the frontier, as the governments instituted policies that excluded the missionaries. Some expressed outrage for both reasons. Canadian and U.S. Protestant missionaries watched their efforts waste away.

Though missionaries worked hard to implement a humane Indian policy, their time ran out. Their governments herded native groups onto reservations and reserves, limiting Indians' freedom and their ability to survive.

INVENTING THE "REDEEMABLE SAVAGE"

As the frontier began to close, the stakes rose for missionaries who believed in justice for the natives. Missionaries realized that if they were to influence and participate in creating a humane native policy, they needed to change the attitudes of the Canadian and American governments and public. Based on ideas gathered from books and popular culture, John Maclean was well aware of how most people viewed the natives: as wretched Indians. After all, he pointed out, readers and policymakers "studied them (natives) from the standpoint of the white man, ignorant of the beautiful languages and traditions, the significant religious ideas, social and political customs, and the native independence and heroism of the dwellers of the wilderness."[58] And as he wrote in 1896 in *Canadian Savage Folk,* "when they [settlers] gazed upon the red men and women, and found the glowing descriptions of prairie life and red men did not agree with the actual vision, . . . there came a revulsion of feeling and hatred dwelt where the romantic ideal had formerly reigned."[59] It became apparent to many missionaries at the end of the nineteenth century that they needed to dissuade the public of the idea that, as Maclean defined it, "red men" were "savages" and "that wisdom was the heritage of the white race."[60] Maclean and others set out to disabuse the public of their belief in one civilization.

As the reserve and the reservation systems became permanent, settlers took control of the Canadian and U.S. frontiers and the governments attempted to separate themselves from mission work. Missionaries in the two countries realized that their governments planned to let the Indians wither and die on the reservations, without the salvation of Christianity. Protestant missionaries needed to prove that the Indians' survival was important and that their work played a pivotal role in this survival. Without natives who needed help, missions would no longer be necessary and missionaries would stop being influential.

To protect their missions, then, missionaries continued to invoke white guilt over the Indians' downfall. In a speech written in 1901, J. D. Mullins patiently explained that contact with white Canadians and Americans had changed the Indian "with his great plume of feathers and his bead covered costume" into someone who is "dependent upon the Trader for everything he wears, and accordingly . . . appears in dirty ill-fitting attempts at European costume." Mullins laid the blame on Canadians and Americans for the destruction of the noble savage, saying that "the godless white men have taught the Indian the white man's vice in addition to his own." These words again raise the image of the wretched Indian. But in an effort to reiterate the positive aspects of mission work, he commented that "civilization has not been a blessing to the Indian where it has come to him apart from the Gospel."[61] Mullins built on the ideas of both the noble savage and the wretched Indian as he tried to lead readers to accept the image of the redeemable savage and establish missionaries as authorities on the Indians. Missionaries hoped such writing would force the governments to limit the number of settlers and use missions to keep Indians from harm. They wanted their native congregations protected, and many wanted to return to or maintain their roles as negotiators for and advisors to the native groups and the governments.

Despite the best efforts of Protestant missionary authors, the idea of the noble savage continued to appear, even in missionary literature. Missionaries and other religious writers condemned the literati, who still portrayed the Indian as a noble savage, covered in fine leathers and with a regal bearing, but a wild creature of nature nonetheless. They wrote their own scholarly works to counter these images. In an 1880 history of native groups and missions, author S. C. Bartlett emphasized the difficult job of the missionaries. He declared that "the rough savage whom the missionaries found was quite a different person from the sentimental red men. . . ."[62] Even at this late date, missionaries and religious writers still sought to justify the missionaries' failures by explaining how different the Indians they encountered were from common perceptions. Yet, missionaries themselves refused to totally abandon the powerful image of the noble savage, which was a valuable recruiting tool. It provided potential missionaries with the idea that the noble savage was redeemable and resonated with the Canadian and American public. Protestant missionary authors simply modified it to specific groups of Indians. But they recognized also that if Canadian and American audiences believed Indians had no redeemable qualities, they might dismiss them as not worth saving, thus ending missionary work among native groups.

Canadian and U.S. missionaries began to realize that previous writings had inspired fear and loathing of Indians among the white population in the two countries. Their efforts to quell this backlash came too late, and two views of the Indians surfaced in the public eye. Egerton Ryerson Young aptly described them in his work of fiction, *Stories from Indian Wigwams and Northern Campfires:* "By some they have been painted in the darkest colors, as possessing every characteristic of fiends without a redeeming feature; and if these chroniclers could have their own way the stronger nations would long ago have civilized them off the face of the earth."[63] This description appears to depict a version of the wretched Indian. Young then writes that others described Indians as dwellers in "the land of Arcadian simplicity and innocence . . . , where the inhabitants were without a vice or defect, and in possession of all those excellencies which make up the perfect ideal character . . ."[64] Here, Young invokes the image of the noble savage. These two images clashed continually not only in the minds of missionaries, who were conflicted about the ideas even in the later crisis years of funding reductions, but also in the minds of white Canadians and Americans. Young played a major role in creating the romantic image of Indians, with seventeen novels to his credit. The first line in *Stories from Indian Wigwams and Northern Campfires* goes: "Around none of the subdivisions of the great human family does there cluster more than the romantic and picturesque than that which is associated with the North American Indian."[65] Despite the fact that he worked only with the Cree, through his fiction Young still projected the idea that he understood and knew all native groups.

Missionaries were not the only ones who were affected by these conflicting ideas about natives. An 1890 article in the *Toronto Globe* exclaimed:

> Too long have the good people of this Province been neglectful of all pertaining to the life history of its aborigines. Our ideas of Indians are, in the main, drawn either from races of the Cooperian stamp, or from the wretched specimens of the race that are occasionally seen on the borders of civilized territory. Nothing is more certain than that the untutored savage was very different from both these types.[66]

As the quote illustrates, for a long time the public had two images of the Indian: the noble savage of Cooperian stamp and the wretched Indian on the borders of civilized territory. But now came the idea that a wholly different kind of Indian existed. Accordingly, journalists and researchers sought to discover the "true Indian" through the scholarly reports and ethnographic works of missionaries and others. Missionaries, needing to recapture the interest and support of the public and the governments, jumped on the idea of the redeemable savage. Some missionaries reacted to the withdrawal of government support by criticizing government policy, while others set out to join the scholarly world to identify the true Indian and find the one group of redeemable savages (preferably the group with which the missionary worked). Some missionaries combined the two pursuits by criticizing the governments' treatment of the redeemable savage. But as more and more information about natives became available, the image of the Indian broke into different renditions concerning individual groups of natives. The new, mutated images of the redeemable savage emerged in an effort to convince Canadian and American societies that specific Indians deserved respect and consideration.

The new image of the redeemable savage combined elements from the noble savage and the wretched Indian. It united the belief in the redeemability of the noble savage with the acceptable flaws from the wretched Indian. But unlike those previous images, missionaries applied the idea of the redeemable savage to specific native groups. For example, to missionaries who worked with the Sioux, that tribe suddenly became the only one worth assimilating and saving from extinction. Thus, when discussing Indians, Canadian and U.S. missionary authors tried to avoid using broad categorizations that could be disputed or disproved by specific images that already existed. The redeemable savage and its narrow focus allowed Protestant missionaries to present themselves as experts on specific groups of Indians who they believed had the necessary qualifications for salvation.

Even the most hackneyed Canadian and U.S. writers launched the idea that there were differences among the North American native groups. Overwhelmingly, though, the authors used the same terminology, "noble savage" versus "wretched Indian," to describe the groups, only fragmenting the image of the Indian, not discrediting it. Writers often mixed the popular images of Indians, appealing to the preconceptions held by Canadian and American audiences. Authors who culled information from missionary reports were particularly guilty of mixing ideas. Belle M. Brain, author of *The Redemption of the Red Man,* stated that "physically and intellectually the Dakotas stood very high," but she also demeaned them as "ignorant and superstitious, and sunk in the lowest heathenism."[67] By combining the idea of the tall, handsome noble savage with that of the ignorant, superstitious wretched Indian, writers continued to pit the two stereotypes against each other, leading to the creation of the redeemable savage.

As more and more Canadian and U.S. Protestant missionaries took up anthropological and ethnographic pursuits, they spent more time cataloging the customs and ideas of different native groups. They edged away from broad terms such as "Indian" and concentrated on discussing specific groups. By focusing on customs, missionaries like Edward Francis Wilson tried to get Canadian and American audiences interested in native groups, hoping to gain support for their protection. In an issue of his pro-native newsletter, *The Canadian Indian,* Wilson emphasized the importance of Indians as part of human history, tying native cultures to ancient civilizations. He bemoaned that "it will be too late when another half century has rolled by to regret the neglect of a collection of Indian lore, and oral traditions, such as those which form the basis of Greek and Roman history, and the race which for thousands of years trod this continent . . ." Here, Wilson invokes the idea of the redeemable savage with a glorious culture worth saving. He then implied that eventually only the image of the wretched Indian would remain, the image of the Indian that white Canadians and Americans ruined: "The recollection of them [Indians] will only be that of the degraded savage, contaminated by the vices of the lowest class of white men, surrounded by squalor and dependent upon charity for his scanty food." Finally, he alluded to the original noble savage concept, which when coupled with the tie to ancient civilization, impressed upon the reader that the Indians deserved to survive. Wilson declared that "the Indian in his manly pride, who first greeted Columbus, will be only a historical myth."[68] The strongest image from the reading, though, is that of the redeemable savage and its combination of elements from the noble savage and the wretched Indian. This article also shows how Wilson appealed to the guilt of Canadian and American societies by mentioning "the lowest class of white men." He relied on such appeals to persuade whites to support his cause of saving the Indians.

In the preface to his 1896 work *Canadian Savage Folk,* John Maclean focused on the richness and importance of native history in order to secure support for their protection. In the first part of the preface, he invokes an exotic image of the natives: "Hidden in the memories of the Red Men of Canada, there lie weird legends and strange stories of bygone years." He then progresses to the importance of natives to human history, stating that "the customs of our savage folk and the wealth of their languages and literature are interesting to us, as belonging to a people who were the pioneers of our land, and they open up a new world of myth, religion, and native culture." Unlike most early missionary translators, like Stephen Return Riggs, who portrayed Indian languages as "barren," Maclean describes the "wealth of their languages." At this point, Maclean appears to be depicting the redeemable savage, claiming that natives were "pioneers" of Canada. Maclean then attacks previous stereotypes of native cultures, declaring that "close contact with our native tribes show us the mistakes we have been making in deciding that ignorance, superstition and cruelty belong to these people, and that there is no wisdom, truth or beauty in their belief and manner of life." Of course, the "we" to whom he refers was largely composed of missionaries. It is also important to note that Maclean credits close contact with a better understanding of the natives, re-emphasizing the importance of missionaries. Finally, Maclean argues that natives are an important part of the human race, stating that "a faithful study of the languages and customs compels us to acknowledge that there are deeper truths than facts, and under the blanket and coat of skin there beats a human heart, as there is beauty, sweetness and wisdom in their [Indians] traditions and courage, liberty and devotion in their lives."[69] This last statement neatly illustrates the idea of the redeemable savage. While "courage, liberty and devotion" were holdovers from early descriptions of the noble savage, Maclean's use of the word "wisdom" to describe their traditions implies they are redeemable, not unlike other ancient civilizations that became Christians.

Actually, throughout his preface, Maclean emphasizes the wisdom of the natives and the depth of their literature, stories, poems, and so forth. These cultural items proved they were like whites, and therefore worth redeeming. Or as Myron Eells declared in his work, *Ten Years of Missionary Work Among the Indians at Skokomish, Washington Territory, 1874–1884,* "There is much of human nature in [the Indians]."[70] The comments of Wilson, Maclean, and Eells stand out from those in other missionary writings. Prior to the 1880s, few missionaries or racial theorists had strongly embraced North American natives as part of the human race. Wilson, Maclean, and Eells not only embraced them but attempted to argue their importance to humankind.

Missionary writings began to reflect these new attitudes toward Indians. The wretched Indian faded and the redeemable savage, with his strong character and powerful customs but misguided ways, appeared. In another of his newsletters, Wilson listed reasons why the Indian was interesting:

> that there appear to be in the Red Indian latent signs of a former greatness, a remarkable self-composure and dignity of manner and readiness to adapt himself to his surroundings, and to behave with the greatest propriety and self-possession, even though translated suddenly from the wigwam to the palace.[71]

Wilson, Maclean, Eells, and others tried to balance their views between assimilation and preservation. In his writings, Wilson implied that natives adapted well to new cultures, yet they inherently possessed qualities worth keeping—qualities admired by Canadian and American societies. Balancing old and new images became standard in missionary texts. The new redeemable savage became a rationalized version of the old images of the Indians, a civilized being ravaged by the uncivilized white man, and a national treasure and aesthetic object worth saving.

As the frontier closed, many missionaries hoped white attitudes toward Indians would soften. Unfortunately, the stereotype of the violent Indian persisted, despite the lack of evidence to support it. As historian of religion Martin Marty accurately states, the "more positive appraisals could never catch up with or counteract the original, more negative pictures that had already come to be accepted."[72] The romantic idea of the dangerous savage endured, even though it was an unrealistic image.

By the late nineteenth century, as Canadian and U.S. native policy reached a crisis, missionaries started to recognize that the images of natives conflicted. They also began to push more intently for preservation of Indians and their rights. In fighting for preservation, missionaries raised specific groups of natives as representatives of certain redeemable aspects of the human race and placed the blame for the degradation of these "savages" on the shoulders of white society. The redeemable savage image portrayed the Indians as remnants of some glorious past civilization that had been degraded by white society and was patiently waiting for help from the missionaries, the government, and the public. Missionaries accused the Canadian and U.S. governments and secular writers of promoting ideas of white superiority. They conveniently forgot that generations of missionaries had provided both secular and religious audiences with many of their ideas about native cultures in the first place.

The concept of the redeemable savage resulted from an effort by missionaries to force the Canadian and U.S. governments and populace to deal more equitably with native groups. Protestant missionaries tried to get involved in the debate about the Indians' future, while still protecting their own role on the frontier. Unfortunately, it was too late for such efforts. By the 1890s and early 1900s, the Canadian and U.S. governments had terminated their relationships with missionaries. Missionaries no longer acted as agents or advisors to the governments. It became apparent around this time also that despite the best efforts of missionary writers, the concept of the wretched Indian remained central in the minds of white Canadians and Americans. Reverend W. Arthur Burman, who worked with the Sioux in Manitoba, addressed this issue in his unpublished work from the 1930s, "Indian Work of the United Church of Canada." Burman acknowledged that, with a few exceptions, ordinary Indians were still wretched: "The historian and the missionary make it quite clear that while there were outstanding noble characters such as Joseph Brant and Tecumseh the rank and file of the Indian Tribes from coast to coast were aboriginal savages in spirit and in life." In this statement, he uses language representative of the noble savage image. He goes on to say that "this statement is no reflection upon the people into whose country we came but it forms a contrast which, in the light of conditions that exist in the native settlements today, throw great credit on them for the progress [toward assimilation into white society] which they have made."[73] Burman dismisses previous derogatory statements about the Indians, implying they are good people beneath their savage exterior. He then praises them for seeing the light and making tremendous efforts to integrate themselves into white society. Burman's statement captures the essence of the redeemable savage image. Even at this late date, both the secular and religious public felt that the savage or wretched Indian had once existed, having been redeemed only by Christianity. While Canadians and Americans blamed missionaries and other writers for propagating these images, they nonetheless accepted them.

Three concerns shaped the way Protestant missionaries portrayed the Indians in the last twenty years of the nineteenth century. First, missionaries faced the aftermath of rapidly expanding frontier settlement. Second, they dealt with Canadian and U.S. government policies that increasingly began to mirror each other. Third, missionaries in both countries found themselves at the end of their financial and political relationships with the governments. These pressures pushed Protestant missionaries to take significant action. Both Canadian and American missionaries quickly became severe critics of their governments' policies toward native groups. They attacked policies that legislated immediate assimilation. They complained about how little policymakers understood the Indians' situation and their responses to white settlement and policy changes. And missionaries accused the governments of allowing and encouraging the misuse of funds earmarked for native groups. These criticisms and complaints helped shape the final image of the Indians—the redeemable savage—as missionaries turned to one last group for financial support: secular research institutions.

CHAPTER SEVEN

"We Are All Savages"

A S THE CANADIAN and U.S. governments reduced financial support to Protestant missionaries toward the end of the nineteenth century, missionaries began to rely more heavily on assistance from the general public. During this time, missionaries also turned to scholarly research institutions and learned societies to help further their work. Just as they had when embarking on lecture tours and seeking to get earlier secular articles printed, missionaries crossed the Canadian-U.S. border in search of publication space and financial assistance in the late 1800s. As more and more missionaries presented their work in both countries on specific groups of redeemable savages, the border between Canada and the United States—along with the discrepancy between Canadian and U.S. missionaries' views on Indians—virtually disappeared. More missionaries published in scholarly journals as opposed to religious ones, helping their ideas become institutionalized across the border.

Even as Canadian and U.S. Indian policies became more similar than different, the imagery of Indians created by missionaries in each country merged faster, quickly producing one image of Indians: that of redeemable savages. Missionaries used this image to argue that specific native groups needed to be protected, effectively preserving some missions in the West from white encroachment. Though the dissolution of their relationships with the missionary societies and governments made the missionaries more autonomous, it also marginalized them. And though missionaries in both countries perceived Canadian and U.S. policies to be different, their own positions remained indistinguishable from each other.

THE ROAD TO THE SCHOLARLY LIFE

Missionaries reacted to the changes in Canadian and U.S. Indian policy in two ways. As previously discussed, some missionaries became highly and visibly critical of Indian policy in the two countries. Others redirected their efforts within the scholarly world. With the governments and missionary societies providing less and less support, missionaries needed to find funding and legitimacy for their work. Moving into the world of scholarship helped. Secular research institutions allowed missionaries to continue working on the frontier by giving them grants and valuing their opinions and information on the Indians.

In 1880, John Maclean rode across the Canadian prairie under very different circumstances than those of his predecessors. He had some financial and political support from his government, rather than having to rely solely on the Methodist Missionary Society. His missionary society no longer defined his role on the frontier. His superior, John McDougall, was negotiating treaties for the Canadian government as well as overseeing missions. Maclean and his contemporaries balanced their work to meet the requirements of their missionary societies and an increasingly secularized Canadian and U.S. public.

Nine years later, John Maclean—minus the entanglements of the Methodist Missionary Society—returned from the frontier as an anthropologist. He had reinvented himself as a scholar of native peoples. In his first book after his career change, *The Indians: Their Manners and Customs,* Maclean described his new position. Whereas most Protestant missionaries made some mention in their writings of their sponsoring missionary society, Maclean did not. Though the Methodist Missionary Society published many of his works, Maclean carefully deleted any overt references to their sponsorship of his nine years of "study." He wrote simply, "Nine years spent among the Blood Indians of the Canadian North-West, studying their language, customs, mythology, and traditions, have given me opportunities of learning much that may prove interesting to young and old."[1] And in fact, by mentioning that after three years, "I was requested to send information on the North-West tribes to the British Association, the Smithsonian Institution, and other learned societies,"[2] he implied that his purpose on the frontier had been scholarly and not spiritual.

In addition to his struggle over the scholarly and spiritual worlds, Maclean struggled to redefine the Indians, both in his own terms and in terms of what Canadian and American audiences expected and demanded. On the one hand, by declaring that "many of the books written [on natives] were of a sensational character,"[3] Maclean railed against previous missionaries and fiction writers such as James Fenimore Cooper. On the other hand, in his desire to write "something that would be reliable and at the same time, interesting to all,"[4] he himself blurred the line between entertainment and scholarship. While he recognized the need to engage the reader by playing upon existing stereotypes, Maclean also wanted to temper the sensationalist view of the wretched Indian with an objective, informative account. In his work, *The Indians,* he wrote that "the strange life of the dwellers in the lodges, the wonderful mythology and traditions, and the peculiar customs which are essentially their own, reveal to us a civilization that is fascinating and yet but little understood."[5] Here Maclean employed—as he often did—broad, descriptive terms to depict the lives of the natives. While he played up the exotic aspects of the Indians, Maclean also tried to portray them as redeemable savages, and thus a civilization that needed to be understood. This attempt to establish native groups as civilized was a shift from previous efforts that focused on the Indians' lack of civilization. Maclean's new audiences in the general public and the scholarly world helped shape his view. Whereas the missionaries of past years had relied on emotion to draw financial support, Maclean, as he straddled the roles of missionary, government informer, and scholar, relied on ethnographic interpretation and fact to prove the worthiness of the native. Maclean thus reinvented the Indians, as he declared their culture a "civilization," a term previously unconnected with the North American natives.

In the nine years Maclean spent on the western frontier, many changes occurred in the field of missionary work. As discussed in the previous chapter, missionary societies continued to reduce financial support to their missions. Consequently, missionaries forged stronger and more binding ties with government agencies, though they later came apart. These relationships had come with advantages and disadvantages. Because of them, missionary writings and lectures began to reach broader sections of Canadian and American societies and to compete more openly with each other. But also they had restricted the missionaries' freedom, as the governments made certain demands of them.

Also during this nine-year period, the tides of settlers onto both the Canadian and U.S. frontiers changed how the two countries' governments regarded missionary work. The settlers demanded a secure frontier, and so the governments pressured the missionaries to increase their pacification of the western lands. As Maclean acknowledged, "The Indian is suffered to exist, but he is regarded as an encumbrance to the country and a strong barrier to its speedy development."[6] Former and present missionaries became more vocal in their criticism of the governments and more willing to recognize the tenuous position of natives on the frontier. Native policy approached an ultimatum: it would steer toward either the assimilation or extinction of the Indians. In 1890, Edward Francis Wilson voiced his thoughts on the subject: "The Indian [Problem] is fraught with difficulties, and as settlement advances in our western territories, . . . the remnants of that race will year by year be more squeezed out, till the reservations even will be absorbed."[7] In the missionaries' minds, the extermination of the natives changed from an abstract idea to a real possibility. This frightening new prospect, combined with the governments' reduction of support, threatened the missionaries' position on the frontier.

Missionaries needed to make a place for themselves in the debate over the Indians if they were to influence government policy and public opinion and thus maintain support for their work. The two governments had become the primary sources of funding for missionary work in the 1860s and 1870s, but now sought to reduce that funding in the 1880s and 1890s. The missionaries needed the governments to consider them as part of the solution to the Indian Problem in order to guarantee funding for and survival of the missions. Also, they still needed the public's financial support and now they hoped that citizens would pressure the governments to include missionaries in policymaking decisions. After all, the missionaries had spent fifty years creating ties and building support with first the literate Christian public and later a secular one.

But times had changed and the methods for securing support needed to change as well. The success of lecture tours in the 1850s had produced an unexpected benefit. Men like William Duncan of Canada and Cyrus Byington of the United States had crisscrossed the two countries to raise awareness of and money for their missions. During their travels, many missionaries made contact with secular institutions like universities, historical societies, and other research organizations. In the 1850s and 1860s, these institutions provided money to publish specific works written by missionaries. Such funds were minimal, but they made missionaries feel like legitimate authorities on the Indians. In his autobiography, Stephen Return Riggs bragged about how the Minnesota Historical Society was interested in publishing his dictionary; he felt that their interest proved his value to institutions other than his own sponsoring missionary society.[8] By the 1880s, more and more scholarly institutions were publishing missionary works. In his 1888 edition of *A Grammar of the Kwagiutl Language,* Canadian Alfred James Hall thanked G. M. Dawson of the United States Geological Survey for recommending that he publish his work with the Royal Society of Canada.[9] At a time when their own missionary societies and governments viewed them as failures, missionaries mitigated the criticism by believing that scholarly institutions desired their knowledge.

By the 1880s, missionaries began to rely on the funds that secular institutions provided to help further their mission work. Many missionaries also worked as interpreters or intermediaries for folklorists, ethnologists, and anthropologists, hoping to be reimbursed for their efforts. Missionaries like Stephen Return Riggs and Edward Francis Wilson published the results of their research in scholarly journals and contracted to do more articles to support their mission work.[10] Secular publications exposed these articles to new audiences and established missionaries as Indian experts in the minds of the literate public.

With this expertise came responsibility. For missionaries like Maclean, Myron Eells, Kate McBeth, and Edward Francis Wilson, emotional appeals in their writing became a thing of the past and a more scientific, authoritative voice appeared. This new voice allowed them to pursue three goals, as stated by historian Curtis Hinsley: to influence a more efficient and humane policy, to gain better knowledge of civilization through study of its antecedent forms, and to procure permanent financial support for their work.[11] Bishop John Horden described how, as "that state of simple innocence in which we now exist" disappeared, missionary writings began to leave the world of sensationalism and enter the world of scholarship in hopes of achieving these goals.[12] But even as missionary articles turned more scholarly and factual, the public remained enamored with the images of the noble savage and the wretched Indian, which had become familiar during the last fifty years.

The transition from missionary to scholar was not an easy one. It was full of contradictions and battles between past and present ideas. The literate public had accepted the idea of the wretched Indian; as discussed previously, they had opened their wallets willingly to support struggling missionaries. Now missionaries needed to prove to the Canadian and U.S. governments and the public that despite the low conversion rates, they had gained something on the frontier— knowledge. Maclean struggled mightily with these issues, as was reflected in his writings about native women. In *The Indians: Their Manners and Customs,* he decried the degraded position of women among the tribes "who have not accepted the civilization resulting from the gospel of the Nazarene."[13] Even though Maclean recognized the existence of Indian civilizations, he still ranked Christian civilization as superior. But he also claimed that "some native confederacies have given her [the woman] a position of equality, while she has become the sole arbiter of those things belonging to her own sex and family."[14] Here Maclean presents some valuable aspects of native societies. Of course, he sees admirable traits only where they mirror those of white Christians. These conflicting ideas—believing that the Indians needed civilization while at the same time proclaiming the existence of a vibrant native culture—caused tension and debate between those who thought the old stereotypes of the Indians were accurate and those who now saw them as redeemable savages.

Many missionary scholars wrestled with these contradictory viewpoints. Even as they moved toward more informative, objective writing during the 1880s and 1890s, sensationalist elements continued to invade their articles. Edward Francis Wilson, creator of the pro-native paper *The Canadian Indian* and a leader of the missionary scholarly movement in Canada, desperately tried to convince the Canadian populace that Indians needed to be preserved. Unfortunately, Wilson remained steeped in tales of the wretched Indian that permeated writings of the time. In the 1890 edition of *The Canadian Indian* he too reprinted William Duncan's story of cannibalism, full of descriptions of wretched, animal-like Indians.

While attempting to be scholarly, Wilson revisited the animalistic image of the wretched Indian because it still resonated with the public. In the 1890 edition of his newspaper, Wilson began an article by stating that "it will be too late in another half century . . . to regret the neglect of a collection of Indian lore, and oral traditions" that "form the basis of Greek and Roman history." However, he quickly slipped into the jargon that equated natives with wild animals. He declared that Indians would "be known only in the same way as the bison, which has so suddenly disappeared."[15] After providing an overview of the Tshimshian Indians, their clan system, progress toward civilization, fishing, beliefs, and language, Wilson launched into Duncan's story of their cannibalism, a "horrible scene" that "used to be far from infrequent."[16] Again, two bands of "furious wretches" appeared, led by a man who "walked with high steps like a proud horse." As in all other versions, when they sighted the corpse, they rushed "around it like so many angry wolves." Though the story was supposedly about only the Tshimshian Indians, and Wilson followed the pattern of most writings on the redeemable savage by not mentioning other native groups, the consistent use of animal metaphors and racist concepts helped readers conjure up horrific images and fed into their preconceived ideas of Indians. In this way, many missionaries attempted to bridge the gap between the wretched Indian and the redeemable savage: by merging successful elements from the two ideas into a new form of the redeemable savage.

During the same period in the United States, Myron Eells recorded parts of this same story of cannibalism in his notebook on the Puget Sound natives. Eells succeeded where others had failed. He carefully had recorded the incidents of cannibalism, separating events that he had witnessed from those he had only heard about. He wrote that *"it is said* that formerly two slaves laughed at the pe formances (of the medicine men), whereupon they were immediately torn into pieces and eaten."[17] Additionally, Eells differentiated between true canni-balism—eating a body—and ritual cannibalism—simply biting people. The Tshimshian fell into the latter category, as they "bit pieces out of living persons in some of their savage orgies."[18] Despite Eells's care and accuracy, he failed to resist employing terms such as "savage orgies" to illustrate his point. (Wilson's ac-count erred on this level as well.) Despite his use of suggestive terms, on the whole Eells avoided traditional portrayals. His relatively objective and informa-tive piece came that much closer to portraying the Indians as redeemable savages. The language of wretchedness lent itself to such discussions, tying the re-deemable savage to past images of the Indians.

The redeemable savage idea conceptualized Indians as remnants of some past glorious civilization that had been degraded by whites and was patiently waiting for help from the missionaries, the government, and the public. The image of the redeemable savage built on the images of the noble savage and the wretched In-dian, both of which continued to exist. From the noble savage, this new image bor-rowed the belief that the Indians had admirable qualities worth preserving. From the wretched Indian, it took the idea that white intrusion had degraded native so-cieties. And by suggesting that the natives needed help, the image of redeemable savages created a place for missionaries and their work in future Indian policy.

While the missionaries wanted to continue their work of saving the natives from their state of sinfulness, they now realized that this argument was not enough. Therefore, missionaries used their roles as authorities and scholars to contend that the preservation of native groups was necessary for the greater good of the nation. Missionaries had to balance their own desire to keep working with the Indians, the governments' need to pacify the frontier, and the public's re-quirement that the Indians serve some purpose, either psychological, symbolic, or political. Missionaries mitigated these different goals by suggesting that a pre-served native civilization could be the linchpin for comparing the successes or failures of Canadian or American society and their own level of civilization. They thought that Indians could become the barometer of civilization in Canada and the United States.

The transition to scholarly writing occurred slowly. Missionaries still relied on their earlier writings to raise public interest and support. Therefore, they could not just reject the ideas in their previous works and expect readers to embrace the new image of redeemable Indians. Hence, they mixed their metaphors, balancing the exotic, romantic natives with the traditional, worthy ones.

Indeed, few missionaries totally abandoned sensationalist writings. Even Maclean, who purged himself of his missionary past, later wrote pieces solely for entertainment that attracted a more secular audience. In 1896, seven years after leaving mission work, he published a book of stories about life among the Indians. Like most fiction written by missionaries, cultural lessons about Indians filled the book. He took the opportunity to reiterate ideas he had stressed in his scholarly works, perhaps hoping to influence the general public with them. In his story "Asokoa, the Chief's Daughter," he repeated a statement about women from *The Indians: Their Manners and Customs:*

> Women had not always been degraded, for in the early years of the history of the Indians she had held equal rights with the men, those of each sex performing their own duties and being honored by the other for the possession of sterling qualities essentially their own.[19]

While portraying the natives in a fictional, adventurous setting, Maclean nonetheless attempted to correct the romantic vision that he thought inhabited just such works. Yet lurid accounts of kidnapping, treachery, and other misdeeds cheapened his own work and emphasized the wretchedness of the Indians by portraying their lives as unpredictable and uncivilized.

There are several examples of the gradual shift in missionary portrayals of the Indians from wretched to redeemable.[20] By trying to create an image that mixed exoticism, hope, and aspects of the Indian character that were worth saving, these writers reworked an old idea. They maintained that native cultures were worthy or redeemable, while acknowledging that the Indians still needed help and direction from a slightly superior group. To make this new imagery more palatable to Canadian and U.S. audiences, they focused on small groups of natives, such as nations, tribes, or language groups, hoping to add new dimensions to the public's conception of the Indians.[21] They struggled to reshape the image of Indians to attract interest and help protect their positions on the frontier.

Maclean's transformation from missionary to scholar was not uncommon. Myron Eells, Stephen Return Riggs, Thomas Crosby, Edward Francis Wilson, and others also made the transition. Myron Eells conducted censuses for the U.S. government, filled out questionnaires for the Centennial Exhibition, acted as an informant for the anthropologist Franz Boas, and published in the *American Anthropologist* and *Antiquarian.*[22] Riggs published with both the Smithsonian Institution and the Minnesota Historical Society as well as serving as an advisor to the Bureau of Ethnology.[23] Crosby, like Eells, supplied information to Franz Boas.[24] Wilson published in the *Journal of American Folklore* and worked for the Smithsonian in the American Southwest and for the Centennial Exhibition.[25] By the late nineteenth century, missionaries—whether out of financial need or simply interest—began to write works in the areas of anthropology, folklore, sociology, and history, boosting their status as experts and going beyond their previous publishing efforts. But none of these men made the transition from missionary to scholar without struggling with their own preconceived ideas. They battled the instinct to dismiss the North American natives as exotic or frightening, to reject them as stupid and unworthy.[26] In trying to examine native cultures objectively, missionaries sought to emphasize positive traits in order to counterbalance negative stereotypes, draw empathy from the white population, prove their worthiness to the governments, and secure financial support. They hoped that this approach would allow them to become an active part of making policy toward the natives more humane. The move to scholarly writing changed the image of the Indians but not without difficulty and not completely, as many Canadians and Americans still focused on the "wretched" aspects of the redeemable savage.

MISSIONARIES AS SCHOLARS

Just as the missionaries' funding crisis began in the 1850s, folklore, ethnology, and anthropology were blossoming into fields of study in Canada and the United States. Clergy, missionaries, and dilettantes embraced these new fields—which blended theology and science—and formed secular research institutions to explore them and to focus on explaining human diversity. Historian Curtis Hinsley comments that as the British and American empires exploded across a previously undiscovered world, scientists and theologians scrambled to try to explain the burgeoning diversity in their ever-expanding world.[27] These early researchers attempted to explain the origin of man, and focused much of their investigation around the monogenetic theory of human origin. Hinsley explains that "for pious Christians fully committed to human unity through the biblical account, historical inquiry backward through time promised to reconcile present diversity with single creation."[28] Missionaries and missionary societies gravitated toward the monogenetic theory. Missionaries in western North America supported this line of inquiry since they had spent decades trying to understand why Indians differed so from their preconceived ideas. Canadian and U.S. missionaries needed to understand the native groups with whom they worked in order to be more efficient in the process of conversion.

Indian cultures often became the focus of discussion and study for these new research institutions. By learning about the decline of Indian cultures, white Canadian and U.S. societies could measure their own level of civilization. Missionaries eagerly participated in this research, because it sought to link the origin of the Indians to that of all other humans. Missionaries could now assert that although Indians had drifted away from Christianity, they could be returned to it if they were enveloped by a Christian environment. This argument, coupled with the learned societies' fascination with the uniqueness of Indians, was the basis for a long-term relationship between secular research institutions and missionaries.[29]

When examining the birth of scholarly institutions and the role missionaries played in their creation, it is important to remember that in the 1850s and 1860s, religion and science remained comfortably intertwined. Specifically, this was true in three ways. First, theology often determined the lines of inquiry used to explore questions of human origin. Like all good scientists, the new folklorists, anthropologists, and ethnographers attempted to prove pre-existing theories. They also used the Bible as their theoretical handbook. Second, research institutions often viewed missionaries as their best source for analysis. Curtis Hinsley points out that "the familiarizing work of the missionaries advanced the tide of Christian fellowship," while "anthropology not only Christianized the heathen Indian but cleanse[d] the White of ignorance and prejudice."[30] The early scholarly institutions made no distinction between Christianity and science, unlike those in the twentieth century. Thus, from the 1850s through the 1870s, these establishments willingly acted as middlemen for missionaries on the frontier and scholars at universities.[31] Third, early anthropological, folklore, and ethnological work became associated with self-sacrifice and a willingness to go unrecognized, which were both considered to be qualities of a good Christian. Or as Hinsley puts it, "In the middle of the nineteenth century, being a scientist in America was still a matter of character and integrity as well as one of the specific academic or laboratory training."[32] Protestant missionaries fit this description and often had already proved themselves after years of unrecognized toil in their field. Thus, the goals of the secular research institutions mirrored those of the missionary societies, and later, the missionaries.

Stephen Return Riggs was one of the first missionaries to begin working with a scholarly association. In *Mary and I,* Riggs fondly remembered his first brush with the scholarly world: "It was about the beginning of the year 1851 when the question of publication [of his Dakota Dictionary] was first discussed. Certain gentlemen in the Legislature of Minnesota, and connected with the Historical Society of Minnesota, became interested in the matter."[33] Eventually, Riggs became one of the foremost linguistic experts for the Bureau of Ethnology.[34] Thus Riggs began a fruitful relationship with various scholarly and governmental institutions. Riggs, one of the primary experts on the Dakotas and translators of their language, used these connections throughout his career to publish his works and fund his research and conversion efforts.[35] Publication with the scholarly organizations rather than with missionary societies led to a broader audience.

In the 1870s and 1880s, there was another boom in the foundation of learned societies.[36] Many of these new institutions, particularly those that specialized in folklore and anthropology, sought to explain how society progressed toward modernity. As historian Simon Bronner explains, "Folklore studies helped to answer how civilization had progressed, measured in middle-class material and technical terms. It answered how 'mechanilized' modern man came to be."[37] Studying the "dying" Indian cultures was important, then, because it provided a window into why one society survived and another did not.

The 1870s and 1880s also led to the professionalization of the fields of anthropology, ethnography, and folklore away from the gentleman scholar and toward the dedicated authority. Rather than excluding missionaries, though, this development led to their deeper involvement with the learned societies. These experts saw missionaries on the frontier as professionals because of their knowledge, dedication, and isolation. Bronner states, "In keeping with the attitude toward learning then, the societies promoted devotion to rather than the practice of, an esoteric, systematic body of knowledge. They called for an exclusive and independent circle of authorities, as a congress of 'scientists,' loosely defined, suggested."[38] Protestant missionaries fit this description. Their time on the frontier and their understanding of linguistics and ethnology designated them as professionals rather than amateurs.

Many Canadian and American missionaries jumped at the chance to discuss their work with others and to share their ideas with new audiences who might respect them for their depth of knowledge. Bishop William Hobart Hare of the Dakotas, Sheldon Jackson of Alaska, and J. Owen Dorsey of Iowa joined the American Folklore Society, which gave them the opportunity to correspond with other scholars.[39] William Duncan in British Columbia subscribed to the *American Antiquarian,* helping him keep current on ethnographic research.[40] Bishop

William Carpenter Bompas received the Smithsonian's annual reports.[41] And Canadian missionary John Black became a member of the Minnesota Historical Society in 1853.[42] These subscriptions exposed the missionaries to scholars in the fields of folklore, anthropology, and ethnology as well as to other missionaries who worked in different regions. The many articles on Indians also inspired missionaries to submit their own work to these publications.

In the 1860s, missionaries began to submit their works to scholarly institutions. Gideon Pond published a piece titled "Dakota Superstitions" in the *Collections of the Minnesota Historical Society*.[43] In the 1880s, several missionaries burst onto the writing scene with a wide variety of scholarly articles. Canadian W. Arthur Burman published "The Sioux Language" in a publication for the Manitoba Historical and Scientific Society in 1883.[44] Four years later, Edward Francis Wilson published two articles in the journal of the British Association for the Advancement of Science.[45] In 1889, Alfred James Hall published "Grammar of the Kwagiutl Language" in the *Proceedings and Transactions of the Royal Society of Canada for the Year of 1888*.[46] Around this same time, John Maclean published "Blackfoot Indian Legends" and "Blackfoot Mythology" for the *Journal of American Folklore,* as well as an article called "The Blackfoot Sun Dance" for the Canadian Institution.[47] In the 1890s, Edward Francis Wilson used the *Journal of American Folklore* to publicize his "Canadian Indian Aid and Research Society," which attempted to raise funds for the defense and preservation of Indians.[48] And also in the 1890s, Myron Eells published an article on Indian doctors of the Puget Sound in *Antiquarian* and one on the Chinook jargon in the *American Anthropologist*.[49] Obviously, scholars accepted these missionaries as their equals.

In addition to writing articles, missionaries also made presentations at the meetings of these learned societies. In 1885, Myron Eells presented a paper to the Victoria Institute in Great Britain titled "The Worship and Traditions of the Aborigines of America; or, Their Testimony to the Religion of the Bible."[50] Eells's paper is particularly interesting because it demonstrates a blending of religious/theological topics and anthropological ones. Also, Edward Francis Wilson presented a paper on the British Columbian Kootenay at the annual meeting of the American Folklore Society in 1890, helping him to develop contacts with folklorists like Franz Boas, with whom he shared information.[51]

Associations with scholarly institutions legitimated many missionaries' work. By humbly referring to the interest that both British and American organizations showed in his work, John Maclean impressed readers with his transnational scholarly credentials. The same held true for Eells and others; their connection with scholarly institutions provided their work with the authenticity previously denied them.

By publishing with research institutions, missionaries added other scholars to their readership. Riggs's publication of his dictionary through the Smithsonian made it available not only to church groups but also to secular audiences. These scholarly organizations provided both guidelines for publication and editors. Reported the American Board of Commissioners for Foreign Missions, "The work [on the Dakota lexicon] has been executed in admirable style, under the auspices of the Smithsonian Institute [*sic*]."[52] By publishing dictionaries, lexicographies, and articles, the scholarly organizations removed a great financial burden from the missionary societies. At the same time, they also decreased the missionary societies' control over the content of these works. Missionaries had more freedom to speculate on racial origins, cultural traditions, and other Indian-related issues. Many missionaries continued to produce fiction and biographies in addition to their intellectual pieces, in order to keep the public interested. They continued to promote the idea of the wretched Indian while also trying to create the new image of the redeemable savage.

The scholarly institutions benefited, too, from publishing missionaries' work. Though often they could defray the costs of missions, these organizations could not afford to send their own men onto the entire frontier. Missionaries did the fieldwork, therefore, just as they had for the governments. Often they performed other duties for the institutions as well, such as filling out questionnaires, completing censuses, and investigating rumored events of incest, cannibalism, and exotic rituals.[53] In 1877, Myron Eells filled out a questionnaire based on interviews with natives for the "Indian Bureau for the Centennial Exhibition and the Smithsonian Institution." He was allowed to add a comment to the study of native demographics, and so wrote that "if it is of any value, it is not altogether because it describes the Indian[s] under their old native habits and customs, but because it gives an account of them in a state of *transition* from their native wildness to civilization."[54] Even in his scholarly work, Eells pushed for recognition of missionary achievements.

These questionnaires often covered everything from average height and weight to accepted sexual practices, and the answers missionaries gave told as much about them as about the natives. The questionnaire completed by Eells requested physical descriptions, as well as information concerning "Rights and Wrongs" and "Surroundings and Environment." Throughout his answers, Eells used whites as the standard of comparison. For example, under "Muscular

Strength," Eells wrote that Indians were "quite inferior to the white man."[55] The redeemable savage construct fulfilled the role of providing a comparison point for whites in Canada and the United States. Despite attempts to be scholarly and objective, all of their writings became a contest between whites and natives, which was not unusual. As historian Robert Berkhofer Jr. points out, "Whites overwhelmingly measured the Indians as a general category against those beliefs, values, or institutions they most cherished themselves at the time."[56] In Eells's work even "Reproductive Powers" were deemed "much less than whites" without considering what the reasons for or consequences of such an assertion might be. That these attributes were even being studied is significant. It shows that the image of the Indian was slowly moving away from the exotic native to the more mundane idea of an everyday person, or, as Curtis Hinsley describes it, from "historical actor to aesthetic object."[57]

Many scholars relied on missionaries to act as go-betweens on the frontier. Franz Boas utilized missionary connections when he embarked on a research trip to the northwest Pacific coast of Canada. He met with W. H. Collison, William Duncan, John Booth Good, and Alfred James Hall in his travels.[58] All of these missionaries later published their own accounts of the Indians of the Northwest Pacific Coast. Collison wrote a famous book, *In the Wake of the War Canoe: A Stirring Record of Forty Years' Successful Labour, Peril and Adventure amongst the Savage Indian Tribes of the Pacific Coast, and the Piratical Head-hunting Haida of the Queen Charlotte Islands, British Columbia,* that portrayed the Haida as vicious and savage. Duncan, while an advocate for the Indians, also produced exaggerated lectures on cannibalism among the Haida and Tshimshian. Missionaries were expert at manipulating their portrayals of Indians to fit the audience. In Canada, Myron Eells entertained traveling researchers while doing census work for the Smithsonian. He too produced a wide variety of works, changing his depictions of natives to fit his many different audiences. And Kate McBeth, while writing her own history of the Nez Perce, worked as an informant to Alice Fletcher. Eventually, Alice Fletcher wrote the foreword for McBeth's 1908 book.[59] In this way, missionaries contributed to research institutions and shaped the way that future anthropologists and folklorists would see the Indians.

Nineteenth-century scholarly institutions were closely linked not only to missionaries themselves but also to their definitions of morality and ethics. Though the move away from emotional writing was difficult, missionaries were still able to pontificate on moral issues. In the "Rights and Wrongs" section of the census, Eells took advantage of this liberty in his examination of "chastity," "immoralities," and "Schoopanism [pederasty] and Sodomy." By his definitions, many natives were unchaste, and their immoralities were universal.[60] Eells consistently saw Indians through the lens of white Protestant Christian society, despite his attempts to view them objectively. Thus, scholarly writing continued to make constant comparisons between the superiority of Christian life and non-Christian life.

By the end of the nineteenth century, both Canadian and U.S. missionaries were crossing the transnational border to publish their work and secure support. Edward Francis Wilson worked in Ontario, but contributed heavily to U.S. scholarly publications. He also actively sought aid from U.S. scholarly institutions. In 1886, he met with Professor Baird and General Powell of the Smithsonian for this purpose.[61] His efforts paid off and in 1892 he helped them prepare for the Chicago Exposition. "On account of my acquaintance with so many Indian tribes the Smithsonian institution asked me to travel for them."[62] During his trip, Wilson measured natives' features and took samples of their hair, weapons, and other items of interest. Though not paid, Wilson felt that the assignment proved his knowledge, and he received a complete set of instruments and all expenses were covered.[63]

As more secular research institutions appeared, they also gave funds to mission work. The Royal Ethnographic Society, the American Anthropological Society, and the American Folklore Society, for example, all became patrons. Besides gaining missionaries some financial support, connections with secular institutions served two other purposes for them. First, they helped expose missionaries' work to a broader audience, allowing missionaries to solicit funds from outside their own regions and denominations. They no longer had to rely solely on the missionary societies or the governments for aid and publicity. The support of these scholarly institutions validated the missionaries' work, though not in the same way that the missionary societies and the governments had. Instead of praising their success in conversion, these organizations focused on missionaries' access to and knowledge of Indians. This kind of recognition allowed missionaries to press for a more humane government policy toward native groups. Second, the connections between research institutions and missionaries provided the latter with opportunities to meet folklorists and other scholars who needed them to act as translators or contacts on the frontier. With the backing of these societies, missionaries pursued work that deviated from religious and sensational writing and focused instead on positive aspects of native civilization that justified their continued presence on the frontier.

Throughout the nineteenth century, missionaries were a conduit for ideas and information between Canadian and U.S. institutions and native ones. The kind of information that missionaries gave changed as their relationships with the missionary societies, governments, and public changed. As the late nineteenth century approached, missionaries' location on the Canadian and U.S. frontiers allowed them access to details not available to scholars back east. Their contacts with natives made missionaries invaluable to institutions such as the Smithsonian and the British Association.[64] They provided enough information about Indians that the institutions did not have to hire and train their own field workers. The benefits for missionaries, of course, were financial support and the chance to pursue interests other than religious ones. As John Maclean wrote in 1889 in *The Indians: Their Manners and Customs*, "The works written concerning the Indians during the last century, and the early part of the present were confined chiefly to a narration of missionary effort among them, but many books of great value on American antiquities have sprung into existence . . ."[65] Without the patronage of the scholarly institutions, men such as Maclean, Wilson, Eells, and Stephen Return Riggs probably would not have pursued such academic works.

INDIANS AS AN ANCIENT CIVILIZATION

As more and more missionaries endeavored to make the transition into the scholarly world, their articles focused on aspects of native culture that paralleled aspects of what they considered to be civilized societies. Both Canadian and U.S. missionary writers tried to link native cultures to other "ancient" ones like those in Egypt, Israel, Wales, Ireland, and Scotland. Their efforts corresponded to the demise of sensationalist writing, as the Indians' history slowly became tied to that of the rest of the human race. Missionaries and scholars began to question and explain the origin of Indians as well as racial differences between the various groups they encountered.[66]

From the moment they arrived on the frontier, Canadian and American Protestant missionaries sought to link ancient cultures and the natives in order to establish the Indians as redeemable savages, just as ancient peoples had been. John West linked native legends and myths about the beginning of the world to "the events which the sacred Scriptures recorded, and which have been corrupted and fabled by different nations" who are the "descendants of Noah, without a written language."[67] The connection of North American native customs to those of the biblical Jews continued for the next seventy years, until the end of the nineteenth century.

As Protestant missionaries sought to be more scientific in their studies, like other scientists of the time they used the Bible to prove their theories about the origin of Indians. The explosion of scholarly publishing at the end of the nineteenth century formalized these ideas for the public. Missionaries searched for any connection between the North American natives and the Bible, often focusing on words or aspects of Indian languages that corresponded to those of Hebrew. In 1892, Bishop William Carpenter Bompas explained that "a readier match for the Hebrew names might be found among the present Indians of the North West."[68] In his treatise on how the Bible related to the North American natives, he drew such weak parallels as: "The father of King Saul was named Fowler or Snarer (I Sam. ix.1). A modern Esquimaux chief was named Grousesnare."[69] Such feeble evidence appears repeatedly in Bompas's letters and books. He seemed particularly obsessed with proving that the natives of the Arctic held some tie to the ancient biblical world. He sought to justify his work by showing that the Indians belonged to some ancient and worthy civilization, and were thus redeemable.

The parallels between native mythology and the Bible fascinated Canadian and American missionaries in the nineteenth century. Referring to the Nez Perce, Kate McBeth wrote in 1908 that "indeed, no other book is so easy for these Indians to understand as the Old Testament . . . 'Oh, so we used to do!' is often heard while they are studying it."[70] McBeth marveled at how much the natives' lives paralleled or once paralleled those of Biblical characters. "There were many customs which must have come from the children of Jacob."[71] She forgot or failed to take into account that both Protestant and Catholic missionaries had worked with the Nez Perce since the mid-eighteenth century. Missionaries often did not remember that other missionaries had come before them and native cultures had adapted to and adopted new cultural ideas. In McBeth's area alone, Jesuits, Methodists, and Congregationalists had attempted to convert the natives for almost two hundred years before her arrival. As they came and went, these missionaries deposited elements of Christianity into native cultures. Just because a native group did not proclaim themselves Christians did not mean they had not been exposed to Christianity or adopted some of its elements.

Other missionaries also sought to prove that the North American natives acted like the ancient Jews, some of whom eventually converted to Christianity. Also, scholars and scientists recognized the Jews as a civilization. Thus, a parallel between the Jews and the Indians raised the Indians to a civilization. Like Bompas, Egerton Ryerson Young also made lists of the parallels between the Indians and the ancient Jews. Unlike others, though, he used fiction to discuss these links. In *Stories from Indian Wigwams and Northern Campfires,* published in 1893, he wrote that "the Indians lived in tribes as did the ancient Israelites."[72] He also declared that "we have seen many Indian faces that were very Jewish indeed."[73] He failed to elaborate on the shared physical features, but probably he was referring to dark skin and black hair. Young also found parallels in their religions: "By some of the tribes the Good Spirit is called *Ahe,* the old Hebrew name for God."[74] And he saw patterns in their rituals, as "the ceremony of the offering of the first kettle of green corn is exactly as the Jewish offering of the first-fruits was."[75] Young considered himself a champion of the Indians and by equating their lives with those of the ancient Jews, he illustrated the value of saving the natives.

This issue constitutes one of the last of the different ways in which native groups were viewed in Canada and the United States. Efforts to connect Indians with Jews appeared more often in Canadian works. Perhaps after the growth of the Mormons in the United States and their persecution for believing that the Indians were the lost tribe of Israel, American missionaries shied away from being associated with such a belief. For whatever reason, American missionaries focused on linking Indians with other ancient groups, but not with Jews.

By comparing North American native religions and customs to those of previously studied groups, missionaries hoped to understand and explain the differences between Protestant Christian whites and heathen Indians. This way, heathenism and other faults might be deciphered. In 1881, *The Foreign Missionary* reported that "among the evidences of an Asiatic origin found among the tribes of North America is the trace of Shamanism, or devil-worship, which they practice in common with the Northern Tartars and the tribes of Siberia."[76] This kind of comparison explained away the differences between the native groups and other "civilized" groups, helping to establish the idea that Indians did have a civilization, if a degraded one.[77] Statements comparing the Indians to other civilizations became more common as more investigation was done into the Indians' past, and as the statements became important in arguing for the protection of the native population.

Missionaries also compared natives with other "savage" groups that eventually converted to Christianity—particularly the early Scots and Britons. John Maclean pointed out in his 1896 work, *Canadian Savage Folk: The Native Tribes of Canada,* that "among the American Indians, belief in amulets is universal" and then provided examples of the same belief from pre-modern Ireland and Scotland.[78] This was in keeping with the scientific movement at the time. By placing native customs alongside those of ancient groups that later adopted Christianity, Maclean softened the criticism of native groups and provided hope for the future of missionary work. This softening helped missionaries make the transition from just writing about the natives to actually studying them as members of a legitimate culture.

By studying native culture within the context of ancient civilizations, missionaries embarked on a journey to understand the Indians' perspective and to explain away aspects of their lifestyle that Canadians and Americans found uncomfortable or exotic. Comparisons allowed missionaries to judge and explain at the same time. Egerton Ryerson Young softened his criticism of scalping by implying that ancestors of Canadians and Americans also may have carried out this ritual: "We know of no other people of this horrid practice unless it was our remote German ancestors and the Vandals and the Huns."[79] Young used this method of comparison to help Canadian and U.S. audiences empathize with the plight of the Indians. Myron Eells, in *Ten Years of Missionary Work Among the Indians at Skokomish, Washington Territory, 1874–1884,* attempted to establish a similar association between native culture and early-nineteenth-century white frontier culture: "In many respects—as in their habits of neatness and industry, their visions, superstitions and the like—I have often been reminded of what I have read of the whites in the Southern and Western States fifty years ago, and of what I have seen among the same class of people in Oregon thirty years ago."[80]

Though descriptions like this made pre–Civil War Southerners and Westerners appear savage, they were one of the primary ways that missionaries tried to generate empathy for native groups. Just as Canadian and American missionaries had linked the North American natives with the urban poor, they tried to link them to the untamed U.S. pioneers of decades past. "When we are able to note the points of similarity and not dwell on the differences, we are drawn closer together and we are able to understand and appreciate one another,"[81] wrote John Maclean in 1896, several years after leaving mission work. By reminding Canadian and American societies of their own "savage" history, missionaries tried to force them to recognize natives as legitimate members of the human race. They were reminded also that Christianity had redeemed other "primitive" groups. Years of reading about the wretched and bizarre Indians had hardened Canadian and American audiences against the preservation of native societies. Missionaries like Maclean, Eells, Bompas, Young, Stephen Return Riggs, McBeth, and Wilson strove to change their opinions by creating empathy and demonstrating a shared past. Perhaps John Maclean's eloquent phrase from

Canadian Savage Folk, "We are all savages in the estimation of somebody," best illustrates how missionaries viewed their role at the end of the nineteenth century: to de-emphasize the savage aspects of Indians and highlight the savage aspects of whites.[82] Using this method, missionaries hoped to change public opinion as well as Indian policy as the frontiers closed.

THE INDIAN AND RACE

The biggest issue addressed in missionary works in the last twenty years of the nineteenth century was race. Canadian and U.S. missionaries tried to categorize Indians into groups using what they deemed "racial characteristics"—personality, physical condition, and language—in an effort to distance native peoples from the stereotype of the wretched Indian. Thus, Thomas Crosby dismissed in his memoir the theory that coastal tribe members were short because they spent much of their lives in a canoe. Instead, he decided their stature must be "inherently racial," not caused by their environment.[83] Just as his predecessors had, Crosby built on existing racial theories when discussing race.

Specifically, missionaries tried to distance the groups they worked with from the stereotype of the wretched Indian. By doing so, they showed that there might still be hope for their Indians, and thus for their missions. An example of such an attempt is found in Kate McBeth's work, *The Nez Perces since Lewis and Clark*. In one passage, McBeth sought to demonstrate how long the Nez Perce had been civilized: "Lewis and Clark did not find the Nez Perces naked savages, but wearing skin dresses."[84] Missionaries focused on local rather than global projects, partly to save their own missions and partly because the withdrawal of missionary society and government funds left them no choice.

Both Canadian and U.S. missionaries considered themselves experts on natives. They chided other writers who failed to meet their standards of accuracy, often forgetting that other missionaries provided the misinformation. Kate McBeth reprimanded those who told the story of the natives coming to St. Louis to request the "Book of Heaven." She declared, "It is strange that historians have made such careless statements about this delegation—that they were Flatheads, or the Flathead branch of the Nez Perces. There is no such branch."[85] Missionaries like McBeth wanted a separation between the stereotyped Indians in books and articles and the real Indians with whom they dealt on an everyday basis. Just as early-nineteenth-century missionaries had searched for the noble savage, their successors now sought to prove that *their* congregations were redeemable ones. They tried to create ideas about the native groups that differed from the noble savage and wretched Indian concepts. To achieve this goal, they highlighted racial differences, implying that certain native groups were inherently superior to others and therefore more worthy of protection.

Bishop William Carpenter Bompas is another good example of a missionary who was aware of what others wrote and used diversity to separate worthy natives from unworthy ones. In addition to reading information published by the Church Missionary Society and other religious groups, in an 1893 letter he told his brother that he also "received Reports of the Smithsonian Institute [*sic*] which are the most scientific volume I see on this side of the ocean."[86] Bompas also illustrated in his writing how porous the border was between Canada and the United States. Claiming that "dwellers on mountains or along the seashore are generally more lively and high-spirited than those located in a plain or valley," he pushed the idea that the Inuit were more intelligent than the natives of the Mackenzie River basin. Whereas those near the Mackenzie basin had a "sluggish disposition," the "races located on the Rocky Mountains and westward down to the Pacific Coast, and the *Esquimaux* at the Arctic sea, are more intelligent, sprightly and active."[87] Of course, Bompas worked with the Inuit and those natives in the Rocky Mountains. Perhaps Bompas, an Anglican, hoped to build upon ideas already propagated by the Church Missionary Society, his sponsoring organization. In 1873, their annual atlas of missions repeated many of his ideas, including that "the Indians of these Northern latitudes are more rigorous and intelligent than those in the South, but they are addicted to cannibalism and other revolting practices of savage life."[88] By omitting the derogatory remarks, Bompas raised the status of the northern Indians immensely. Missionaries hoped such simple differences in presentation would encourage the public to hold one tribe in higher regard than another. Thus, missionaries aspired to protect their missions from white Canadian and American encroachment by establishing clear differences between the native groups. Each missionary attempted to prove that the Indians he or she worked with were redeemable and should be preserved above all other native groups against the tide of emigration. Unfortunately, the public was comfortable with the broad, all-encompassing image of the wretched Indian, and chose to keep it.

In their attempts to categorize natives by racial characteristics, missionaries invariably provided valuable ethnographic and anthropological data. As they concentrated on specific groups, their work became more detailed and informative, not unlike the early dictionaries and lexicographies first produced on frontier missions. Missionaries began to turn out comprehensive works that discussed both present-day natives and their ancestors. Just as early missionaries had located themselves within Canadian and American societies, listing their own genealogies, their successors began to locate natives within their own societies. Thus, the statement that Cree "are of the same race as the Ojibwas, belonging to the great Algonquin family" appeared in the 1898 biography of John Black instead of in a handbook on natives themselves.[89] By recognizing that natives had a history just as whites did, missionaries acknowledged their value as members of the human race. Thus, missionaries began to raise Indians to the same social status as themselves simply by considering them human.

In their efforts to prove the similarities between whites and natives, Canadian and American missionaries dismissed ideas that whites and Indians should be treated differently because of race.[90] In a startling complaint to the attorney general of Victoria, British Columbia, William Duncan outlined the limits of separation by race: "Does an individual born in an indian [*sic*] camp . . . exercising their savage customs and in no sense a civilized person; yet manifesting signs of not being a pure indian [*sic*] by blood—no longer remain under the restrictions of the Indian liquor law?"[91] It is clear why Duncan became a thorn in the Church Missionary Society's side during the late nineteenth century. He also asked whether "the Law proscribing the sale of liquor to the Indians rests on a moral or blood distinction," which raised other uncomfortable questions about the future. But his query was valid: how would cultural and racial assimilation affect the laws created by governments? As the lines between native and white societies blurred, as they were supposed to, Canadian and American missionaries questioned the inherent separations legally prescribed by the governments. They used racial arguments and their wealth of knowledge to criticize government policies and their effects on the Indians.

As missionaries began to validate the natives as people, they furthered this new perspective by publishing studies on native groups in scholarly papers. They no longer wanted to rely on fictional accounts and biographies to spark interest in the Indians. Now missionary writers portrayed the Cherokee or the Haida or other groups as noble and ancient, thereby making them redeemable, and other groups as wretched.

As the nineteenth century came to a close and their work ended, missionaries left behind their most important contribution to Canadian and American societies—their ideas, opinions, and evaluations of native groups and the frontier.

Their observations became part of the scholarly literature and were discussed often throughout the twentieth century. Though Protestant missionaries had failed to convert the majority of the Indians, or to protect them from Canadian and U.S. government policies, they did manage to preserve various images of the Indians in the minds of the public and in government policies. Even as the field of mission work faded away with the dawn of the twentieth century, missionaries' contributions to scholarship and to the public imagination continued to grow and thrive.

CONCLUSION

THIS BOOK has compared how Canadian and U.S. missionary attitudes toward the natives on the western frontiers developed in the nineteenth century. By examining the changing images of Indians, I have shown how the missionary societies, governments, and research institutions influenced the process of image formation for missionary authors and scholars. Within this context, the book has demonstrated that despite important institutional differences and the varied perceptions of both past missionaries and current scholars, Canadian and U.S. images of and attitudes toward the Indians were similar during the nineteenth century.

There is no denying that Canada and the United States had different relationships with and policies toward their native populations. Such differences have been examined closely throughout this book. From the 1830s through the 1850s—the early period of missionary frontier work—major distinctions existed between the Canadian and U.S. governments. Canada remained a British colony, governed by both British and colonial laws. The United States was an independent nation whose western frontier was overseen only by its federal government, if at all. The pre-Confederation Canadian government adopted a protectionist policy toward native groups, attempting to keep their environment secure and the frontier regulated. The U.S. government focused on removing the natives from the path of white settlement. And while the U.S. government viewed its frontier as porous, allowing for constant westward movement, the Canadian government saw its as solid and secure, partially because of the Hudson's Bay Company. The Canadian government relied on the Company to preserve the sanctity and peace of its frontier, and historians today credit it with having accomplished this. The United States lacked such an institution to regulate its frontier.

Missionaries and missionary society policies also varied between the two countries during this early period. Canadian missionaries tended to be Anglican, Methodist, and Presbyterian while American missionaries were Presbyterian, Congregationalist, Methodist, and Baptist. Most of the early Canadian missionaries came from England whereas the American ones were born primarily in the United States. British missionary societies and their Canadian subsidiaries discouraged male missionaries from taking wives with them to the frontier, while American missionary societies encouraged marriage and allowed wives as well as single women to work on missions. Canadian missionary societies expected their missionaries to teach the gospel first and assumed that civilization of the Indians would follow. American missionary societies wanted their missionaries to teach civilization by example, so that it would come as they taught Christianity. Missionaries in Canada answered to different authorities than those in the United States. The Hudson's Bay Company supported much of the early missionary work in western Canada, whereas the U.S. government, with its Civilization Fund, was the only other early institutional sponsor in that country besides the missionary societies. Finally, missions spread across Canada from the south to the north and northwest, while in the United States they spread from east to west. All these disparities suggest that early missionaries should have perceived Indians differently depending on which side of the border they worked.

Canadian and American missionaries in the early period regarded Indians in the same way, however. Missionaries in both countries began their work assuming that they would find noble savages, willing and eager to convert. All missionaries were excited about heading to the frontier, but expressed disappointment when they actually encountered the native groups. And though missionaries reacted differently to this frustration, no national patterns appear. Some missionaries in both countries attempted to debunk the idea of the noble savage. Some continued to try to employ the image in their own work. Some used terms associated with the noble savage even as they bemoaned the existence of the image. And all missionaries blamed the disappearance of the noble savage on the disreputable whites who had preceded them on the frontier. In addition to these parallels, Protestant missionaries in both countries had to contend with the unrealistic expectations of the missionary societies: quick conversion, tithing converts, and self-supporting missions.

Early Canadian and U.S. Protestant missionaries shared another major problem. The missionary societies sent them to Christianize heathens who differed dramatically from those in Africa, India, and China, where conversion had been largely successful. To the missionary societies, the native groups in Canada and the United States were simply more heathens waiting for conversion. But North American missionaries quickly discovered that their experiences with these groups was going to be very different from those of their colleagues across the world. Canadian and U.S. missionaries had no incentives to offer converts, unlike those who worked in Africa and India. Also, the North American Indians were not one large nation but many small ones, with no outside groups looking for a way to take them over. And, Canadian and U.S. missionaries dealt with a largely rural, somewhat mobile population, as opposed to the extensive urban populations in China and India. Finally, missionaries sent to Africa, India, and China did not have to compete with the governments' and settlers' desires to exploit the land. From the moment the first Protestant missionaries arrived at the Red River settlement in Canada in 1820 and in Tennessee in 1825, the clock began ticking toward the closing of the frontiers in Canada and the United States.

The second period of missionary work on the western frontiers, which lasted from the 1850s to the 1880s, also saw great differences between Canada and the United States. Canada established itself as a confederacy just as the United States emerged from the Civil War. The new Canadian government faced land issues with its Métis community, while the U.S. government simply ignored its half-breed population. The U.S. government experimented with the Peace Policy, formally including missionary concerns in the legislative process. The Canadian government used missionaries for specific jobs, but never officially considered them when making policy decisions. Also, Canada began to split its Indian policies into two different types during this period. One set of policies, similar to those in the United States, appeared in British Columbia, while the other set, an extension of previous policies, surfaced in the prairie provinces. Lastly, the United States experienced a rising number of bloody encounters between the native and white populations, something Canada apparently avoided. Overall, this period seemed bloodier in the United States than in Canada.

For Protestant missionaries and their sponsoring missionary societies, though, many of these dissimilarities became muted by their own problems. Even with denominational differences, life for Canadian and U.S. missionaries appeared strikingly similar. Missionary societies in both countries faced the rising cost of conversion. Consequently, missionaries were met with the disappointment of their missionary societies when they failed to produce significant numbers of converts (who would have contributed financially to the mission). Canadian and U.S. missionary societies sought to reduce their expenditures by limiting funds to North American missionaries, focusing on the rest of the heathen world, and forming stronger financial ties to their governments. Later in this period, missionaries in both countries followed the leads of the missionary societies and also forged financial relationships with their governments. In addition, missionaries began to take their demands for money and support directly to the literate Christian public, bypassing the missionary societies altogether. This approach became more and more necessary, and missionaries began to propagate the wretched Indian image in order to gain public support. Though it never completely dislodged the idea of the noble savage, this new image gained ground in direct proportion to the rising pressure from both the missionary societies and governments to produce converts and pacify the frontier for white settlement.

In the final twenty years of the nineteenth century, four major differences between Canada and the United States were evident regarding Indian policy. Canada created the North-West Mounted Police to enforce law and order on the frontier. The United States used its army to wage conventional war against its native population. Canada experienced a second rebellion of its Métis population, though this time a sizable native population participated as well. The United States endured the last of its Indian wars. Finally, the United States passed the Dawes Act, which effectively abrogated earlier treaties and sought to legislate assimilation. Again, the U.S. frontier seemed bloodier and more violent than the Canadian one, suggesting that Canadians treated their native population differently than the United States treated theirs.

As far as Protestant missionary experiences are concerned, though, the border between the two countries effectively disappeared by 1880. Missionaries in both countries faced the intrusion of white settlements into native territories. Both governments gave the missionaries ultimatums: pacify the Indians or leave the frontier. Canadian and U.S. missionaries became vocal critics of their governments' policies. In order to regain power and support, missionaries sought more assistance from the public and became affiliated with scholarly secular institutions. Associations with academic organizations transformed the missionaries from marginalized players into legitimate authorities on the natives, at the same time that missionaries introduced the image of the redeemable savage, which combined aspects of the noble savage with the wretched Indian while not displacing either idea.

This book has sought to add to the literature on stereotype creation. Several scholars of American history (e.g., Robert Berkhofer Jr., Bernard Sheehan, and Brian Dippie) have attempted to discuss the racial attitudes of white Americans toward Indians. But most of their works have focused on texts whose authors did not have first-hand contact with Indians and rarely applied their theories to the frontier. This book looks at sources by those who interacted daily with Indians. It also examines the societal and structural institutions that affected missionary attitudes and their portrayals of native groups. Furthermore, this book applies many of the categories used in analyzing images of the Indians to missionaries who employed them to describe their experiences on the Canadian and U.S. frontiers.

Protestant missionaries and their attitudes toward Indians and the frontier are important not just within the context of Canadian and American nineteenth-century history, but because they provide a window into the attitudes of colonial institutions around the world during this time, as well. While this book focused on North America, it raises questions that could be asked of the frontiers in Africa, India, and China. How did Protestant missionaries in those areas create similar stereotypes about native groups to justify their own work? How did colonial institutions reward missionaries who produced images that justified colonialism? Much more comparative work is needed if we are to understand the underlying racial concepts that have shaped not just North American and European history, but world history as well.

Nineteenth-century Canadian and U.S. Protestant missionaries shared more attitudes toward the Indians than previously believed, though these attitudes first appear to have been quite different. The structural differences between Canada and the United States during this time suggest that Canadian missionaries viewed Indians in a kinder manner than their American colleagues. And, more regulation of the Canadian frontier implies that missionaries in Canada treated natives more fairly than those in the United States. American missionaries, while bemoaning their poor relations with and treatment of the native populations, had always seen Canada as an imperialist power, and therefore different from the United States. All of these perceptions prove false when compared to the attitudes expressed by those who actually worked with the native population during the nineteenth century. In a blind reading of newsletter articles, journal entries, and other documents, one would be hard-pressed to find attitudinal differences between Canadian and American Protestant missionaries. No matter how much kinder the Canadian frontier nor how much more democratic the American one, Protestant missionaries in both countries viewed Indians as wretched, degraded, and, most importantly, not white, as they attempted to change them into Canadians and Americans.

NOTES

INTRODUCTION

1. Throughout this book, the term "missionary societies" refers to corporate Protestant missionary societies only.

2. This book does not include a discussion of Catholic missionaries, though similar work on the Catholics would be illuminating. Catholic missionaries are excluded for two primary reasons. First, adding the various Catholic orders to the study would have greatly increased the length of both the research process and the manuscript. Second, Protestant missionaries interacted with secular society more regularly, as many of them left missionary work altogether after several years and returned to mainstream society. Catholic missionaries either remained on their missions, relocated to other missions, or moved within the Catholic Church, thus limiting the dissemination of their ideas about race to the secular public.

3. Robin Winks, *The Relevance of Canadian History: U.S. and Imperial Perspectives* (Toronto: Mcmillan of Canada, 1979), p. 3.

4. Seymour Martin Lipset, *Continental Divide: The Values and Institutions of the United States and Canada* (New York: Routledge, 1990); Paul Sharp, *Whoop-Up Country: The Canadian and American West, 1865–1885* (Minneapolis: University of Minnesota Press, 1955); and Winks, *Relevance of Canadian History*.

5. Lipset, *Continental Divide*, p. 174.

6. Sharp, *Whoop-Up Country*, p. 133.

7. Winks, *Relevance of Canadian History*, p. 19.

8. Lipset, *Continental Divide*, p. 91.

9. Winks, *Relevance of Canadian History*, p. 16.

10. Lipset, *Continental Divide*, p. 91 fn. 10.

11. Brian Dippie, *The Vanishing American: White Attitudes and U.S. Indian Policy* (Middletown: Wesleyan University Press, 1982); Robert F. Berkhofer Jr., *White Man's Indian: Images of the American Indian from Columbus to the Present* (New York: Vintage Books, 1978); Reginald Horsman, *Race and Manifest Destiny: The Origins of Ameri-*

can Racial Anglo-Saxonism (Cambridge: Harvard University Press, 1981); and Bernard Sheehan, *Savagism and Civility: Indians and Englishmen in Colonial Virginia* (London: Cambridge University Press, 1980).

12. Ontario has been included throughout the book as part of western Canada because many of the missionary societies viewed it as part of their Indian frontier. Reports from missionaries in Ontario were lumped together with those from Manitoba and British Columbia.

13. In this book, the term "Métis" refers to people with one native parent and one French parent. In general, members of this groups were the descendants of Indian and white parentage "but more specifically . . . the French- and Cree-speaking descendants of Red River métis." The Métis demanded political recognition in the middle of the nineteenth century. Jacqueline Peterson and Jennifer S. H. Brown, eds. *The New Peoples: Being and Becoming Métis in North America* (Lincoln: University of Nebraska Press, 1985), p. 5. Also, this book does not explicitly discuss the Métis and their relations with the missionaries. It does use the experience of the Red River Métis to highlight the fact that the United States did not recognize a similar group within its boundaries. Several excellent books exist that cover the Métis in Canada. Among them are: Peterson and Brown, *New Peoples;* D. N. Sprague, *Canada and the Métis, 1869–1885* (Waterloo, Canada: Wilfred Laurier University Press, 1988); and Marcel Giraud, *The Métis in the Canadian West,* vols. 1–2, trans. George Woodcock (Lincoln: University of Nebraska Press, 1986).

14. Missionaries considered any work outside the boundaries of "civilized society" to be in a foreign field.

15. Oscar Handlin, *Truth in History* (Cambridge: Belknap Press, 1979), pp. 176–177.

16. This book does not attempt to explore the complex issue of how natives responded to missionary activity. Most of the accounts of native responses uncovered while researching this book present numerous problems. These articles, written primarily by missionaries in published form, depict the Indian as either resistant to conversion, therefore bolstering the missionary's request for more funds, or as the rare convert who clearly demonstrates that more money would produce more converts. Either way, the accounts are tainted.

17. F. H. Duvernet, "Canadian Indians," *Montreal Weekly Witness,* 1894, item in scrapbook, Egerton Ryerson Young Papers, Archives of Ontario, Toronto.

18. John Harns, *The Great Commission; or the Christian Church Constituted and Charged to Convey the Gospel to the World* (Boston: Gould, Kendall, and Lincoln, 1842), p. 196. This book is significant because it appears to be one of the only works that covers British, Canadian, and American Protestant missions.

19. Harns, *Great Commission,* p. 194.

20. See chapter 6.

21. Alvin J. Torry, *Autobiography of Reverend Alvin Torry, First Missionary to the Six Nations and the Northwestern Tribes of British North America* (Auburn, Ala.: William J. Moses, 1861), p. 63.

CHAPTER ONE: THE GREAT COMMISSION

1. For recent histories of the Catholics in North America, see Rupert Costo and Jeanette Henry Costo, *The Missions of California: A Legacy of Genocide* (San Francisco: The Indian Historian Press for the American Indian Historical Society, 1987); Christopher Vecsey, *The Paths of Kateri's Kin* (Notre Dame, Ind.: University of Notre Dame Press, 1997); and Herbert Eugene Bolton, *The Mission as a Frontier Institution in the Spanish-American Colonies* (El Paso: Texas Western College Press for Academic Reprints, 1960).

2. Margaret Szasz, *Indian Education in the American Colonies, 1607–1783* (Albuquerque: University of New Mexico Press, 1988); and Robert F. Berkhofer Jr., *Salvation and the Savage: An Analysis of Protestant Missions and American Indian Response, 1787–1862* (Lexington: University of Kentucky Press, 1965).

3. For histories of the various Protestant missionary societies in Canada, see John Webster Grant, *Moon of Wintertime: Missionaries and the Indians of Canada in Encounter Since 1534* (Toronto: University of Toronto Press, 1989); S. Gould, *INASMUCH: Sketches of the Beginning of the Church of England in Canada in the Relation to the Indian and Eskimo Races* (Toronto: n.p., 1917); and Richard Lovett, *The History of the London Missionary Society, 1795–1895*, 2 vols. (London: Henry Frowde, 1899).

4. For in-depth histories of the early-eighteenth- through nineteenth-century U.S. Protestant missionary societies, see Robert Pierce Beaver, *Church, State and the American Indians: Two and a Half Centuries of Partnership in Missions between Protestant Churches and the Government* (St. Louis: Concordia, 1966); Berkhofer, *Salvation and the Savage;* Henry Warner Bowden, *American Indians and Christian Missions: Studies in Cultural Conflict* (Chicago: University of Chicago Press, 1981); Clifford Drury, *Presbyterian Panoram: One Hundred and Fifty Years of National Missions History* (Philadelphia: Board of Christian Education, Presbyterian Church of the U.S.A., 1952); Oliver W. Elsbree, *The Rise of the Missionary Spirit in America, 1790–1815* (Williamsport, Penn.: Williamsport Printing and Binding, 1928); and Martin Marty, *Righteous Empire: The Protestant Experience in America* (New York: Dial Press, 1970).

5. For brief histories of the founding of these missionary societies, see Berkhofer, *Salvation and the Savage,* pp. 161–178; Walter Posey, *Frontier Mission: A History of Religion West of the Southern Appalachians to 1861* (Lexington: University of Kentucky Press, 1966), pp. 157–190; Arthur Judson Brown, *One Hundred Years: A History of the Foreign Missionary Work of the Presbyterian Church in the U.S.A., with Some Account of the Countries, Peoples and the Policies and Problems of Modern Missions,* 2nd ed. (New York: Fleming H. Revell, 1936); Samuel Hall Chester, *Behind the Scenes: An Administrative History of the Foreign Work of the Presbyterian Church in the United States* (Austin, Tex.: Press of Von Boeckmann-Jones, 1928); and S. F. Smith, *Missionary Sketches: A Concise History of the Work of the American Baptist Missionary Union* (Boston: W. G. Corthell, 1881).

6. Harns, *Great Commission,* p. 188.

7. To provide context and continuity, native groups east of the Mississippi River are included prior to their removal to the West.

8. For in-depth discussions of these societies, see Posey, *Frontier Mission*, pp. 157–190; and Berkhofer, *Salvation and the Savage*, pp. 161–178.

9. Beaver, *Church, State and the American Indians*, pp. 60–61.

10. Berkhofer, *Salvation and the Savage*, pp. 3–4.

11. Marty, *Righteous Empire*, p. 54.

12. Harns, *Great Commission*, p. 189.

13. Ibid., p. 201. The missionary's denomination influenced this choice. This will be discussed in-depth in chapter 3.

14. Ibid., pp. 202–203.

15. Berkhofer, *Salvation and the Savage*, p. 67.

16. Harns, *Great Commission*, pp. 228–240.

17. Ibid., pp. 206–213.

18. Board of Foreign Missions of the Presbyterian Church, *The Foreign Missionary: Published for the Board of Foreign Missions of the Presbyterian Church* 1, no. 2 (1842): p. 15.

19. Berkhofer, *Salvation and the Savage*, pp. 7–10, 22; George W. Stocking, *Victorian Anthropology* (New York: Free Press, 1987), p. 87; and Dippie, *Vanishing American*, p. 10.

20. Berkhofer, *Salvation and the Savage*, p. 97.

21. Information on the structure of large corporate missionary societies has been drawn from the following primary sources: Baptist General Convention, *Proceedings and Annual Report of the Board of Managers of the Baptist General Convention* (Boston: Missionary Rooms, 1833–1850); Board of Foreign Missions of the Presbyterian Church, *The Foreign Missionary*, vols. 1–44 (1842–1885); Church Missionary Society, *The Church Missionary Intelligencer and Record*, n.s., vols. 2–3 (London: Seeley, Jackson and Halliday, 1866–1867); Church Missionary Society, *The Church Missionary Intelligencer and Record*, n.s., vols. 1–49 (London: Church Missionary House, 1876–1898); Harns, *Great Commission;* John C. Lowrie, *A Manual of Missions; or, Sketches of the Foreign Missions of the Presbyterian Church . . .* , 3rd ed. (New York: Randolph, 1854); John C. Lowrie, *A Manual of Foreign Missions of the Presbyterian Church in the United States of America*, 3rd ed. (New York: Rankin, 1868); Methodist Episcopal Church, *Annual Report of the Missionary Society of the Methodist Episcopal Church* (1844–1884); Methodist Episcopal Church, South, *Annual Report of the Missionary Society of the Methodist Episcopal Church, South* (1846–1891); *The Missionary Register for 1820; Containing the Principal Transactions of the Various Institutions for Propagating the Gospel: With the Proceedings, at Large, of the Church Missionary Society* (London: L. B. Seeley, 1820); and *Reports of the American Board of Commissioners for Foreign Missions* (1820–1881).

22. Beaver, *Church, State and the American Indians*, p. 76.

23. Ibid., p. 102.

24. Ibid.

25. Harns, *Great Commission*, p. 190.

26. Beaver, *Church, State and the American Indians,* p. 153.

27. Richard Slotkin, *Regeneration Through Violence: The Mythology of the American Frontier, 1600–1860* (Middletown, Conn.: Wesleyan University Press, 1973), p. 66.

28. *Report of the American Board of Commissioners for Foreign Missions Compiled from Documents Laid Before the Board at the Twentieth Annual Meeting* (Boston: Crocker and Brewster, 1829), p. 65.

29. *Report of the American Board of Commissioners for Foreign Missions Read at the Twenty-Fifth Annual Meeting* (Boston: Crocker and Brewster, 1834), p. 106.

30. *Report of the American Board of Commissioners for Foreign Missions Presented at the Twenty-Eighth Annual Meeting* (Boston: Crocker and Brewster, 1837), p. 108.

31. Bureau of Census, "Membership of Selected Religious Bodies: 1790–1970," in *Historical Statistics of the United States: Colonial Times to 1970,* pt. 1 (Washington, D.C.: U.S. Government Printing Office, 1976), p. 392.

32. *Report of the American Board of Commissioners for Foreign Missions Presented at the Fifty-First Annual Meeting* (Boston: T. R. Marvin and Son, 1860), p. 37; Bureau of Census, "Selected Religious Bodies," p. 392.

33. Robert Keller, *American Protestantism and United States Indian Policy, 1869–1882* (Lincoln: University of Nebraska Press, 1983), pp. 4, 5.

34. Curtis Hinsley, "Ethnographic Charisma and Scientific Routine: Cushing and Fewkes in the American Southwest, 1879–1893," in *Observers Observed: Essays in Ethnographic Fieldwork,* ed. George W. Stocking Jr. (Madison: University of Wisconsin, 1983), pp. 58, 60.

35. Throughout the nineteenth century, missionary societies clung to this idea, while politicians and scientists argued its validity. For a detailed version of the debate in the United States, see Dippie, *Vanishing American.*

36. Harns, *Great Commission,* p. 198.

37. Berkhofer, *White Man's Indian,* p. 117.

38. For a discussion of the concept of the "vanishing Indian," see Dippie, *Vanishing American.* Unfortunately, Dippie, as well as many other scholars, examines only the attitudes of politicians, anthropologists, and bureaucrats in eastern North America. He devotes less than ten pages to the impact of missionaries on the Indians and excludes them entirely from his discussions on policy (including the Peace Policy). Also, he examines only American policy, deeming it unique, without considering its similarities to Canadian policy.

39. Harns, *Great Commission,* p. 205.

40. *Twenty-Fifth Annual Meeting,* p. 111.

41. Thomas Crosby, *Up and Down the North Pacific Coast by Canoe and Mission Ship* (Toronto: The Missionary Society of the Methodist Church, 1914), p. 270.

42. W. H. Withrow, ed., *The Native Races of North America* (Toronto: Methodist Mission Rooms, 1895), p. 69.

43. John Booth Good, "Nanaimo and Comox Indian Mission. Extracts from the

Journal of Rev. J. B. Good and his Catechist, Mr. Cane for 1864," in *Sixth Annual Report of the Columbia Mission, with List of Subscriptions, 1864* (London: Rivingtons, 1865), p. 30.

44. Methodist Episcopal Church, *35th Annual Report of the Missionary Society of the Methodist Episcopal Church* (New York: Conference Office, 1854), p. 39.

45. "The Preservation of the Indians," in *Report of the American Board of Commissioners of Foreign Missions Presented at the Forty-Fourth Annual Meeting* (Boston: T. R. Marvin, 1853), p. 22.

46. John Maclean, *Canadian Savage Folk: The Native Tribes of Canada* (Toronto: William Briggs, 1896), p. 549.

47. Harns, *Great Commission*, p. 198; and Lucy Maddox, *Removals: Nineteenth-Century American Literature and the Politics of Indian Affairs* (New York: Oxford University Press, 1991), p. 24.

48. Harns, *Great Commission*, p. 203.

49. Ibid., p. 200.

50. Berkhofer, *Salvation and the Savage*, pp. 36–37.

51. Myron Eells, *Ten Years of Missionary Work Among the Indians at Skokomish, Washington Territory, 1874–1884* (Boston: Congregational Sunday-School and Publishing Society, 1886), p. 91.

52. Egerton Ryerson Young to Sam Young, 25 September 1868, Young Papers.

53. Egerton Ryerson Young, journal, 1868–1876, from the Rossville and Berens River, Young Papers.

54. Roy Harvey Pearce, *The Savages of America: A Study of the Indian and the Idea of Civilization* (Baltimore: Johns Hopkins University Press, 1953), pp. 61–66.

55. Harns, *Great Commission*, p. 189.

56. Eells, *Ten Years of Missionary Work*, p. 256.

57. Belle M. Brain, *Fuel for Missionary Fires* (Boston: United Society of Christian Endeavor, 1894). See also Harns, *Great Commission*.

58. Miss Weagart, "The American Indian," *The Canadian Church Magazine and Mission News* 1, no. 23 (1888).

59. Berkhofer, *Salvation and the Savage*, p. 104.

60. John Smithurst, journal, 9 July 1840, John Smithurst Collection, National Archives of Canada, Ottawa.

61. The term "pre-Confederation Canadian government" refers to the British imperial and Canadian colonial governments that ruled Canadian territory until Confederation in 1867.

62. Bishop of Saskatchewan, "Journal of a Visit to the CMS Mission of Stanley, English River," *The Church Missionary Intelligencer and Record*, n.s., 8 (London: Church Missionary House, 1883), p. 92.

63. Berkhofer, *Salvation and the Savage*, pp. 70, 72–73, 77.

64. John Hines, *The Red Indians of the Plains* (London: Society for Promoting Christian Knowledge, 1915).

65. John Booth Good, "The Thompson River Mission," in *Eleventh Annual Report of the Columbia Mission for the Year 1869* (London: Rivingtons, 1870), p. 22.

66. Stephen Return Riggs, *Mary and I: Forty Years with the Sioux* (Boston: Congregational Sunday-School and Publishing Society, 1880), p. 28.

67. Ibid.

68. Marty, *Righteous Empire*, p. 11.

69. Stocking, *Victorian Anthropology*, p. 87.

70. Tetsuo Miyakawa, *Protestants and Pioneers: Individualism and Conformity on the American Frontier* (Chicago: University of Chicago Press, 1964), p. 13; and John Horden to Mr. Grove, 21 February 1884, Moosonee Collection, Anglican Church of Canada–General Synod Archives, Toronto.

71. Miyakawa, *Protestants and Pioneers*, p. 47.

72. Ibid., pp. 13, 90.

73. Ibid., pp. 47, 93–94.

74. Berkhofer, *Salvation and the Savage*, pp. 2–3.

75. William Rankin, *Handbook and Incidents of Foreign Missionaries of the Presbyterian Church, U.S.A.* (Newark, N.J.: W. H. Shorts, 1893), p. 102.

76. Stuart Piggin, *Making Evangelical Missionaries, 1789–1858: The Social Background, Motives and Training of the British Protestant Missionaries in India* (Abingdon, England: Sutton Courtenay Press, 1984), pp. 1–20.

77. Though a greater number of the missionaries sent to Canada were unmarried, the majority of those who left the diaries, journals, and autobiographies used in this book were married.

78. Brown, *One Hundred Years*, appendix A.

79. This statistic includes only those officially listed with the missionary boards as missionaries. It excludes the various teachers and lay workers who often stayed on the frontier for a year or less. The information given here was compiled from the primary sources listed in note 21 of this chapter.

80. Niel Gunson, *Messengers of Grace: Evangelical Missionaries in the South Seas, 1797–1860* (New York: Oxford University Press, 1978), pp. 32–43.

81. Riggs, *Mary and I*, p. 25.

82. James Axtell, *The European and the Indian: Essays in the Ethnohistory of Colonial North America* (New York: Oxford University Press, 1981), pp. 252, 269.

CHAPTER TWO: NOBLE SAVAGES AND WRETCHED INDIANS

1. Berkhofer, *White Man's Indian;* Horsman, *Race and Manifest Destiny;* Francis Jennings, *The Invasion of America: Indians, Colonialism, and the Cant of Conquest* (New York:

Norton, 1976); Pearce, *Savages of America;* Sheehan, *Savagism and Civility;* William Stanton, *The Leopard's Spots: Scientific Attitudes Toward Race in America, 1815–1859* (Chicago: University of Chicago Press, 1960); and Ronald Takaki, *Iron Cages: Race and Culture in Nineteenth-Century America* (New York: Alfred A. Knopf, 1979).

2. George Catlin was an artist who traveled among the Indians west of the Mississippi in the United States. His paintings and drawings have been used to illustrate Indians in works of fiction and non-fiction since the early nineteenth century.

3. Sandra Myres, *Westering Women and the Frontier Experience, 1800–1915* (Albuquerque: University of New Mexico Press, 1982), p. 48; and Dippie, *Vanishing American,* p. 19.

4. Herbert L. Malchow, *Gothic Images of Race in Nineteenth-Century Britain* (Stanford: Stanford University Press, 1996), p. 10.

5. Takaki, *Iron Cages,* p. 11.

6. Pearce, *Savages of America,* p. 22.

7. Dippie, *Vanishing American,* p. 18.

8. Gaile McGregor, *The Noble Savage in the New World Garden: Notes Toward a Syntactics of Place* (Toronto: University of Toronto Press, 1988), p. 77.

9. Pearce, *Savages of America,* p. 189.

10. Berkhofer, *White Man's Indian,* p. 42.

11. Horsman, *Race and Manifest Destiny,* p. 62.

12. Ibid., p. 137.

13. Takaki, *Iron Cages,* p. 11; Horsman, *Race and Manifest Destiny,* p. 62; and Pearce, *Savages of America.*

14. For some excellent examples of this trend, see Stanton, *Leopard's Spots.*

15. John Booth Good, "Mission Gleanings in British Columbia," in *Mission Life,* vol. 6, pt. 2, ed. J. J. Halcombe (London: W. Wells Gardner, 1875), p. 401.

16. See Stelio Cro, *The Noble Savage: Allegory of Freedom* (Waterloo, Canada: Wilfrid Laurier University Press, 1990); and Dippie, *Vanishing American,* p. 19.

17. Robert Surtees, "Canadian Indian Policies," vol. 4, *Handbook of North American Indians: History of Indian-White Relations* (Washington, D.C.: Smithsonian Institution, 1988), p. 81.

18. Ibid., p. 82.

19. Jean Barman, *The West Beyond the West: A History of British Columbia,* rev. ed. (Toronto: University of Toronto Press, 1996), pp. 24, 39.

20. Olive Dickason, *Canada's First Nations: A History of Founding Peoples from Earliest Times* (Tulsa: University of Oklahoma Press, 1992), p. 247.

21. Ibid., p. 249.

22. For more information on the Civilization Fund, see Keller, *American Protestantism,* pp. 6–10; and Beaver, *Church, State and the American Indians.*

23. Francis Paul Prucha, *The Great Father: The United States Government and the American Indians* (Lincoln: University of Nebraska Press, 1984), vol. 1, pp. 151–154.

24. Marty, *Righteous Empire*, p. 7.

25. Samuel Francis Smith, *Missionary Sketches: A Concise History of the Work of the American Baptist Missionary Union* (Boston: W. G. Corthell, 1881), p. 387.

26. *Twentieth Annual Meeting*, p. 76. For similar comments, see *Report of the American Board of Commissioners for Foreign Missions: Compiled from Documents Laid Before the Board at the Twenty-First Annual Meeting* (Boston: Crocker and Brewster, 1830), p. 79.

27. See *Report of the American Board of Commissioners for Foreign Missions Presented at the Sixty-Sixth Annual Meeting* (Boston: Riverside Press, 1876), p. 89; and *Report of the American Board of Commissioners for Foreign Missions Read at the Twenty-Second Annual Meeting* (Boston: Crocker and Brewster, 1831), p. 93.

28. *Twenty-Second Annual Meeting*, p. 85.

29. Prucha, *Great Father*, p. 206.

30. Horsman, *Race and Manifest Destiny*, p. 105.

31. Ibid., p. 100.

32. Marty, *Righteous Empire*, p. 9.

33. For works on first contact, see Gregory Nobles, *American Frontiers: Cultural Encounters and Continental Conquest* (New York: Hill and Wang, 1997); Bruce Trigger, *Natives and Newcomers: Canada's "Heroic Age" Reconsidered* (Kingston, Canada: McGill-Queen's University Press, 1985); Colin Calloway, *New Worlds for All: Indians, Europeans, and the Remaking of Early America* (Baltimore: Johns Hopkins University Press, 1997); Karen Kupperman, *Settling with the Indians: The Meeting of English and Indian Cultures in America, 1580–1640* (Totowa, N.J.: Rowman and Littlefield, 1980); Carl Sauer, *Seventeenth Century North America* (Berkeley, Calif.: Turtle Island, 1980); and Ian Steele, *Warpaths: Invasions of North America* (New York: Oxford University Press, 1994).

34. Slotkin, *Regeneration Through Violence*, p. 357.

35. The North-West Territories included Manitoba and Saskatchewan during this time.

36. Winks, *Relevance of Canadian History*, p. 14.

37. Dippie, *Vanishing American*, p. 25.

38. Riggs, *Mary and I*, p. 147.

39. According to legend, Marcus married his wife Narcissa simply because he was heading west. Julie Roy Jeffrey refutes this belief in *Converting the West: A Biography of Narcissa Whitman* (Norman: University of Oklahoma Press, 1991), pp. 50–60. For other opinions on the Whitman marriage, see Clifford Drury, *Marcus Whitman, M.D.: Pioneer and Martyr* (Caldwell, Idaho: Caxton Printers, 1937), pp. 89, 121; and Drury, *Henry Harmon Spalding* (Caldwell, Idaho: Caxton Printers, 1936), pp. 96, 104.

40. *Report of the American Board of Commissioners for Foreign Missions: Compiled from Documents Laid Before the Board at the Thirteenth Annual Meeting* (Boston: Crocker and Brewster, 1822), p. 60; *Report of the American Board of Commissioners for Foreign Missions: Compiled from Documents Laid Before the Board at the Fifteenth Annual Meeting* (Boston: Crocker and Brewster, 1825), pp. 63, 67, 69.

41. W. H. Collison, *In the Wake of the War Canoe: A Stirring Record of Forty Years' Successful Labour, Peril, and Adventure amongst the Savage Indian Tribes of the Pacific Coast, and the Piratical Head-Hunting Haida of the Queen Charlotte Islands, British Columbia* (London: Seeley, Service and Company, 1915), p. 37.

42. Sylvia Van Kirk, *Many Tender Ties: Women in Fur-Trade Society, 1670–1870* (Norman: University of Oklahoma Press, 1983), pp. 173–175.

43. *Fifteenth Annual Meeting*, p. 75.

44. Rankin, *Handbook and Incidents*, p. 102.

45. Belle M. Brain, *The Redemption of the Red Man: An Account of Presbyterian Missions to the North American Indians of the Present Day* (New York: The Board of Home Missions of the Presbyterian Church in the U.S.A, 1904), p. 43. As Susan Armitage points out, "women did not have to *do* anything; they simply had to be there, and men would build communities around them." Susan Armitage, "Through Women's Eyes: A New View of the West," in *The Women's West*, ed. Susan Armitage and Elizabeth Jameson (Norman: University of Oklahoma Press, 1987), p. 13.

46. Jeffrey, *Converting the West*, p. 36.

47. *Fifteenth Annual Meeting*, p. 72; and Jane Hunter, *The Gospel of Gentility: American Women Missionaries in Turn-of-the-Century China* (New Haven: Yale University Press, 1984), p. 31.

48. Carroll Smith-Rosenberg, *Disorderly Conduct: Visions of Gender in Victorian America* (New York: Alfred A. Knopf, 1985), p. 133; and Nancy Cott, *The Bonds of Womanhood: "Woman's Sphere" in New England, 1780–1835* (New Haven: Yale University Press, 1977), pp. 84–98.

49. Harns, *Great Commission*, p. 248.

50. Rankin, *Handbook and Incidents*, p. 102.

51. For the best quick reference to this, see *Dictionary of Canadian Biography*, s.v. "West, John."

52. Grant, *Moon of Wintertime*, pp. 98–99.

53. Horsman, *Race and Manifest Destiny*, pp. 88–89.

54. For an example of this apocryphal story, see Thomas Crosby, *Among the An-ko-me-nums or Flathead Tribes of Indians of the Pacific Coast* (Toronto: William Briggs, 1907), pp. 13–15.

55. For the Congressional hearings reprinted, see United States Bureau of Indian Affairs, *Letter from the Secretary of the Interior Communicating, in Compliance with the Resolution of the Senate of the 2nd Instant, Information in Relation to the Early Labors of the Missionaries of the American Board of Commissioners for Foreign Missions, Commencing in 1856* (Washington, D.C.: Government Printing Office, 1871). For a different perspective, see Barman, *West Beyond the West*, p. 48.

56. Riggs, *Mary and I*, p. 36.

57. S. M. Irvin, "Iowa Mission, March 7, 1863," *Foreign Missionary* 22, no. 12 (1863).

58. Good, "Mission Gleanings in British Columbia," p. 350.

59. H. A. Cody, "Indians of the Yukon," ca. 1900–1910, Anglican Church of Canada–General Synod Archives, Toronto.

60. Brain, *Redemption of the Red Man*, p. 1.

61. Methodist Episcopal Church, South, *9th Annual Report of the Missionary Society of the Methodist Episcopal Church, South* (Louisville, Ky.: Morton and Griswold, 1854), p. 95.

62. Bishop Mclean, "Journal of a Visit to the Church Missionary Society Mission of Stanley, English River," *The Church Missionary Intelligencer and Record*, n.s., 8 (1883): p. 92.

63. Board of Foreign Missions of the Presbyterian Church, *The Foreign Missionary* 44, no. 5 (1885): p. 211.

64. John Booth Good, "The Utmost Bounds of the West," n.d., British Columbia Archives, Victoria.

65. Methodist Episcopal Church, South, *10th Annual Report of the Methodist Episcopal Church, South* (Louisville, Ky.: Morton and Griswold, 1855), p. 106.

66. Good, "Mission Gleanings in British Columbia," p. 401. Also regarding this subject, Gaile McGregor states that "the gap between the pioneers' hopeful expectations and the ugly reality, distressing enough in any case, was, of course, made doubly distressing by the mythical concept which shaped those expectations." McGregor, *New World Garden*, p. 115.

67. Good, "Mission Gleanings in British Columbia," p. 401.

68. Ibid.

69. Mary C. Greenleaf, *Life and Letters of Miss Mary C. Greenleaf* (Boston: Massachusetts Sabbath School Society, 1858), p. 337.

70. Caroline Sarah Tate, Lecture given in Cincinnati, 1913, Tate Family Collection and Papers, British Columbia Archives, Victoria.

71. For a more complete list of these terms, see Appendix C in George Catlin, *The Manners, Customs and Condition of the North American Indians*, vol. 2 (London: Published at the Egyptian Hall, Picadilly, 1841).

72. Berkhofer, *Salvation and the Savage*, p. 12.

73. John Douse to Richard Reese, 26 August 1834, John Douse Papers, Archives of Ontario, Toronto.

74. Maclean, *Canadian Savage Folk*, pp. 106–107. In particular, Maclean worked in present-day Saskatchewan and Manitoba.

75. Malchow, *Gothic Images of Race*, p. 14.

76. William Duncan, journal, no. 2, 1857, reel 2154, William Duncan Papers, Special Collections, University of British Columbia, Vancouver. Though these journals were never published, they must have been read by various people as sections of them appeared in other missionaries' books.

77. Methodist Episcopal Church, South, *1st Annual Report of the Missionary Society of the Methodist Episcopal Church, South* (Louisville, Ky.: Morton and Griswold's Power Press, 1846), p. 37.

78. Slotkin, *Regeneration Through Violence,* p. 357.

79. Ibid., p. 35.

80. Marty, *Righteous Empire,* p. 52.

81. Dippie, *Vanishing American,* p. 12.

82. Pearce, *Savages of America,* p. 59.

83. John West, "The British North American Indians with Free Thoughts on the Red River Settlement, 1820–1823," p. 6, Provincial Archives of Manitoba, Winnipeg.

84. Samuel Pond, *Two Volunteer Missionaries Among the Dakotas or the Story of the Labors of Samuel W. and Gideon H. Pond* (Boston: Congregational Sunday-School and Publishing Society, 1893), p. 19.

85. West, "British North American Indians," p. 5.

86. Sherman Hall, "Report of the Ojibway Mission," in *Report of the American Board of Commissioners for Foreign Missions Presented at the Thirty-Eighth Annual Meeting* (Boston: T. R. Marvin, 1847), p. 195.

87. Alfred James Hall, *The Church Missionary Intelligencer and Record,* n.s., 4 (1879): p. 162. This same quote can be found in Alfred James Hall, "New Work in the Far West," *The Church Missionary Gleaner* 6, no. 1061 (1879): p. 10.

88. Dippie, *Vanishing American,* p. 25.

89. Roy Harvey Pearce observed that "as the frontier advanced the Indian came more and more to be celebrated as the pathetic victim of the frontiersman, and the frontiersman as the blind agent of civilized life." Pearce, *Savages of America,* p. 59.

90. John Maclean, *The Indians: Their Manners and Customs* (Toronto: Methodist Mission Rooms, 1889), p. 130.

91. Pearce, *Savages of America,* p. 195.

CHAPTER THREE: SPEAKING IN TONGUES

1. S. F. Smith, *Missionary Sketches: A Concise History of the Work of the American Baptist Missionary Union* (Boston: W. G. Corthell, Publisher, 1879), p. 385.

2. Riggs, *Mary and I,* p. 40.

3. John Horden, "News from the Great Lone Land: Letter from the Bishop of Moosonee," 28 January 1892, Jervois Newnham Papers, National Archives of Canada, Ottawa.

4. Berkhofer, *Salvation and the Savage,* p. 10.

5. Stocking, *Victorian Anthropology,* p. 87.

6. Anna Eliza Robertson, "Translating into the Muskogee or Creek," *Oklahoma School Herald* 1, no. 6 (1893).

7. W. David Baird, "Cyrus Byington and the Presbyterian Choctaw Mission," in *Churchmen and the Western Indians, 1820–1920*, ed. Clyde A. Milner and Floyd O'Neil (Norman: University of Oklahoma Press, 1985), p. 10; Berkhofer, *Salvation and the Savage*, pp. 10, 33; Keller, *American Protestantism*; and Miyakawa, *Protestants and Pioneers*.

8. Abraham Cowley to Ebenezer Robson, 13 June 1863, Ebenezer Robson Collection, British Columbia Archives, Victoria. See also "William Duncan's Recollections, n.d.," Reminiscences, reel 2158, Duncan Papers.

9. Horden, "Great Lone Land," Newnham Papers.

10. "Report on the Missions to the Cherokees," in *Thirteenth Annual Meeting*, p. 34.

11. *Twentieth Annual Meeting*, p. 73.

12. Isaac McCoy, *History of the Baptist Indian Missions* (Washington, D.C.: William M. Morrison, 1840), p. 215.

13. Instructions delivered to Reverend J. W. Tims on his proceeding to the Saskatchewan mission, 5 June 1883, Archdeacon John William Tims Collection, Glenbow-Alberta Institute, Calgary, Canada.

14. *Foreign Missionary* 1, no. 2, p. 15.

15. Board of Foreign Missions of the Presbyterian Church, *The Foreign Missionary of the Presbyterian Church* 37, no. 4 (1878): p. 109.

16. *Twenty-Fifth Annual Meeting*, p. 173.

17. William Hobart Hare, *Eleventh Annual Report of the Missionary Bishop of Niobrara* (n.p., 1883), p. 3.

18. Berkhofer, *Salvation and the Savage*, p. 10.

19. Gould, *INASMUCH*, p. 54.

20. Berkhofer, *Salvation and the Savage*, pp. 31–34.

21. While Chinook is technically a jargon—an amalgam of English, French, and several native languages—missionaries often considered it a legitimate native language.

22. Myron Eells, comp., *Hymns in the Chinook Jargon Language*, 2nd ed. (Portland, Ore.: David Steel, successor to Hines the Printer, 1889), p. 7.

23. See also the translation of "Nearer my God to Thee" in Reverend John Hawksley to Abraham Cowley, 18 December 1908, Reverend H. A. Cody Papers, Anglican Church of Canada–General Synod Archives, Toronto.

24. Eells, *Ten Years of Missionary Work*, p. 245.

25. Eells, *Chinook Jargon Language*, p. 9.

26. Harns, *Great Commission*, p. 201.

27. Ibid.

28. *Foreign Missionary* 1, no. 2, p. 15; *Foreign Missionary* 37, no. 4, p. 109; and *Twenty-Fifth Annual Meeting*, p. 173. Italics mine.

29. *9th Annual Report*, p. 123.

30. Clifford M. Drury, *A Tepee in His Front Yard: A Biography of H. T. Cowley, One of*

the Four Founders of the City of Spokane, Washington (Portland, Ore.: Binfords and Mort, 1949), p. 46.

31. Greenleaf, *Life and Letters,* p. 393.

32. Eells, *Ten Years of Missionary Work,* p. 33.

33. Stephen Return Riggs, *Tah-koo Wah-kan; or the Gospel among the Dakotas* (1869; reprint, New York: Arno Press, 1974), p. 10.

34. Riggs, *Tah-koo Wah-kan,* p. 10.

35. John Horden to Dr. Wright, 10 April 1890, correspondence and letterbooks, John Horden Papers, Moosonee Collection.

36. *Report of the American Board of Commissioners for Foreign Missions Read at the Twenty-Fourth Annual Meeting* (Boston: Crocker and Brewster, 1833), p. 109.

37. Stocking, *Victorian Anthropology,* p. 80.

38. Archdeacon Farrar, "Archdeacon Farrar on Foreign Missions," *Our Mission News* 1, no. 7 (1887): p. 163.

39. *Foreign Missionary* 37, no. 4, p. 111.

40. Board of Foreign Missions of the Presbyterian Church, *The Foreign Missionary of the Presbyterian Church* 37, no. 2 (1878): p. 44.

41. Isaac McCoy, *The Annual Register of Indian Affairs within the Indian (or Western) Territory* (Shawanoe Baptist Mission, Indian Territory: J. Meeker, 1836), p. 26.

42. Chinook, Micmac, Beaver, Blackfoot, Chipewyan, Cree, Eskimo, Loucheux, Ojibwa, Saulteux, and Slave transliterated with syllabics by missionaries to Canada. For examples, see Karen Evans, comp., *Masinahikan: Native Language Imprints in the Archives and Libraries of the Anglican Church of Canada* (Toronto: Anglican Book Centre, 1985), p. 315.

43. *Twenty-Fourth Annual Meeting,* p. 109.

44. *Fifteenth Annual Meeting,* pp. 72, 45; and Hunter, *Gospel of Gentility,* p. 95.

45. For examples, see Riggs, *Mary and I,* pp. 41, 61; Gould, *INASMUCH,* p. 54; John Horden to Mr. Grove, 26 January 1883, Moosonee Collection; and John William Tims, comp., *Grammatical Dictionary of the Blackfeet Language in the Dominion of Canada: For the Use of Missionaries, School-Teachers and Others* (London: Society for Promoting Christian Knowledge, 1889), p. vii.

46. Gary Clayton Anderson, "Joseph Renville and the Ethos of Biculturism," in *Being and Becoming Indian: Biographical Studies of North American Frontiers,* ed. James Clifton (Prospect Heights, Ill.: Waveland Press, 1993), pp. 60–65.

47. Riggs, *Mary and I,* p. 63.

48. McCoy, *Baptist Indian Missions,* p. 47.

49. Reverend Edwin Watkins completed a six-thousand-word dictionary of the Cree language according to John S. Long in his article, "Reverend Edwin Watkins: Missionary to the Cree, 1852–1857," in *Papers of the Sixteenth Algonquin Conference,* ed. William Cowan (Ottawa: Carleton University Press, 1985), p. 101. Other major translators of the period who wrote dictionaries were John Booth Good, Alfred Hall James, Stephen Re-

turn Riggs, Bishop John Horden, John William Tims, John Maclean, and Archdeacon McDonald.

50. For other examples, see Tims, *Grammatical Dictionary of the Blackfeet;* Archdeacon McDonald, *A Grammar of the Tukudh Language* (London: Society for Promoting Christian Knowledge, 1911); and John William Tims, "Notebook on the Sarcee Indians (1897)," Tims Collection.

51. Riggs, *Mary and I,* p. 130.

52. Ibid., p. 81.

53. Horden to Grove, 26 January 1883, Moosonee Collection.

54. Riggs, *Mary and I,* pp. 59–60.

55. Alfred J. Hall, "Grammar of the Kwakiutl Language," *Proceedings and Transactions of the Royal Society of Canada for the Year 1888,* vol. 6, pt. 2 (Montreal: Dawson Brothers, 1889), p. 59.

56. Riggs, *Tah-koo Wah-kan,* p. 414; and *Report of the American Board of Commissioners for Foreign Missions Presented at the Forty-Third Annual Meeting* (Boston: T. R. Marvin, 1852), p. 149.

57. Riggs, *Mary and I,* p. 130.

58. Newton Chittenden, *Official Report of the Exploration of the Queen Charlotte Islands for the Government of British Columbia* (Victoria: Printed by Authority of the Government at Victoria, 1884), p. 18. Italics mine.

59. *Twenty-Eighth Annual Meeting,* p. 116.

60. Riggs, *Tah-koo Wah-kan,* p. 13. Italics mine.

61. Sarah Tuttle, *Letters and Conversations on the Chickasaw and Osage Missions* (Boston: T. R. Marvin, 1831), p. 77. This book is designed to mirror a casual correspondence describing life with the Chickasaw and Osage, when it is clearly a contrived format. Italics mine.

62. S. C. Bartlett, "Historical Sketch of the Missions of the American Board among the North American Indians," 1880, Young Papers.

63. Mary Riggs, *An English and Dakota Vocabulary, by a Member of the Dakota Mission* (New York: R. Craighead, 1852), p. 3.

64. John Booth Good, *A Vocabulary and Outlines of Grammar of the Nitlakapamuk or Thompson Tongue, together with a Phonetic Chinook Dictionary, Adapted for Use in the Province of British Columbia* (Victoria, B.C.: St. Paul's Mission Press, 1880), p. 6.

65. Good, *Grammar of the Nitlakapamuk,* p. 38.

66. William Carpenter Bompas, *Diocese of Mackenzie River* (London: Society for Promoting Christian Knowledge, 1888), p. 52.

67. Robertson, "Translating into the Muskogee or Creek."

68. Ibid.

69. Ibid.

70. W. A. Burman, "The Sioux Language," publication no. 5 (Winnipeg: Manitoba

Historical and Scientific Society, 1883), p. 4. Despite his disbelief in a connection between Dakota and Hebrew, Burman found Dakota to be a language whose "melody and grace it is not surpassed by any language in the North-West whether barbarous or otherwise" (ibid.).

71. For an example, see Hines, *Red Indians of the Plains,* p. 112.

72. Hinsley, "Ethnographic Charisma and Scientific Routine," p. 53.

73. *Fifteenth Annual Meeting,* p. 86.

74. S. A. Archer, comp., *A Heroine of the North: Memoirs of Charlotte Selina Bompas* (Toronto: The Macmillan Company of Canada Limited, 1929), p. 27.

75. William Carpenter Bompas, "Narrative of a Journey to Metlakatla: A Race with Winter," 1877, p. 4, Anglican Church of Canada–General Synod Archives, Toronto.

76. Torry, *Autobiography,* p. 51.

77. By 1834, *The Christian Advocate,* a Methodist publication, had "acquired a readership of 25,000, while children's magazines published by the Methodists routinely had a circulation of 12,000. This circulation increased during the nineteenth century." James Penn Pilkington, *The Methodist Publishing House,* vol. 1 (Nashville: Abingdon Press, 1968), pp. 210, 256.

78. [Beatrice Batty], ed., *The Coral Missionary Magazine,* n.s., 148 (1890): p. 98.

79. *Twenty-Eighth Annual Meeting,* p. 116.

80. Walter Ong, *Orality and Literacy: The Technologizing of the World* (London: Methuen, 1982), pp. 78–116.

81. Crosby, *Among the An-ko-me-nums,* p. 58. Reverend Thomas Crosby referred to this lack of expressive terms as a "peculiarity," a rather kind word to convey his frustration with the language.

82. McCoy, *Baptist Indian Missions,* p. 17.

83. Myron Eells, "The Chinook Jargon," *The American Anthropologist* 7, no. 3 (1894): p. 303.

84. *Twenty-Eighth Annual Meeting,* p. 116.

85. Good, *Grammar of the Nitlakapamuk,* p. 38.

86. Berkhofer, *Salvation and the Savage,* pp. 31–33.

87. Stocking, *Victorian Anthropology,* p. 87.

88. See these works of fiction by Egerton Ryerson Young: *The Battle of the Bears and Reminiscences of Life in the Indian Country* (London: Robert Culley, n.d.); *Indian Life in the Great North-West* (London: Robert Culley, n.d.); *On the Indian Trail* (London: Religious Tract Society, n.d.); *Stories from Indian Wigwams and Northern Campfires* (London: Charles H. Kelly, 1893); *Three Arrows, the Young Buffalo Hunter* (London: R. T. S. Office, n.d.); *Three Boys in the Wild North Land* (Toronto: William Briggs, 1897); *When the Blackfeet Went South and Other Stories* (London: The Boy's Own Paper Office, n.d.). See also the work of fiction by John Maclean, *The Warden of the Plains and Other Stories of Life in the Canadian Northwest* (Toronto: William Briggs, 1896).

89. Margaret T. Applegarth, *Missionary Stories for Little Folks, First Series: Primary* (New York: George H. Doran, 1917), p. 285.

CHAPTER FOUR: MANY TENDER TITHES

1. For an in-depth discussion of this process, see chapter 1.

2. George Catlin commented that "all of the Indians tribes . . . are worshipful—and many of them go to incredible lengths . . . in worshiping the Great Spirit, denying and humbling themselves before Him for the same purpose and in the same hope *as we do,* perhaps in a more rational and accepting way." Catlin, *Manners, Customs and Conditions,* vol. 1, p. 156. Italics mine.

3. Marty, *Righteous Empire,* p. 11. For histories of Protestant missions to other parts of the world, see John Comaroff and Jean Comaroff, *Of Revelation and Revolution* (Chicago: University of Chicago Press, 1991); Richard Garett, *The History of the London Missionary Society, 1795–1895,* 2 vols. (London: Henry Frowde, 1899); Gunson, *Messengers of Grace;* Hunter, *Gospel of Gentility;* Kenneth S. Latourette, *A History of the Expansion of Christianity,* vol. 4 of *The Great Century in Europe and the United States of America, A.D. 1800–A.D. 1914* (New York: Harper, 1941); and Piggin, *Making Evangelical Missionaries.*

4. David Mandelbaum, *Society in India* (Berkeley: University of California Press, 1970).

5. Van Kirk, *Many Tender Ties,* pp. 106–109. The term "half-breed" is used throughout this book for its historical accuracy to refer to peoples of mixed Euro-American and native parentage.

6. For differences in conversion rates between the western United States and the rest of the world, see the appendices in *Report of the American Board of Commissioners for Foreign Missions* (1850–1880). The appendices show cost as well as number of converts for each mission. For differences in conversion rates between Canada and the rest of the world, see the appendices in Church Missionary Society, *The Church Missionary Society Intelligencer and Record* (1866–1880).

7. *Report of the American Board of Commissioners for Foreign Missions Presented at the Forty-Ninth Annual Meeting* (Boston: T. R. Marvin and Son, 1858), p. 131.

8. Riggs, *Mary and I,* p. 156.

9. William Hobart Hare, *The Indians* (Philadelphia: Indian Rights Association, 1890).

10. *Twenty-Fifth Annual Meeting,* p. 111.

11. Horden, "Great Lone Land," Newnham Papers.

12. *Report of the American Board of Commissioners for Foreign Missions: Compiled from Documents Laid before the Board at the Eleventh Annual Meeting* (Boston: Crocker and Brewster, 1820), p. 65.

13. *Report of the American Board of Commissioners for Foreign Missions Read at the Twenty-Third Annual Meeting* (Boston: Crocker and Brewster, 1832), p. 104.

14. Methodist Episcopal Church, South, *43rd Annual Report of the Board of Missions of the Methodist Episcopal Church, South* (Nashville: Publishing House of the Methodist Episcopal Church, South, 1889), p. 23.

15. Harns, *Great Commission,* p. 190.

16. *Report of the American Board of Commissioners for Foreign Missions Presented at the Forty-Sixth Annual Meeting* (Boston: T. R. Marvin, 1855), p. 19; Margaret Whitehead, *Now You Are My Brother: Missionaries in British Columbia,* Sound Heritage Series no. 34 (Victoria, B.C.: Provincial British Columbia Archives and Record Service, 1981), p. 1.

17. *Report of the American Board of Commissioners for Foreign Missions Presented at the Fifty-Fifth Annual Meeting* (Boston: T. R. Marvin and Son, 1865), p. 148.

18. Berkhofer, *Salvation and the Savage,* p. 2.

19. Hare, *Missionary Bishop of Niobrara,* p. 4.

20. Marty, *Righteous Empire,* p. 12.

21. Kenneth Coates, "Anglican Clergy in the Yukon," *Journal of the Canadian Church Historical Society* (1990).

22. Methodist Episcopal Church, *44th Annual Report of the Missionary Society of the Methodist Episcopal Church* (New York: Printed for the Society, 1863), pp. 47, 53. In 1872, Reverend Hu Young Mi of Fooching City wrote to *The Foreign Missionary of the Presbyterian Church* (31, no. 9 [1873]: p. 280), saying that "we are all agreed in the opening that the Christian Church in China must become self-supporting." He went on to suggest that native ministers received less each year from missionary societies and that native congregations made up the difference. Thus, the Chinese missions seemingly followed the proper scenario of achieving self-support.

23. *Report of the American Board of Commissioners for Foreign Missions Presented at the Fifty-First Annual Meeting* (Boston: T. R. Marvin and Son, 1860), p. 138.

24. *Report of the American Board of Commissioners for Foreign Missions Presented at the Fiftieth Annual Meeting* (Boston: T. R. Marvin and Son, 1859), p. 21.

25. *Fiftieth Annual Meeting,* p. 141.

26. Methodist Episcopal Church, *54th Annual Report of the Missionary Society of the Methodist Episcopal Church for the Year 1872* (New York: Printed for the Society, 1873), p. 139.

27. Berkhofer, *Salvation and the Savage,* p. 25.

28. For histories of Protestant missionary relationships with the governments, see Berkhofer, *Salvation and the Savage;* Dippie, *Vanishing American;* J. R. Miller, *Shingwauk's Vision: A History of Native Residential Schools* (Toronto: University of Toronto Press, 1997); and Grant, *Moon of Wintertime.*

29. Regarding this issue, Frederick O'Meara commented that "the New England Company, the Society for the Promoting of the Gospel in Foreign Parts, the Society for the Promoting of Christian Knowledge and the Colonial Church and School Society

[have] given aid in this work; besides which some of our Missions have been supported wholly or in part from the Imperial grant for civilizing the Indians." O'Meara, *Report of the Committee on Indian Missions,* n.d., Bishop Strachan Papers, reel 9, Archives of Ontario, Toronto. See also references throughout the American Board of Commissioners for Foreign Missions reports about the Civilization Fund regulated by the U.S. Congress. For a history of this fund in the United States, see Beaver, *Church, State and the American Indians;* and Prucha, *Great Father.* For government money to missionaries in Canada, see Miller, *Shingwauk's Vision;* and Grant, *Moon of Wintertime.*

30. Dippie, *Vanishing American,* p. 97.

31. *Report of the American Board of Commissioners for Foreign Missions: Compiled from Documents Laid before the Board at the Twelfth Annual Meeting* (Boston: Crocker and Brewster, 1821), p. 50.

32. *Fifteenth Annual Meeting,* p. 72.

33. Rankin, *Handbook and Incidents,* p. 84.

34. Church Missionary Society, *The Church Missionary Intelligencer and Record,* n.s., 5 (1880): p. 515.

35. *Twelfth Annual Meeting,* p. 72.

36. Rankin, *Handbook and Incidents,* p. 84.

37. Riggs, *Mary and I,* p. 79.

38. *Report of the American Board of Commissioners for Foreign Missions Presented at the Fortieth Annual Meeting* (Boston: T. R. Marvin, 1849), p. 215.

39. Riggs, *Mary and I,* p. 79.

40. Rankin, *Handbook and Incidents,* p. 84.

41. Isaac McCoy, *The United States and the Indians* (Washington, D.C.: 22nd Congress, 1832), p. 171, D'Arcy McNickle Collection, Newberry Library, Chicago.

42. British Columbia was an exception to this rule. In the 1850s, several treaties relinquishing native land were negotiated here, but the discussions had ceased by Confederation. See Barman, *West Beyond the West,* p. 58.

43. Miller, *Shingwauk's Vision,* pp. 99–105.

44. Minutes of the Methodist Central Missionary Board, 1872, p. 170, John Maclean Collection, United Church of Canada/Victoria University Archives, Toronto.

45. *Twenty-Second Annual Meeting,* p. 85; and *Twenty-Third Annual Meeting,* p. 103.

46. *Twenty-Fourth Annual Meeting,* p. 108.

47. Methodist Episcopal Church, *37th Annual Report of the Missionary Society of the Methodist Episcopal Church* (New York: Printed for the Society, 1856), p. 64.

48. Reverend James Nisbet to Governor Alexander Morris, 22 July 1873, Alexander Morris Papers, Provincial Archives of Manitoba, Winnipeg. See also Barman, *West Beyond the West,* p. 161.

49. Reverend John William Tims to the Indian Commissioner, 4 July 1892, correspondence, 1883–1895, Tims Collection.

50. Jervois Newnham to Mr. Lang, 14 September 1898, regarding meeting with Lord Strathcona, letterbooks and journal, 1892–1898, Newnham Papers.

51. "Appeal for the Native Race, Settlers, and Miners of British Columbia" (n.p., 1871), British Columbia Archives, Victoria.

52. Jervois Newnham, journal, p. 26, Newnham Papers.

53. Methodist Episcopal Church, South, *43rd Annual Report,* p. 24.

54. Baptist Missionary Union, *34th Annual Report of the Board of Missions of the American Baptist Missionary Union* (Boston: Missionary Rooms, 1848), p. 18.

55. H. A. Cody, *An Apostle of the North: Memoirs of the Right Reverend William Carpenter Bompas, D.D.,* 2nd ed. (n.p., 1910), p. 225.

56. *Forty-Third Annual Meeting,* pp. 27, 34.

57. Dickason, *Canada's First Nations,* p. 251.

58. Dickason, *Canada's First Nations,* p. 248; Barman, *West Beyond the West,* p. 58.

59. George F. Stanley, *The Birth of Western Canada: A History of the Riel Rebellions* (Toronto: University of Toronto Press, c1963), pp. 37–38.

60. Barman, *West Beyond the West,* pp. 52–53, 61.

61. Ibid., p. 82.

62. Ibid., pp. 156–157.

63. Stanley, *Birth of Western Canada;* Thomas Flanagan, *Louis 'David' Riel: Prophet of the New World,* rev. ed. (Buffalo, N.Y.: University of Toronto Press, c1996).

64. The push for settlement in British Columbia did not occur until the 1880s. For a discussion of this, see Barman, *West Beyond the West,* pp. 104–110.

65. Dickason, *Canada's First Nations,* p. 274.

66. Keller, *American Protestantism,* p. 61. For more on the peace policy, see Prucha, *Great Father,* pp. 479–533.

67. J. Reynard, "The Victoria Mission," in *Ninth Annual Report of the Columbia Mission for the Year 1867* (London: Rivingtons, 1868), p. 21.

68. Malchow, *Gothic Images of Race,* p. 14.

69. Riggs, *Mary and I,* p. 66.

70. Hall, "New Work in the Far West," p. 10.

71. Abraham Cowley, journal, 18 October 1852, original letters, journals, and papers, reel 86, Church Missionary Society, Northwest America Mission, Provincial Archives of Manitoba, Winnipeg.

72. Crosby, *Up and Down,* p. 116.

73. [William Rankin], *Memorials of Foreign Missionaries of the Presbyterian Church U.S.A.* (Philadelphia: Presbyterian Board of Publications of Sabbath School Work, 1895), p. 141.

74. Marty, *Righteous Empire,* p. 52.

75. Riggs, *Mary and I,* pp. 249–250.

76. Withrow, *Native Races of North America,* p. 67.

CHAPTER FIVE: COURTING THE PUBLIC

1. Berkhofer, *Salvation and the Savage,* pp. 154–156; Keller, *American Protestantism,* pp. 5–6; and Dippie, *Vanishing American,* p. 50.

2. Rankin, *Handbook and Incidents,* pp. 85–86.

3. Archdeacon Reece, "Indifference of the Government to the Welfare of the Native Race," in *Twelfth Annual Report of the Columbia Mission for the Year 1870* (London: Rivingtons, 1871), p. 24.

4. Good, "Mission Gleanings in British Columbia," p. 350.

5. Eells, *Ten Years of Missionary Work,* p. 133; Riggs, *Mary and I,* p. 212; John McDougall, *Opening the Great West: Experiences of a Missionary in 1875–1876* (Calgary: Glenbow-Alberta Institute, 1970), p. 18. See also Alex Morris to Reverend George McDougall, 9 August 1875, George and John McDougall Papers, Glenbow-Alberta Institute, Calgary, Canada. William Duncan, "North Pacific Mission," *The Church Missionary Intelligencer and Record,* n.s., 1 (1876): p. 430.

6. For examples of these hearings, see *Testimony Taken by the Joint Committee Appointed to Take into Consideration the Expediency of Transferring the Indian Bureau to the War Department* (Washington, D.C.: Government Printing Office, 1879); *Testimony Taken by a Select Committee for the Senate Concerning the Condition of the Indian Tribes in the Territories of Montana and Dakota under Resolution of the Senate* (Washington, D.C.: Government Printing Office, 1884); *Testimony before the Select Committee on Removal of Northern Cheyenne as to the Removal and Situation of the Poncas* (Washington, D.C.: Government Printing Office, 1882); and *Hearing of the Chippewa Indians of Minnesota before the Committee of Indian Affairs, House of Representatives* (Washington, D.C.: Government Printing Office, 1899).

7. *Hearing of the Chippewa Indians,* p. 5.

8. For an example, see *The Church Missionary Intelligencer and Record,* n.s. 1 (1876): p. 430. William Duncan's letters and visits to Canadian government officials concerning native policy in British Columbia are reprinted and described here.

9. "Letter from W. F. Richardson, Superintendent of Indian Affairs, to *The Foreign Missionary,* September 16, 1842," *The Foreign Missionary* 1, no. 10 (1843).

10. *42nd Annual Report of the Board of Missions of the Methodist Episcopal Church, South* (Nashville: Publishing House of the Methodist Episcopal Church, South, 1888), p. 62. See also Rankin, *Handbook and Incidents,* p. 32; *9th Annual Report,* p. 95; *12th Annual Report of the Missionary Society of the Methodist Episcopal Church, South* (Nashville: E. Stevenson and F. A. Owen, 1857), p. 70.

11. The Minister of Finance of Canada to Egerton Ryerson Young, 30 March 1885, Young Papers.

12. "Recommendations from William Duncan to the Government, [1860]," reminiscences, reel 2158, Duncan Papers.

13. Archdeacon John William Tims to the Indian Commissioner, 7 August 1890, Tims Collection.

14. Tims to Indian Commissioner, 4 July 1892, Tims Collection.

15. Ibid.

16. John Horden to the Honorable Edward Dewdney, Superintendent General of Indian Affairs, 27 August 1889, Moosonee Collection.

17. Reverend T. Clark to Hayter Reed, 11 July 1891, Hayter Reed Papers, National Archives of Canada, Ottawa.

18. Edward Francis Wilson, *Missionary Work among the Ojebway Indians* (London: Society for Promoting Christian Knowledge, 1886), p. 222.

19. Wilson, *Ojebway Indians,* p. 222.

20. Jervois Newnham to Reverend C. C. Fenn, 2 June 1894, letterbooks and journal, 1892–1898, Newnham Papers.

21. *Report of the American Board of Commissioners for Foreign Missions Presented at the Thirty-Ninth Annual Meeting* (Boston: T. R. Marvin, 1848), p. 260. Italics mine.

22. Methodist Episcopal Church, *53rd Annual Report of the Missionary Society of the Methodist Episcopal Church for the Year 1871* (New York: Printed for the Society, 1872), p. 118.

23. Maclean, *Manners and Customs,* pp. 264–265.

24. Marty, *Righteous Empire,* p. 52.

25. Greenleaf, *Life and Letters,* pp. 26–84.

26. David A. Nock, *A Victorian Missionary and Canadian Indian Policy: Cultural Synthesis vs. Cultural Replacement* (Waterloo, Canada: Published for the Canadian Corporation for Studies in Religion by Wilfrid Laurier University Press, 1988), p. 25.

27. Harns, *Great Commission,* p. 239.

28. William Duncan, miscellaneous papers, reel 2156, and notes on speeches, reel 2157, Duncan Papers.

29. Crosby, *Up and Down,* p. 29.

30. [William Duncan?], *The Metlakahtlan* 1, no. 6 (1890).

31. Young, *Indian Wigwams and Northern Campfires,* p. 125.

32. Brain, *Fuel for Missionary Fires.*

33. *The Western Methodist Recorder* 1, no. 6 (1899): p. 4.

34. Ibid.

35. Whitehead, *Now You Are My Brother,* p. 2.

36. Crosby, *Up and Down,* p. 116.

37. JPH, "Thomas Crosby's Jubilee," *The Western Methodist Recorder* 13, no. 11 (1912): p. 6–10.

38. Crosby, *Up and Down,* p. 29.

39. J. D. Mullins, "Lectures to the North West Canada 'T' Slides," November 1900, given at the Diocese of Athabasca about Mackenzie River and Selkirk, I. O. Stringer Papers, Anglican Church of Canada–General Synod Archives, Toronto.

40. For examples of tour sponsorship from a later period, see the flyers for William Duncan's lectures in 1870. On two of the three flyers, the Church Missionary Society is prominently displayed as a supporter. See Duncan, miscellaneous papers, reel 2156, Duncan Papers.

41. Egerton Ryerson Young, list and dates of lectures, Young Papers. John Maclean also traveled to Maryland during one of his lecture tours.

42. William Duncan, list of places lectured, Duncan Papers.

43. Brain, *Redemption of the Red Man*, p. 35. See also Archer Butler Hulbert and Dorothy Printup, *The Oregon Crusade* (Denver: The Stewart Commission of Colorado College, 1935); Hugh Kerr, *Children's Missionary Story Sermons* (New York: Fleming H. Revell, 1915); and John C. Lowrie, *A Manual of Missions; or, Sketches of the Foreign Missions of the Presbyterian Church . . .* , 3rd ed. (New York: Randolph, 1854).

44. For a complete record of the U.S. congressional debates concerning Whitman, see United States Bureau of Indian Affairs, *Letter from the Secretary of the Interior.*

45. *Elmira Herald*, 5 December 1870, in United States Bureau of Indian Affairs, *Letter from the Secretary of the Interior*, p. 45.

46. H. H. Spalding, "Narrative of an Overland Journey to Fort Vancouver and Lapwai in 1836 together with an Account of the Beginning of the American Protestant Missions Beyond the Rockies," Typescript copy, Western Americana Collection, Beinecke Rare Book Library, Yale University.

47. Asa Bowen Smith to Elkanah Walker, 20 April 1839, Asa Bowen Smith Collection, Beinecke Rare Book Library, Yale University.

48. Letter from Asa Bowen Smith, 12 October 1840, Smith Collection.

49. Though there are known cases of violence in missions elsewhere in the world, few show up in the records for North American missions. In Spalding's case, it was unfortunate for him that the other missionaries' papers survived; they complained about his violent tendencies in their letters to the American Board of Commissioners for Foreign Missions. The Board never published any of these letters, nor any news of Spalding's dismissal. Much to the disgust of the Board, Spalding's fame rose as the lone male survivor of the Whitman Massacre.

50. Hines, *Red Indians of the Plains*, p. 19.

51. *Extracts from the New York Christian Advocate and Journal*, 18 April 1834, Clarence Booth Bayley Papers, British Columbia Archives, Victoria.

52. John Smithurst, letterbook, 1839–1840, p. 5, Smithurst Collection.

53. Horsman, *Race and Manifest Destiny*, pp. 98–99.

54. Brian Fagan, *The Great Journey: The Peopling of Ancient America* (London: Thames and Hudson, 1987), p. 16.

55. *Report of the American Board of Commissioners of Foreign Missions Presented at the Thirtieth Annual Meeting* (Boston: Crocker and Brewster, 1839), p. 142.

56. Fagan, *Great Journey*, p. 9.

57. Wilson, *Ojebway Indians,* pp. 95–108.

58. Horsman, *Race and Manifest Destiny,* p. 98.

59. William Duncan, notes on speeches, 21st February [no year], Duncan Papers.

60. Duncan, notes on speeches, 30 January 1887, Duncan Papers.

61. Duncan, notes on speeches, 6 February 1887, Duncan Papers.

62. Berkhofer, *White Man's Indian,* p. 28.

63. From a flyer announcing lectures by Egerton Ryerson Young, Young Papers.

64. Jervois Newnham, "Great but Lonely: The Land of Moosonee and its 'Metropolis,' Moose Fort" (excerpts of a talk given with slides, n.d.), Newnham Papers.

65. Newnham, "Great but Lonely," Newnham Papers.

66. For an example of this increased publishing activity, see Pilkington, *Methodist Publishing House,* pp. 386–435.

67. William Duncan, journal, no. 2, 1857–1858, Duncan Papers.

68. Ibid.

69. Ibid.

70. William Duncan, "Baptism of a Cannibal Chief," *The Foreign Missionary* 22, no. 12 (1864): p. 303. Italics mine.

71. J. J. Halcombe, *Stranger than Fiction,* 3rd ed. (London: Society for Promoting Christian Knowledge, 1873), p. 2.

72. Halcombe, *Stranger than Fiction,* p. 3.

73. *Metlahkatla and the North Pacific Mission* (London: Church Missionary House, 1881), p. 6, Duncan Papers, Special Collections.

74. [Edward Francis Wilson], *The Canadian Indian* 1, no. 3 (1890): p. 81.

75. Malchow, *Gothic Images of Race,* p. 41.

76. Bishop William Carpenter Bompas, "A Plea for the Wild Sheep of the Rocky Mountains," *The Church Missionary Gleaner* (November 1893): p. 171.

77. Bompas, "Plea for the Wild Sheep," p. 171.

78. Myron Eells, *Justice to the Indian* (Portland, Ore.: George H. Hines, 1883), p. 7.

CHAPTER SIX: LET NO MAN REND ASUNDER

1. James Nisbet to William Mclaren, 26 June 1870, James Nisbet Papers, United Church of Canada/Victoria University Archives, Toronto; see also Berkhofer, *Salvation and the Savage,* pp. 89–90.

2. Nisbet to McLaren, 29 September 1868, Nisbet Papers.

3. Greenleaf, *Life and Letters,* p. 393.

4. James Nisbet, "Memorandum of Matters to Be Submitted for the Consideration of His Honorable Secretary Governor Morris," 1 August 1873, Morris Papers.

5. Ibid.

6. Archer, *Heroine of the North,* p. 101.

7. Methodist Episcopal Church, South, *39th Annual Report of the Board of Missions of the Methodist Episcopal Church, South* (Nashville: Southern Methodist Publishing House, 1885), p. 30.

8. Hall, "Report of the Ojibway Mission," p. 195.

9. Ibid.

10. John Horden to A. Campbell, 14 February 1883, Moosonee Collection, National Archives of Canada, Ottawa.

11. See United States Bureau of Indian Affairs, *Letter from the Secretary of the Interior,* p. 2.

12. Riggs, *Mary and I,* p. 147.

13. McDougall, *Opening the Great West,* p. 13.

14. Myron Eells, "What Made Oregon," *The Foreign Missionary* 42, no. 9 (1884): p. 377.

15. R. C. Macleod, *The NWMP and Law Enforcement, 1873–1905* (Toronto: University of Toronto Press, 1976), pp. 84–86.

16. Dickason, *Canada's First Nations,* p. 306; Macleod, *NWMP and Law Enforcement,* p. 21.

17. Dickason, *Canada's First Nations,* p. 281.

18. Stanley, *Birth of Western Canada,* pp. 350–380.

19. Dickason, *Canada's First Nations,* p. 307.

20. Dickason, *Canada's First Nations,* p. 313.

21. Stanley, *Birth of Western Canada,* pp. 240–242, 378.

22. Dickason, *Canada's First Nations,* pp. 286–289, 315.

23. Barman, *West Beyond the West,* p. 129.

24. Barman, *West Beyond the West,* p. 160; Dickason, *Canada's First Nations,* p. 286.

25. Takaki, *Iron Cages,* p. 188.

26. Dippie, *Vanishing American,* p. 177.

27. Brain, *Redemption of the Red Man,* p. 56.

28. Riggs, *Mary and I,* p. 273.

29. Thomas Crosby, "Record of the Chilliwack Indian Mission B.C. Methodist Church of Canada," Robert Clyde Scott Papers, British Columbia Archives, Victoria.

30. For a comparison of Canadian and U.S. policy, see J. R. Miller, *Skyscrapers Hide the Heavens: A History of Indian-White Relations* (Toronto: University of Toronto Press, 1989); Barman, *West Beyond the West,* p. 156.

31. Maclean, *Manners and Customs,* p. 264.

32. Reverend A. Sutherland to J. S. Corcoran, 24 August 1888, United Church of Canada/Victoria University Archives, Toronto.

33. Reverend A. Sutherland to Honorable Superintendent General of Indian Affairs, 20 May 1889, United Church of Canada/Victoria University Archives, Toronto.

34. L. Vankoughnet to Reverend John William Tims, 20 June 1887, Tims Collection.

35. Jervois Newnham to the Minister of the Interior, 15 September 1892, Newnham Papers.

36. Whitehead, *Now You Are My Brother*, p. 3.

37. Methodist Episcopal Church, *61st Annual Report of the Missionary Society of the Methodist Episcopal Church for the Year 1879* (New York: Printed for the Society, 1880), p. 185.

38. Methodist Episcopal Church, *65th Annual Report of the Missionary Society of the Methodist Episcopal Church for the Year 1883* (New York: Printed for the Society, 1884), p. 199.

39. Riggs, *Tah-koo Wah-kan*, pp. 386–401.

40. Berkhofer, *Salvation and the Savage*, pp. 90–91.

41. Rankin, *Handbook and Incidents*, p. 88.

42. John Maclean, "The Canadian Indian Problem," *Methodist Magazine* (n.d.): p. 167, John Maclean Collection, United Church Archives, Toronto.

43. Eells, *Justice to the Indian*, p. 8.

44. Edward Francis Wilson, *Canadian Gazette*, 4 December 1890, in *The Canadian Indian* 1, no. 5 (1891): p. 133.

45. Eells, *Justice to the Indian*, p. 1.

46. Ibid., p. 3.

47. Thomas Crosby, "Letter from Reverend Thomas Crosby to the Superintendent General of Indian Affairs, John A. MacDonald," 1882, reprinted in *Letter from the Methodist Missionary Society to the Superintendent-General of Indian Affairs Respecting British Columbia Troubles*, [1889], British Columbia Archives, Victoria.

48. [Edward Francis Wilson], *The Canadian Indian* 1, no. 6 (1891).

49. John McDougall, "Among the Bloods: Reverend John MacDougall [*sic*] on the Indians and their Government," n.d., Young Papers.

50. Berkhofer, *Salvation and the Savage*, pp. 105–106.

51. Kate C. McBeth, *The Nez Perces Since Lewis and Clark* (New York: Fleming H. Revell, 1908).

52. William Duncan "7th Letter," n.d., miscellaneous papers, reel 2156, Duncan Papers.

53. Thomas Crosby, "Letter from Reverend Thomas Crosby."

54. Board of Foreign Missions of the Presbyterian Church, *The Foreign Missionary* 40, no. 2 (1881): p. 49.

55. Withrow, *Native Races of North America*, p. 67.

56. Board of Foreign Missions of the Presbyterian Church, *The Foreign Missionary* 40, no. 2 (1881): p. 49.

57. Thomas Crosby, "Statement of Thomas Crosby," reprinted in *Letter from the Methodist Missionary Society to the Superintendent-General of Indian Affairs Respecting British Columbia Troubles*, [1889], British Columbia Archives, Victoria.

58. Maclean, *Canadian Savage Folk,* p. 307.

59. Ibid., p. 307.

60. Ibid., p. 307.

61. Mullins, "Lectures to the North West Canada," p. 34, Stringer Papers.

62. Bartlett, "Historical Sketch of the Missions," p. 39, Young Papers.

63. Young, *Stories from Indian Wigwams,* p. 18.

64. Ibid.

65. Ibid., p. 17.

66. Excerpted in [Edward Francis Wilson], *The Canadian Indian* 1, no. 1 (1890): p. 3.

67. Brain, *Redemption of the Red Man,* p. 114.

68. [Edward Francis Wilson], *The Canadian Indian* 1, no. 3 (1890): p. 57.

69. Maclean, *Canadian Savage Folk,* preface.

70. Eells, *Ten Years of Missionary Work,* p. 270.

71. Beatrice Batty, ed., *The Coral Missionary Magazine,* n.s., 152 (1890): p. 175.

72. Marty, *Righteous Empire,* p. 52.

73. Arthur Burman, "Indian Work of the United Church of Canada," ca. 1931, Stephenson Collection, United Church of Canada/Victoria University Archives, Toronto.

CHAPTER SEVEN: "WE ARE ALL SAVAGES"

1. Maclean, *Manners and Customs,* p. vii.

2. Ibid. For more information on the British Association, see Stocking, *Victorian Anthropology.*

3. Maclean, *Manners and Customs,* p. vii.

4. Ibid., p. viii.

5. Ibid.

6. Ibid., p. 275.

7. [Edward Francis Wilson], *The Canadian Indian* 1, no. 1 (1890).

8. Riggs, *Mary and I,* pp. 141–142.

9. Hall, "Grammar of the Kwagiutl Language."

10. Stephen Return Riggs, "The Dakota Mission," in *Collections of the Minnesota Historical Society,* vol. 3, pt. 1 (St. Paul: Minnesota Historical Society, 1880), pp. 115–127; Riggs, "Dakota Portraits," *Minnesota History Bulletin* 2 (1917–1918); Riggs, "A Dog's Revenge: A Dakota Fable by Michel Renville," in *First Annual Report of the Bureau of Ethnology to the Secretary of the Smithsonian Institution, 1879–1880* (Washington, D.C.: Government Printing Office, 1881).

11. Hinsley, "Ethnographic Charisma and Scientific Routine," p. 54; see also Gunson, *Messengers of Grace,* p. 214.

12. Horden to Campbell, 14 February 1883, Moosonee Collection.

13. Maclean, *Manners and Customs,* p. 25.

14. Ibid., p. 24.

15. Wilson, *The Canadian Indian* 1, no. 3 (1890): p. 57.

16. Ibid., p. 81.

17. Myron Eells, *The Indians of Puget Sound: The Notebooks of Myron Eells,* ed. George Pierce Castile (Seattle: University of Washington Press, 1985), pp. 403–404. Italics mine.

18. Ibid.

19. Maclean, *Warden of the Plains,* p. 55.

20. For comparisons, see Maclean, *Canadian Savage Folk;* Maclean, *Warden of the Plains;* Edward Francis Wilson, "Report on the Blackfeet Tribes," in *Reports on the North Western Tribes of Canada, 1885–1891,* vol. 1 (n.p.: British Association for the Advancement of Science, 1887); any volume of Wilson, *The Canadian Indian,* from 1890 to 1891; Egerton Ryerson Young, "Life among the Red Men of America," *The Missionary Review of the World* 18, no. 7 (1895): pp. 481–489; Young, *Oowikapun; or, How the Gospel Reached the Nelson River Indians* (London: Charles H. Kelly, 1895); Myron Eells, *The Twana Indians of the Skokomish Reservation in Washington Territory* (Washington, D.C.: Bulletin of the Survey of the U.S. Geological and Geographical Survey, 1877); and Eells, *Marcus Whitman, M.D.: Proofs of His Work in Saving Oregon to the United States and in Promoting the Immigration of 1843* (Portland, Ore.: George H. Himes, 1883).

21. For a discussion of how anthropologists such as Franz Boas also referred to specific tribes in speaking about all Indians, see Berkhofer, *White Man's Indian,* p. 26.

22. Eells, *Ten Years of Missionary Work,* p. 133; Eells, "Indian Doctors of the Puget Sound," *Northwest Anthropological Research Notes* 4, no. 2 (1970); and Eells, "The Chinook Jargon."

23. Neil Judd, *The Bureau of American Ethnology: A Partial History* (Norman: University of Oklahoma Press, 1967), pp. 10–11.

24. The best evidence for this relationship comes from Diamond Jenness's work *The Indians of Canada* (6th ed., Bulletin 65, Anthropological Series, no. 15 [Toronto: National Museum of Canada, 1963], p. 107). In this book, he recalls that Boas cited Thomas Crosby as an expert on design flaws in Nootka canoes. See also Crosby, *Up and Down,* p. 128; and Franz Boas, "The Kwakiutl Vancouver Island," American Museum of Natural History, Memorial 8.

25. See Edward Francis Wilson, "Autobiography of Edward Francis Wilson," p. 98, Anglican Church of Canada–General Synod Archives, Toronto; Wilson, "The Canadian Indian Aid and Research Society," *Journal of American Folklore* 4 (1891): p. 87; and Wilson, *Journal of American Folklore* 3 (1890): p. 10.

26. According to Robert Berkhofer, anthropologists such as Franz Boas battled the same instincts. Missionaries were generally the first to struggle with this problem, though, as they had lived "inside" native cultures for fifty years or more when anthropologists began studying Indians. For a complete discussion, see Berkhofer, *White Man's Indian,* pp. 65–66.

27. Curtis Hinsley, *The Smithsonian and the American Indian: Making a Moral Anthropology in Victorian America* (Washington, D.C.: Smithsonian Institution Press, 1981), pp. 34–35.

28. Ibid.

29. Ibid., p. 22; Rosemary Zumwalt, *American Folklore Scholarship: A Dialogue of Dissent* (Bloomington: Indiana University Press, 1988), p. 5.

30. Hinsley, *Smithsonian and the American Indian,* p. 50.

31. Ibid., pp. 48–50.

32. Ibid., pp. 34–35.

33. Riggs, *Mary and I,* pp. 141–142; see also Riggs, *Tak-koo Wah-kan,* p. 414; and *Forty-Third Annual Meeting,* p. 51.

34. Judd, *Bureau of American Ethnology,* pp. 10–11.

35. Hinsley, *Smithsonian and the American Indian,* pp. 49–50.

36. Simon Bronner, *American Folklore Studies* (Lawrence: University Press of Kansas, 1986), pp. 17–20.

37. Ibid., p. 32.

38. Ibid., p. 18.

39. *Journal of American Folklore* 2 (1889); *Journal of American Folklore* 3 (1890); *Journal of American Folklore* 4 (1891); *Journal of American Folklore* 5 (1892).

40. William Duncan, list of books ordered, reel 2159, Duncan Papers.

41. William Carpenter Bompas to George Cox Bompas, August 1893, William Carpenter Bompas Papers, Anglican Church of Canada–General Synod Archives, Toronto.

42. Minnesota Historical Society, "Certificate Designating John Black as a Corresponding Member," 6 October 1853, Reverend John Black Collection, Provincial Archives of Manitoba, Winnipeg.

43. Gideon Pond, "Dakota Superstitions," in *Collections of the Minnesota Historical Society* (St. Paul: Pioneer Printing, 1867), pp. 32–62.

44. W. A. Burman, "The Sioux Language," Publication no. 5 (Winnipeg: Manitoba Historical and Scientific Society, 1883).

45. Wilson, "Report on the Blackfeet Tribes"; Wilson, "Report on the Sarcee Indians," *Reports on the North Western Tribes of Canada, 1885–1891* 1 (1887).

46. Hall, "Grammar of the Kwakiutl Language."

47. John Maclean, "Blackfoot Indian Legends," *Journal of American Folklore* 3 (1890): pp. 296–298; Maclean, "Blackfoot Mythology," *Journal of American Folklore* 6 (1893): pp. 165–171; John Maclean, "The Blackfoot Sun Dance," *Proceedings of Canadian Institution,* 3rd ser., 6 (1887–1888): pp. 231–237.

48. Wilson, "The Canadian Indian Aid and Research Society," p. 87.

49. Eells, "Indian Doctors of the Puget Sound"; Eells, "The Chinook Jargon."

50. Myron Eells, "The Worship and Traditions of the Aborigines of America; or, Their Testimony to the Religion of the Bible," paper read before the Victoria Institute, or Philosophical Society of Great Britain, 1885, British Columbia Archives, Victoria.

51. Edward Francis Wilson, untitled paper, *Journal of American Folklore* 3 (1890): p. 10.

52. *Forty-Third Annual Meeting*, p. 151.

53. George Stocking, "The Ethnographer's Magic: Fieldwork in British Anthropology from Tylor to Malinowski," in *Observers Observed: Essays in Ethnographic Fieldwork*, ed. George W. Stocking (Madison: University of Wisconsin, 1983), p. 74.

54. Eells, *Twana Indians*, p. 57.

55. Ibid., p. 58.

56. Berkhofer, *White Man's Indian*, p. 27.

57. Hinsley, "Ethnographic Charisma and Scientific Routine," p. 53.

58. Ronald Rohner, ed., *The Ethnography of Franz Boas* (Chicago: University of Chicago Press, 1969), pp. 155–160, 48, 51, 70–71, 43–46. Rohner misidentifies John Booth Good as a Catholic priest in this volume.

59. McBeth, *Nez Perces*.

60. Eells, *Twana Indians*, p. 102.

61. Wilson, "Autobiography," p. 98.

62. Ibid.

63. Ibid.

64. Stocking, "Ethnographer's Magic," p. 74.

65. Maclean, *Manners and Customs*, p. 237.

66. Marty, *Righteous Empire*, p. 6; Fagan, *Great Journey*, p. 9.

67. West, "British North American Indians," p. 58.

68. William Carpenter Bompas, *Northern Lights on the Bible, Drawn from a Bishop's Experience During Twenty-Five Years in the Great North-West* (London: J. Nisbet, 1892), p. 82.

69. Bompas, *Northern Lights*, p. 82.

70. McBeth, *Nez Perces*, p. 17.

71. Ibid.

72. Young, *Indian Wigwams and Northern Campfires*, p. 83.

73. Ibid.

74. Ibid.

75. Ibid.

76. Board of Foreign Missions of the Presbyterian Church, *The Foreign Missionary* 40, no. 2 (1881): p. 51.

77. Robert Bieder, *Science Encounters the Indian, 1820–1880: The Early Years of American Ethnology* (Tulsa: University of Oklahoma Press, 1986), p. 11.

78. Maclean, *Canadian Savage Folk*, pp. 200–205.

79. Young, *Indian Wigwams and Northern Campfires*, p. 23.

80. Eells, *Ten Years of Missionary Work*, p. 270.

81. Maclean, *Canadian Savage Folk*, p. 308.

82. Ibid.

83. Crosby, *Up and Down,* p. 7.

84. McBeth, *Nez Perces,* p. 19.

85. Ibid.

86. William Carpenter Bompas to George Cox Bompas, August 1893, Bompas Papers.

87. Bompas, *Northern Lights,* pp. 102–103.

88. Church Missionary Society, *The Church Missionary Atlas. Map of the Various Missions of the Church Missionary Society, with Illustrative Letter Press,* 5th ed. (London: Church Missionary House, 1873), p. 57.

89. George Bryce, *John Black: The Apostle of the Red River; or, How the Blue Banner Was Unfurled on Manitoba Prairies* (Toronto: William Briggs, 1898), p. 94.

90. Dippie, *Vanishing American,* p. xxi.

91. William Duncan to the Attorney General of Victoria, reel 2159, 25 January 1872, Duncan Papers.

BIBLIOGRAPHY

PRIMARY SOURCES: PUBLISHED

"Appeal for the Native Race, Settlers, and Miners of British Columbia." N.p., 1871. British Columbia Archives, Victoria.

Applegarth, Margaret T. *Missionary Stories for Little Folks, First Series: Primary.* New York: George H. Doran, 1917.

———. *Missionary Stories for Little Folks, First Series: Secondary.* New York: George H. Doran, 1917.

Archer, S. A., comp. *A Heroine of the North: Memoirs of Charlotte Selina Bompas.* Toronto: The Macmillan Company of Canada Limited, 1929.

Baptist General Convention. *Proceedings and 14th Annual Report of the Board of Managers of the Baptist General Convention.* New York: n.p., 1828.

———. *Proceedings and 19th Annual Report of the Board of Managers of the Baptist General Convention.* Boston: John Putnam, 1833.

———. *Proceedings and 20th Annual Report of the Board of Managers of the Baptist General Convention.* Boston: John Putnam, 1839.

Baptist Missionary Union. *34th Annual Report of the Board of Missions of the American Baptist Missionary Union.* Boston: Missionary Rooms, 1848.

———. *35th Annual Report of the Board of Managers of the American Baptist Missionary Union.* Boston: Missionary Rooms, 1849.

———. *36th Annual Report: With the Proceedings of the Annual Meetings.* Boston: Missionary Rooms, 1850.

Batty, Beatrice. *Forty-Two Years amongst the Indians and Eskimo: Pictures from the Life of the Right Reverend John Horden, First Bishop of Moosonee.* London: Religious Tract Society, 1893.

[———], ed. *The Coral Missionary Magazine,* n.s., 148 (1890).

Board of Foreign Missions of the Presbyterian Church. *The Foreign Missionary: Published for the Board of Foreign Missions of the Presbyterian Church* 1, no. 2 (1842).

———. *The Foreign Missionary* 1, no. 4 (1842).

―――. *The Foreign Missionary* 1, no. 6 (1842).

―――. *The Foreign Missionary* 1, no. 10 (1843).

―――. *The Foreign Missionary* 1, no. 12 (1843).

―――. *The Foreign Missionary* 2, no. 1 (1843).

―――. *The Foreign Missionary* 2, no. 2 (1843).

―――. *The Foreign Missionary* 3, no. 7 (1844).

―――. *The Foreign Missionary* 4, no. 1 (1845).

―――. *The Foreign Missionary* 21, no. 4 (1862).

―――. *The Foreign Missionary* 21, no. 8 (1863).

―――. *The Foreign Missionary* 21, no. 12 (1863).

―――. *The Foreign Missionary* 22, no. 6 (1863).

―――. *The Foreign Missionary* 22, no. 12 (1864).

―――. *The Foreign Missionary* 30, no. 9 (1872).

―――. *The Foreign Missionary of the Presbyterian Church* 31, no. 3 (1872).

―――. *The Foreign Missionary of the Presbyterian Church* 31, no. 9 (1873).

―――. *The Foreign Missionary of the Presbyterian Church* 31, no. 12 (1873).

―――. *The Foreign Missionary of the Presbyterian Church* 32, no. 9 (1874).

―――. *The Foreign Missionary of the Presbyterian Church* 33, no. 2 (1874).

―――. *The Foreign Missionary of the Presbyterian Church* 34, no. 2 (1875).

―――. *The Foreign Missionary of the Presbyterian Church* 35, no. 7 (1876).

―――. *The Foreign Missionary of the Presbyterian Church* 35, no. 11 (1876).

―――. *The Foreign Missionary of the Presbyterian Church* 37, no. 2 (1878).

―――. *The Foreign Missionary of the Presbyterian Church* 37, no. 4 (1878).

―――. *The Foreign Missionary of the Presbyterian Church* 38, no. 2 (1879).

―――. *The Foreign Missionary of the Presbyterian Church* 39, no. 2 (1880).

―――. *The Foreign Missionary* 40, no. 2 (1881).

―――. *The Foreign Missionary* 41, no. 2 (1882).

―――. *The Foreign Missionary* 41, no. 6 (1882).

―――. *The Foreign Missionary* 42, no. 2 (1883).

―――. *The Foreign Missionary* 42, no. 9 (1884).

―――. *The Foreign Missionary* 44, no. 1 (1885).

―――. *The Foreign Missionary* 44, no. 2 (1885).

―――. *The Foreign Missionary* 44, no. 3 (1885).

―――. *The Foreign Missionary* 44, no. 4 (1885).

―――. *The Foreign Missionary* 44, no. 5 (1885).

Bompas, Charlotte Selina. "Cumberland Mission, River Saskatchewan." *The Church Missionary Gleaner* 5: 56.

Bompas, William Carpenter. *Diocese of Mackenzie River.* London: Society for Promoting Christian Knowledge, 1888.

———. *Lessons and Prayers in the Tenni or Slavi Language of the Indians of the Mackenzie River.* London: Society for Promoting Christian Knowledge, 1892.

———. *Northern Lights on the Bible, Drawn from a Bishop's Experience during Twenty-five Years in the Great North-west.* London: J. Nisbet, 1892.

———. "A Plea for the Wild Sheep of the Rocky Mountains." *The Church Missionary Gleaner* November 1893: 171.

Brain, Belle M. *Fuel for Missionary Fires.* Boston: United Society for Christian Endeavor, 1894.

———. *The Redemption of the Red Man: An Account of Presbyterian Missions to the North American Indians of the Present Day.* New York: The Board of Home Missions of the Presbyterian Church in the U.S.A., 1904.

Bryce, George. *John Black: The Apostle of the Red River; or, How the Blue Banner Was Unfurled on Manitoba Prairies.* Toronto: William Briggs, 1898.

Buckland, Augustus. *The Heroic in Missions: Pioneers in Six Fields.* London: Isbister, 1894.

Bureau of Census. "Membership of Selected Religious Bodies: 1790–1970." In *Historical Statistics of the United States: Colonial Times to 1970,* pt. 1. Washington, D.C.: U.S. Government Printing Office, 1976.

Burman, W. A. "The Sioux Language." Publication no. 5. Winnipeg: Manitoba Historical and Scientific Society, 1883.

The Canadian Church Magazine and Mission News 1, no. 17 (1887).

The Canadian Church Magazine and Mission News 1, no. 23 (1888).

The Canadian Church Magazine and Mission News 1, no. 28 (1888).

Catlin, George. *The Manners, Customs and Condition of the North American Indians.* 2 vols. London: Published at the Egyptian Hall, Picadilly, 1841.

Chittenden, Newton. *Official Report of the Exploration of the Queen Charlotte Islands for the Government of British Columbia.* Victoria: Printed by Authority of the Government at Victoria, 1884.

The Church in Story and Pageant: Indian Tribes and Missions. Hartford, Conn.: Church Missions Publishing, 1926.

Church Missionary Society. *The Church Missionary Atlas. Map of the Various Missions of the Church Missionary Society, with Illustrative Letter Press.* 5th ed. London: Church Missionary House, 1873.

———. *The Church Missionary Intelligencer and Record,* n.s., 2 (1866).

———. *The Church Missionary Intelligencer and Record,* n.s., 3 (1867).

———. *The Church Missionary Intelligencer and Record,* n.s., 1 (1876).

———. *The Church Missionary Intelligencer and Record,* n.s., 1 (1877).

———. *The Church Missionary Intelligencer and Record,* n.s., 3 (1878).

———. *The Church Missionary Intelligencer and Record,* n.s., 4 (1879).

———. *The Church Missionary Intelligencer and Record,* n.s., 5 (1880).

———. *The Church Missionary Intelligencer and Record,* n.s., 6 (1881).

———. *The Church Missionary Intelligencer and Record,* n.s., 8 (1883).

———. *The Church Missionary Intelligencer and Record,* n.s., 9 (1884).

———. *The Church Missionary Intelligencer and Record,* n.s., 10 (1885).

———. *The Church Missionary Intelligencer and Record,* n.s., 12 (1887).

———. *The Church Missionary Intelligencer and Record,* n.s., 49 (1898).

Cody, H. A. *An Apostle of the North: Memoirs of the Right Reverend William Carpenter Bompas, D.D.* 2nd ed. N.p., 1910.

———. *On Trail and Rapid By Dog-Sled and Canoe: The Life of Bishop Bompas.* Toronto: Musson Book Company, 1911.

Collison, W. H. *In the Wake of the War Canoe: A Stirring Record of Forty Years' Successful Labour, Peril, and Adventure amongst the Savage Indian Tribes of the Pacific Coast, and the Piratical Head-hunting Haida of the Queen Charlotte Islands, British Columbia.* London: Seeley, Service, 1915.

Coolidge, Grace. *Teepee Neighbors.* Norman: University of Oklahoma Press, 1984.

Cowley, Abraham. "Which of the Three? A Hard Question for Chippeway Indian." *The Church Missionary Gleaner* (1874).

Crosby, Thomas. *Among the An-ko-me-nums or Flathead Tribes of Indians of the Pacific Coast.* Toronto: William Briggs, 1907.

———. "Letter from Thomas Crosby, 20 January 1875." *Missionary Notices of the Methodist Church of Canada,* 3rd ser., no. 2 (April 1875).

———. *Up and Down the North Pacific Coast by Canoe and Mission Ship.* Toronto: The Missionary Society of the Methodist Church, 1914.

Dempsey, Hugh, ed. *The Rundle Journals, 1840–1846.* Calgary: Alberta Records Publication Board, 1977.

Diocese of New Westminster. *Heroes of the Church in British Columbia.* N.p.: Board of Religious Education, 1958.

Drake, Samuel. *The Book of Indians of North America: Book II, Biography and History of the Northern or New England Indians.* 5th ed. Boston: Antiquarian Institute, 1837.

Drury, Clifford M. *A Tepee in His Front Yard: A Biography of H. T. Cowley, One of the Four Founders of the City of Spokane, Washington.* Portland, Ore.: Binfords and Mort, 1949.

[Duncan, William?]. *The Metlakahtlan* 1, no. 6 (1890).

Dundas, R. J. "Mission Work in British Columbia." In *The Emigrant and the Heathen or Sketches of Missionary Life,* edited by J. J. Halcombe. London: Society for Promoting Christian Knowledge, 1870.

Eells, Edwin. "Heroes and Heroines of the Long Ago." *The Washington Historical Quarterly* 2, no. 2 (1908).

Eells, Myron. "The Chinook Jargon." *The American Anthropologist* 7, no. 3 (1894).

———. *History of the Congregational Association of Oregon, and Washington Territory; The Home Missionary Society of Oregon and Adjoining Territories; and the Northwestern Asso-*

ciation of Congregational Ministers. Portland, Ore.: Publishing House of Himes the Printer, 1881.

———. *History of Indian Missionaries on the Pacific Coast, Oregon, Washington, and Idaho.* Philadelphia: The American Sunday-School Union, 1882.

———. "Indian Doctors of the Puget Sound." *Northwest Anthropological Research Notes* 4, no. 2 (1970). First published in *Antiquarian* 1, no. 2 (1891).

———. *The Indians of Puget Sound: The Notebooks of Myron Eells.* Edited by George Pierre Castile. Seattle: University of Washington Press, 1985.

———. *Justice to the Indian.* Portland, Ore.: George H. Himes, 1883.

———. *Marcus Whitman, M.D.: Proofs of His Work in Saving Oregon to the United States and in Promoting the Immigration of 1843.* Portland, Ore.: George H. Himes, 1883.

———. *A Reply to Professor Bourne's "The Whitman Legend."* Walla Walla, Wash.: Statesman Printing, 1902.

———. *Ten Years of Missionary Work Among the Indians at Skokomish, Washington Territory, 1874–1884.* Boston: Congregational Sunday-School and Publishing Society, 1886.

———. *The Twana Indians of the Skokomish Reservation in Washington Territory.* Washington, D.C.: Bulletin of the Survey of the U.S. Geological and Geographical Survey, 1877.

———. "What Made Oregon." *The Foreign Missionary* 42, no. 9 (1884). New York: Presbyterian Mission House.

———, comp. *Hymns in the Chinook Jargon Language.* 2nd ed. Portland, Ore.: David Steel, successor to Himes the Printer, 1889.

Eighth Annual Report of the Columbia Mission for the Year 1866. London: Rivingtons, 1867.

Ellinwood, F. F. *The "Great Conquest"; or, Miscellaneous Papers on Missions.* New York: Rankin, 1876.

Elmira Herald (5 December 1870). In United States Bureau of Indian Affairs, *Letter from the Secretary of the Interior.*

Epworth League. "The Apostle of the North." *Epworth League Program.* Pamphlet Collection. Stephenson Collection. United Church of Canada/Victoria University Archives, Toronto, 11 February 1901.

Epworth League Institute. "Woodstock District, Epworth League Institute, For the Study of the Bible and Missions." Pamphlet Collection. Stephenson Collection. United Church of Canada/Victoria University Archives, Toronto.

Extracts from New York Christian Advocate and Journal. Clarence Booth Bayley Papers, British Columbia Archives, Victoria, 18 April 1834.

Faris, John T. *The Alaskan Pathfinder: The Story of Sheldon Jackson for Boys.* New York: Fleming H. Revell, 1913.

A Friend to the Indians. "Indian Affairs." *The Christian Guardian* (11 August 1858): 179.

Garrioch, Andrew. *The Far and Furry North: A Story of Life and Love and Travel in the Days of the Hudson's Bay Company.* Winnipeg: Douglas-McIntyre Printing and Binding, 1925.

———. *A Hatchet Mark in Duplicate.* Toronto: Ryerson, 1929.

Gay, Theressa. *Life and Letters of Mrs. Jason Lee: First Wife of Reverend Jason Lee of the Oregon Mission.* Portland, Ore.: Metropolitan, 1936.

Gladfelter, Katherine. *Many Moons Ago and Now.* New York: Friendship, 1932.

Good, John Booth. "Gleanings in British Columbia." *Mission Life; or, Home and Foreign Church Work,* n.s., vol. 40, pts. 1 and 2. London: Wells Gardner, Darton, 1880.

———. "Mission Gleanings in British Columbia." Vol. 6, pt. 2, *Mission Life,* edited by J. J. Halcombe. London: W. Wells Gardner, 1875.

———. "The Thompson River Mission." In *Eleventh Annual Report of the Columbia Mission for the Year 1869.* London: Rivingtons, 1870.

———. *A Vocabulary and Outlines of Grammar of the Nitlakapamuk or Thompson Tongue, together with a Phonetic Chinook Dictionary, Adapted for Use in the Province of British Columbia.* Victoria, B.C.: St. Paul's Mission Press, 1880.

Gordon, Reverend Charles. Foreword to *Boys and Girls from Far Away,* by Louise MacDougall. N.p.: Committee on Literature and Missionary Education of the United Church of Canada, 1928.

Greenleaf, Mary C. *Life and Letters of Miss Mary C. Greenleaf.* Boston: Massachusetts Sabbath School Society, 1858.

Halcombe, J. J., ed. *Mission Life: An Illustrated Magazine of Home and Foreign Church Work,* n.s., vol. 3, pt. 1. London: W. Wells Gardner, 1872.

———. *Stranger than Fiction.* 3rd ed. London: Society for Promoting Christian Knowledge, 1873.

Hall, Alfred J. "Grammar of the Kwagiutl Language." *Proceedings and Transactions of the Royal Society of Canada for the Year 1888.* Vol. 6, pt. 2. Montreal: Dawson Brothers, 1889.

———. "New Work in the Far West." *The Church Missionary Gleaner* 6, no. 1061 (1879).

A Handbook of the Church's Mission to the Indians. Hartford, Conn.: Church Missions Publishing, 1894.

Hare, William Hobart. *Bishop Hare's "Rehearsal of Facts" in the case of Samuel D. Hinman, Presbyter, with Mr. Hinman's Reply.* Friends of the Missions, 1879.

———. *Eleventh Annual Report of the Missionary Bishop of Niobrara.* N.p., 1883.

———. *The Indians.* Philadelphia: Indian Rights Association, 1890.

———. *Reminiscences. An Address.* Philadelphia: William F. Fell, 1888.

———. *Second Annual Report of the Missionary Bishop of the Niobrara / Third Annual Report of the Indian Commission.* New York: n.p., 1874.

———. *Third Annual Report of the Missionary Bishop of the Niobrara / Third Annual Report of the Indian Commission.* New York: n.p., 1875.

Harns, John. *The Great Commission; or, the Christian Church Constituted and Changed to Convey the Gospel to the World.* Boston: Gould, Kendall, and Lincoln, 1842.

Harrison, William. *Hymns in the Omaha Language.* New York: American Tract Institute, 1887.

Hearing of the Chippewa Indians of Minnesota before the Committee of Indian Affairs, House of Representatives. Washington, D.C.: Government Printing Office, 1899.

Hewitt, Ethel Erford. *Into the Unknown: An Historical Novel.* New York: Pageant, 1957.

Hines, John. *The Red Indians of the Plains.* London: Society for Promoting Christian Knowledge, 1915.

Hinman, S. D., *Bible and Gospel History of the Language of the Cree Indians of North-West America.* London: Society for Promoting Christian Knowledge, 1892.

———. *A Collection of Psalms and Hymns in the Language of the Cree Indians of North-West America.* London: Society for Promoting Christian Knowledge, 1902.

———. *A Grammar of the Cree Language, as Spoken by the Cree Indians of North America.* London: Society for Promoting Christian Knowledge, 1881.

———. *The Iowa Band.* Boston: Congregation Publishing Society, 1870.

———. "Journal Written at the Mission in Nebraska." In *Taopi and his Friends; or, the Indians' Wrongs and Rights.* Philadelphia: Claxton, Remsen and Haffelfinger, 1869.

———. "News from the Great Lone Land: Letter from the Bishop of Moosonee (Dr. Horden)." Unknown newspaper, 28 January 1892. Jervois Newnham Papers. National Archives of Canada, Ottawa.

Hulbert, Archer Butler, and Dorothy Printup. *The Oregon Crusade.* Denver: The Stewart Commission of Colorado College, 1935.

Hurlburt, Thomas. "Letter to the Editor." *The Christian Guardian* (15 December 1885): 150.

"The Indian Department." *The Christian Guardian* (5 August 1857): 175.

Jackson, Sheldon. *Alaska: Its People, Villages, Missions and Schools.* New York: Women's Executive Committee of Home Missions of the Presbyterian Church, 1887.

———. "The Native Tribes of Alaska." *American Indian Problem: Christian Educators in Council.* N.p., n.d.

Journal of American Folklore 2 (1889).

Journal of American Folklore 3 (1890).

Journal of American Folklore 4 (1891).

Journal of American Folklore 5 (1892).

JPH. "Thomas Crosby's Jubilee." *Western Methodist Recorder* 13, no. 11 (1912): 6–10.

Kerr, Hugh. *Children's Missionary Story Sermons.* New York: Fleming H. Revell, 1915.

Lee, Jason. "Diary of Reverend Jason Lee." *The Quarterly of the Oregon Historical Society* 17, no. 1 (1916).

Letter from the Methodist Missionary Society to the Superintendent-General of Indian Affairs respecting British Columbia Troubles. N.p., n.d. British Columbia Archives, Victoria.

Lewis, Arthur. *The Life and Work of the Rev. E. J. Peck among the Eskimos.* New York: A. C. Armstrong, 1904.

Lowrie, John C. *A Manual of Missions; or, Sketches of the Foreign Missions of the Presbyterian Church. . . .* 3rd ed. New York: Randolph, 1854.

———. *A Manual of Foreign Missions of the Presbyterian Church in the United States of America.* 3rd ed. New York: Rankin, 1868.

Maclean, John. "The Blackfoot Sun Dance." *Proceedings of Canadian Institution,* 3rd ser., 6 (1887–1888).

———. "The Canadian Indian Problem." *Methodist Magazine* (n.d.): 167. John Maclean Collection. United Church Archives, Toronto.

———. *Canadian Savage Folk: The Native Tribes of Canada.* Toronto: William Briggs, 1896.

———. *The Indians: Their Manners and Customs.* Toronto: Methodist Mission Rooms, 1889.

———. *The Warden of the Plains, and Other Stories of Life in the Canadian Northwest.* Toronto: William Briggs, 1896.

McBeth, Kate C. *The Nez Perces since Lewis and Clark.* New York: Fleming H. Revell, 1908.

McBeth, Sue. *Seed Scattered Broadcast; or, Incidents in a Camp Hospital.* 2nd ed. London: Hunt, 1871.

McCoy, Isaac. *The Annual Register of Indian Affairs within the Indian (or Western) Territory.* Shawanoe Baptist Mission, Indian Territory: J. Meeker, 1835.

———. *The Annual Register of Indian Affairs within the Indian (or Western) Territory.* Shawanoe Baptist Mission, Indian Territory: J. Meeker, 1836.

———. *The Annual Register of Indian Affairs within the Indian (or Western) Territory.* Shawanoe Baptist Mission, Indian Territory: J. Meeker, 1837.

———. *History of the Baptist Indian Missions.* Washington, D.C.: William M. Morrison, 1840.

———. *Remarks of the Practicability of Indian Reform, Embracing their Colonization.* Boston: Lincoln and Edmands, 1827.

———. *The United States and the Indians.* Washington, D.C.: 22nd Congress, 1832. D'Arcy McNickle Collection. Newberry Library, Chicago.

McDonald, Archdeacon Robert. *A Grammar of the Tukudh Language.* London: Society for Promoting Christian Knowledge, 1911.

McDougall, John. *Opening the Great West: Experiences of a Missionary in 1875–1876.* Calgary: Glenbow-Alberta Institute, 1970.

"The Memorial of the Indians to the Queen." *The Christian Guardian* (5 September 1860): 142.

Merian, Lewis, and George Hinman. *An Adult Study Book on Christian Missions among the American Indians.* N.p.: Council of Women for Home Missions and the Missionary Education Movement, 1932.

Methodist Episcopal Church. *25th Annual Report of the Missionary Society of the Methodist Episcopal Church.* New York: J. Collard, 1844.

———. *27th Annual Report of the Missionary Society of the Methodist Episcopal Church.* New York: J. Collard, 1846.

———. *28th Annual Report of the Missionary Society of the Methodist Episcopal Church.* New York: Joseph Longking, 1847.

———. *32nd Annual Report of the Missionary Society of the Methodist Episcopal Church.* New York: Joseph Longking, 1851.

———. *35th Annual Report of the Missionary Society of the Methodist Episcopal Church.* New York: Conference Office, 1854.

———. *36th Annual Report of the Missionary Society of the Methodist Episcopal Church.* New York: Printed for the Society, 1855.

———. *37th Annual Report of the Missionary Society of the Methodist Episcopal Church.* New York: Printed for the Society, 1856.

———. *39th Annual Report of the Missionary Society of the Methodist Episcopal Church.* New York: Printed for the Society, 1858.

———. *43rd Annual Report of the Missionary Society of the Methodist Episcopal Church.* New York: Printed for the Society, 1862.

———. *44th Annual Report of the Missionary Society of the Methodist Episcopal Church.* New York: Printed for the Society, 1863.

———. *45th Annual Report of the Missionary Society of the Methodist Episcopal Church.* New York: Printed for the Society, 1864.

———. *52nd Annual Report of the Missionary Society of the Methodist Episcopal Church for the Year 1870.* New York: Printed for the Society, 1871.

———. *53rd Annual Report of the Missionary Society of the Methodist Episcopal Church for the Year 1871.* New York: Printed for the Society, 1872.

———. *54th Annual Report of the Missionary Society of the Methodist Episcopal Church for the Year 1872.* New York: Printed for the Society, 1873.

———. *55th Annual Report of the Missionary Society of the Methodist Episcopal Church for the Year 1873.* New York: Printed for the Society, 1874.

———. *56th Annual Report of the Missionary Society of the Methodist Episcopal Church for the Year 1874.* New York: Printed for the Society, 1875.

———. *61st Annual Report of the Missionary Society of the Methodist Episcopal Church for the Year 1879.* New York: Printed for the Society, 1880.

———. *65th Annual Report of the Missionary Society of the Methodist Episcopal Church for the Year 1883.* New York: Printed for the Society, 1884.

Methodist Episcopal Church, South. *1st Annual Report of the Missionary Society of the Methodist Episcopal Church, South.* Louisville, Ky.: Morton and Griswold's Power Press, 1846.

———. *2nd Annual Report of the Missionary Society of the Methodist Episcopal Church, South.* Louisville, Ky.: Morton and Griswold's Power Press, 1847.

———. *9th Annual Report of the Missionary Society of the Methodist Episcopal Church, South.* Louisville, Ky.: Morton and Griswold, 1854.

———. *10th Annual Report of the Missionary Society of the Methodist Episcopal Church, South.* Louisville, Ky.: Morton and Griswold, 1855.

————. *12th Annual Report of the Missionary Society of the Methodist Episcopal Church, South.* Nashville: E. Stevenson and F. A. Owen, 1857.

————. *39th Annual Report of the Board of Missions of the Methodist Episcopal Church, South.* Nashville: Southern Methodist Publishing House, 1885.

————. *42nd Annual Report of the Board of Missions of the Methodist Episcopal Church, South.* Nashville: Publishing House of the Methodist Episcopal Church, South, 1888.

————. *43rd Annual Report of the Board of Missions of the Methodist Episcopal Church, South.* Nashville: Publishing House of the Methodist Episcopal Church, South, 1889.

————. *45th Annual Report of the Board of Missions of the Methodist Episcopal Church, South.* Nashville: Publishing House of the Methodist Episcopal Church, South, 1891.

The Mission Field, A Monthly Record of the Proceedings of the Society for the Propagation of the Gospel, at Home and Abroad. Vol. 14. London: Bell and Daldy, 1869.

The Missionary Register for 1820; Containing the Principal Transactions of the Various Institutions for Propagating the Gospel: With the Proceedings, at Large, of the Church Missionary Society. London: L. B. Seeley, 1820.

Ninth Annual Report of the Columbia Mission for the Year 1867. London: Rivingtons, 1868.

"An Obstructive Policy." *The Christian Guardian* (28 July 1858): 170.

An Occasional Paper of the Columbia Mission with Letters from the Bishop. June 1860. London: Rivingtons, 1860.

Oliver, Frank. "The Blackfeet." *MacLean's Magazine* (15 March 1931). Stephenson Collection. United Church of Canada/Victoria University Archives, Toronto.

Our Mission News 1, no. 1 (1886).

Our Mission News 1, no. 6 (1886).

Our Mission News 1, no. 7 (1887).

Our Mission News 1, no. 9 (1887).

Phillips, S. Ashton. *Heroes of Lonely Trails.* Toronto: The General Board of Religious Education in the Church of England in Canada, n.d.

Pond, G. H. "Dakota Superstitions." In *Collections of the Minnesota Historical Society.* St. Paul, Minn.: Pioneer Printing, 1867.

Pond, Samuel. *The Dakota or Sioux in Minnesota as They Were in 1834.* St. Paul: Minnesota Historical Society Press, 1986.

————. *Two Volunteer Missionaries among the Dakotas; or, The Story of the Labors of Samuel W. and Gideon H. Pond.* Boston: Congregational Sunday-School and Publishing Society, 1893.

Rankin, William. *Handbook and Incidents of Foreign Missionaries of the Presbyterian Church, U.S.A.* Newark, N.J.: W. H. Shorts, 1893.

[————]. *Memorials of Foreign Missionaries of the Presbyterian Church U.S.A.* Philadelphia: Presbyterian Board of Publications of Sabbath School Work, 1895.

Report of the American Board of Commissioners for Foreign Missions: Compiled from Documents Laid before the Board at the Eleventh Annual Meeting. Boston: Crocker and Brewster, 1820.

Report of the American Board of Commissioners for Foreign Missions: Compiled from Documents Laid before the Board at the Twelfth Annual Meeting. Boston: Crocker and Brewster, 1821.

Report of the American Board of Commissioners for Foreign Missions: Compiled from Documents Laid before the Board at the Thirteenth Annual Meeting. Boston: Crocker and Brewster, 1822.

Report of the American Board of Commissioners for Foreign Missions: Compiled from Documents Laid before the Board at the Fifteenth Annual Meeting. Boston: Crocker and Brewster, 1825.

Report of the American Board of Commissioners for Foreign Missions: Compiled from Documents Laid before the Board at the Eighteenth Annual Meeting. Boston: Crocker and Brewster, 1827.

Report of the American Board of Commissioners for Foreign Missions: Compiled from Documents Laid before the Board at the Nineteenth Annual Meeting. Boston: Crocker and Brewster, 1828.

Report of the American Board of Commissioners for Foreign Missions: Compiled from Documents Laid before the Board at the Twentieth Annual Meeting. Boston: Crocker and Brewster, 1829.

Report of the American Board of Commissioners for Foreign Missions: Compiled from Documents Laid before the Board at the Twenty-First Annual Meeting. Boston: Crocker and Brewster, 1830.

Report of the American Board of Commissioners for Foreign Missions Read at the Twenty-Second Annual Meeting. Boston: Crocker and Brewster, 1831.

Report of the American Board of Commissioners for Foreign Missions Read at the Twenty-Third Annual Meeting. Boston: Crocker and Brewster, 1832.

Report of the American Board of Commissioners for Foreign Missions Read at the Twenty-Fourth Annual Meeting. Boston: Crocker and Brewster, 1833.

Report of the American Board of Commissioners for Foreign Missions Read at the Twenty-Fifth Annual Meeting. Boston: Crocker and Brewster, 1834.

Report of the American Board of Commissioners for Foreign Missions Read at the Twenty-Sixth Annual Meeting. Boston: Crocker and Brewster, 1835.

Report of the American Board of Commissioners for Foreign Missions Read at the Twenty-Seventh Annual Meeting. Boston: Crocker and Brewster, 1836.

Report of the American Board of Commissioners for Foreign Missions Presented at the Twenty-Eighth Annual Meeting. Boston: Crocker and Brewster, 1837.

Report of the American Board of Commissioners for Foreign Missions Presented at the Twenty-Ninth Annual Meeting. Boston: Crocker and Brewster, 1838.

Report of the American Board of Commissioners for Foreign Missions Presented at the Thirtieth Annual Meeting. Boston: Crocker and Brewster, 1839.

Report of the American Board of Commissioners for Foreign Missions Presented at the Thirty-First Annual Meeting. Boston: Crocker and Brewster, 1840.

Report of the American Board of Commissioners for Foreign Missions Presented at the Thirty-Second Annual Meeting. Boston: Crocker and Brewster, 1841.

Report of the American Board of Commissioners for Foreign Missions Presented at the Thirty-Third Annual Meeting. Boston: Crocker and Brewster, 1842.

Report of the American Board of Commissioners for Foreign Missions Presented at the Thirty-Fourth Annual Meeting. Boston: Crocker and Brewster, 1843.

Report of the American Board of Commissioners for Foreign Missions Presented at the Thirty-Fifth Annual Meeting. Boston: T. R. Marvin, 1844.

Report of the American Board of Commissioners for Foreign Missions Presented at the Thirty-Seventh Annual Meeting. Boston: T. R. Marvin, 1846.

Report of the American Board of Commissioners for Foreign Missions Presented at the Thirty-Eighth Annual Meeting. Boston: T. R. Marvin, 1847.

Report of the American Board of Commissioners for Foreign Missions Presented at the Thirty-Ninth Annual Meeting. Boston: T. R. Marvin, 1848.

Report of the American Board of Commissioners for Foreign Missions Presented at the Fortieth Annual Meeting. Boston: T. R. Marvin, 1849.

Report of the American Board of Commissioners for Foreign Missions Presented at the Forty-First Annual Meeting. Boston: T. R. Marvin, 1850.

Report of the American Board of Commissioners for Foreign Missions Presented at the Forty-Second Annual Meeting. Boston: T. R. Marvin, 1851.

Report of the American Board of Commissioners for Foreign Missions Presented at the Forty-Third Annual Meeting. Boston: T. R. Marvin, 1852.

Report of the American Board of Commissioners for Foreign Missions Presented at the Forty-Fourth Annual Meeting. Boston: T. R. Marvin, 1853.

Report of the American Board of Commissioners for Foreign Missions Presented at the Forty-Fifth Annual Meeting. Boston: T. R. Marvin, 1854.

Report of the American Board of Commissioners for Foreign Missions Presented at the Forty-Sixth Annual Meeting. Boston: T. R. Marvin, 1855.

Report of the American Board of Commissioners for Foreign Missions Presented at the Forty-Seventh Annual Meeting. Boston: T. R. Marvin and Son, 1857.

Report of the American Board of Commissioners for Foreign Missions Presented at the Forty-Ninth Annual Meeting. Boston: T. R. Marvin and Son, 1858.

Report of the American Board of Commissioners for Foreign Missions Presented at the Fiftieth Annual Meeting. Boston: T. R. Marvin and Son, 1859.

Report of the American Board of Commissioners for Foreign Missions Presented at the Fifty-First Annual Meeting. Boston: T. R. Marvin and Son, 1860.

Report of the American Board of Commissioners for Foreign Missions Presented at the Fifty-Second Annual Meeting. Boston: T. R. Marvin and Son, 1862.

Report of the American Board of Commissioners for Foreign Missions Presented at the Fifty-Third Annual Meeting. Boston: T. R. Marvin and Son, 1863.

Report of the American Board of Commissioners for Foreign Missions Presented at the Fifty-Fifth Annual Meeting. Boston: T. R. Marvin and Son, 1865.

Report of the American Board of Commissioners for Foreign Missions Presented at the Fifty-Sixth Annual Meeting. Boston: T. R. Marvin and Son, 1866.

Report of the American Board of Commissioners for Foreign Missions Presented at the Fifty-Seventh Annual Meeting. Cambridge, Mass.: Riverside Press, 1867.

Report of the American Board of Commissioners for Foreign Missions Presented at the Sixtieth Annual Meeting. Cambridge, Mass.: Riverside Press, 1870.

Report of the American Board of Commissioners for Foreign Missions Presented at the Sixty-First Annual Meeting. Boston: Riverside Press, 1871.

Report of the American Board of Commissioners for Foreign Missions Presented at the Sixty-Second Annual Meeting. Boston: Riverside Press, 1872.

Report of the American Board of Commissioners for Foreign Missions Presented at the Sixty-Third Annual Meeting. Boston: Riverside Press, 1873.

Report of the American Board of Commissioners for Foreign Missions Presented at the Sixty-Fourth Annual Meeting. Boston: Riverside Press, 1875.

Report of the American Board of Commissioners for Foreign Missions Presented at the Sixty-Sixth Annual Meeting. Boston: Riverside Press, 1876.

Report of the American Board of Commissioners for Foreign Missions Presented at the Sixty-Seventh Annual Meeting. Boston: Riverside Press, 1877.

Report of the American Board of Commissioners for Foreign Missions Presented at the Sixty-Eighth Annual Meeting. Boston: Riverside Press, 1878.

Report of the American Board of Commissioners for Foreign Missions Presented at the Sixty-Ninth Annual Meeting. Boston: Riverside Press, 1879.

Report of the American Board of Commissioners for Foreign Missions Presented at the Seventy-First Annual Meeting. Boston: Riverside Press, 1881.

Riggs, Mary. *An English and Dakota Vocabulary, by a Member of the Dakota Mission.* New York: R. Craighead, 1852.

Riggs, Mary Buel. *Early Days at Santee: The Beginnings of Santee Normal Training School.* Santee, Nebr.: Santee Normal Training School Press, 1928.

Riggs, Stephen Return. "The Dakota Mission." In *Collections of the Minnesota Historical Society.* Vol. 3, pt. 1. St. Paul: Minnesota Historical Society, 1880.

———. "Dakota Portraits." *Minnesota History Bulletin* 2 (1917–1918).

———. "A Dog's Revenge: A Dakota Fable by Michel Renville." In *First Annual Report of the Bureau of Ethnology to the Secretary of the Smithsonian Institution, 1879–1880.* Washington, D.C.: Government Printing Office, 1881.

———. "The Indian Question. Review of Address before the Minnesota Historical Society, by the Honorable H. H. Sibley." *New Englander* 15 (1857): 250–274.

———. *Mary and I: Forty Years with the Sioux.* Boston: Congregational Sunday School and Publishing Society, 1880.

———. "Narrative of Paul Mazakootemane." In *Collections of the Minnesota Historical Society.* Vol. 3. St. Paul: Minnesota Historical Society, 1880.

———. "Protestant Missions in the Northwest." In *Collections of the Minnesota Historical Society.* Vol. 6. St. Paul: The Pioneer Press, 1894.

———. *Tah-koo Wah-kan; or the Gospel among the Dakotas.* 1869. Reprint, New York: Arno Press, 1974.

Robertson, Anna Eliza. "Translating into the Muskogee or Creek." *Oklahoma School Herald* 1, no. 6 (1893).

Ruttan, R. H. "Letter from Reverend R. H. Ruttan." *Missionary Notices of the Methodist Church of Canada,* 3rd ser., no. 5 (January 1876).

Scouller, James Brown. *A Manual of the United Presbyterian Church of North America, 1751–1887.* Pittsburgh: United Presbyterian Publication, 1887.

Sixth Annual Report of the Columbia Mission for the Year 1864. London: Rivingtons, 1865.

Sixth Annual Report of the Columbia Mission with List of Subscriptions. 1864. London: Rivingtons, 1865.

Smith, S. F. *Missionary Sketches: A Concise History of the Work of the American Baptist Missionary Union.* Boston: W. G. Corthell, 1879.

Smith, Timothy. *Missionary Abominations Unmasked; or, A View of Carey Mission. Containing an Unmasking of the Missionary Abominations, Practised among the Indians of the St. Joseph Country, at the Celebrated Missionary Establishment Known as Carey Mission under the Superintendance of the Rev. Isaac McCoy.* South Bend, Ind.: Beacon Office, 1833.

Spalding, H. H. "Early Missionary Labors among the Indians of Oregon." *Pacific* (14 September–9 November 1865).

———. "Excerpts from Lectures by Dr. Spalding." In *Memoirs of the West: The Spaldings,* by Eliza Spalding Warren. Portland, Ore.: Marsh Printing, 1917.

Speer, Robert C. *Servants of the King.* New York: Young People's Missionary Movement of the United States and Canada, 1909.

Thirty-Second Annual Report of the Missionary Society of the Wesleyan-Methodist Church. Toronto: For the Society, 1857.

Tims, John William, comp. *Grammatical Dictionary of the Blackfeet Language in the Dominion of Canada: For the Use of Missionaries, School-Teachers and Others.* London: Society for Promoting Christian Knowledge, 1889.

Torry, Alvin. *Autobiography of Reverend Alvin Torry, First Missionary to the Six Nations and the Northwestern Tribes of British North America.* Auburn, Ala.: William J. Moses, 1861.

Tuttle, Sarah. *History of the American Mission to the Pawnee Indians.* Boston: Massachusetts Sabbath School Society, 1838.

———. *Letters and Conversations on the Cherokee Mission.* 2 vols. Boston: T. R. Marvin, 1830.

———. *Letters and Conversations on the Chickasaw and Osage Missions.* Boston: T. R. Marvin, 1831.

Twelfth Annual Report of the Columbia Mission for the Year 1870. London: Rivingtons, 1871.

Twelfth Annual Report of the Columbia Mission with List of Subscriptions, 1870. London: Rivingtons, 1871.

Twenty-Seventh Annual Report of the Missionary Society of the Wesleyan-Methodist Church in Canada. Toronto: Missionary Society of the Wesleyan Methodist Church, 1852.

United States Bureau of Indian Affairs. *Letter from the Secretary of the Interior Communicating, in Compliance with the Resolution of the Senate of the 2nd Instant, Information in Relation to the Early Labors of the Missionaries of the American Board of Commissioners of Foreign Missions, Commencing in 1856.* Washington, D.C.: Government Printing Office, 1871.

———. *Letter from the Secretary of the Interior Transmitting, in Compliance with the Resolution of the House of the 15th Instant, the Report of J. Ross Browne, in the Subject of the Indian War in Oregon and Washington Territories.* Washington, D.C.: Government Printing Office, 1858.

Vandusen, Reverend C. "Letter from Reverend C. Vandusen to J. S. Hogan, M.P.P., April 15, 1858." *The Christian Guardian* (28 July 1858): 170.

Wallace, Archer. *Blazing New Trails.* Toronto: Musson Book Company, 1928.

Weagart, Miss. "The American Indian." *The Canadian Church Magazine and Mission News* 1, no. 23 (1888).

The Western Methodist Recorder 1, no. 6 (1899).

Whipple, Bishop. "An Appeal for the Red Man." In *History of the Sioux War and the Massacres of 1862 and 1863.* New York: Harper and Brothers, 1865.

———. "Peace with the Sioux: Letter to the New York Tribune, Second Month 17, 1877." In *Indian Civilization: A Lecture,* edited by Stanley Pumphrey. Philadelphia: The Bible and Tract Distributing Society, 1877.

White, Stanley. *The Call and Qualifications for Missionary Service.* New York: Board of Foreign Missions, n.d.

Whitman, Narcissa. *The Letters of Narcissa Whitman.* Fairfield, Wash.: Ye Galleon, [1986].

———. *My Journal.* Fairfield, Wash.: Ye Galleon, 1982.

Wilcox, Helen. *Two Thousand Miles for a Book.* New York: Missionary Education Movement of the United States and Canada, 1913.

Williamson, T. S. "Dakota Scalp Dances." In *Collections of the Minnesota Historical Society.* Vol. 6. St. Paul: The Pioneer Press, 1894.

[Wilson, Edward Francis]. *The Canadian Indian* 1, no. 1 (1890).

[———]. *The Canadian Indian* 1, no. 2 (1890).

[————]. *The Canadian Indian* 1, no. 3 (1890).

[————]. *The Canadian Indian* 1, no. 4 (1891).

[————]. *The Canadian Indian* 1, no. 5 (1891).

[————]. *The Canadian Indian* 1, no. 6 (1891).

[————]. *The Canadian Indian* 1, no. 8 (1891).

[————]. *The Canadian Indian* 1, no. 10 (1891).

————. "The Indians of North America." *The Canadian Church Magazine and Mission News* 3, no. 35 (1889): 107.

————. *The Missionary Diocese of Algoma: An Address.* Toronto: Roswell and Hutchinson, 1892.

————. *Missionary Work among the Ojebway Indians.* London: Society for Promoting Christian Knowledge, 1886.

————. "The Northwest Indians." *The Canadian Church Magazine and Mission News* 3, no. 33 (1889): 53–54.

————. "Report on the Blackfeet Tribes." *Reports on the North Western Tribes of Canada, 1885–1891* 1 (1887).

————. "Report on the Sarcee Indians." *Reports on the North Western Tribes of Canada, 1885–1891* 1 (1887).

————. *Shingwauk Extension. "Red-Hot Shot" No. 1.* Edward Francis Wilson Papers. Anglican Church of Canada Archives, Toronto.

Withrow, W. H., ed. *The Native Races of North America.* Toronto: Methodist Mission Rooms, 1895.

Wright, Julia McNair. *Among the Alaskans.* Philadelphia: Presbyterian Board of Publications, 1883.

Young, Egerton Ryerson. *The Apostle of the North: Reverend James Evans.* London: Marshall Brothers, 1899.

————. *The Battle of the Bears and Reminiscences of Life in the Indian Country.* London: Robert Culley, n.d.

————. *Indian Life in the Great North-West.* London: Robert Culley, n.d.

————. "Life Among the Red Men of America." *The Missionary Review of the World* 18, no. 7 (1895): 481–489.

————. *On the Indian Trail.* London: Religious Tract Society, n.d.

————. *Oowikapun; or, How the Gospel Reached the Nelson River Indians.* London: Charles H. Kelly, 1895.

————. *Stories from Indian Wigwams and Northern Campfires.* London: Charles H. Kelly, 1893.

————. *Three Arrows, the Young Buffalo Hunter.* London: R. T. S. Office, n.d.

————. *Three Boys in the Wild North Land.* Toronto: William Briggs, 1897.

————. *When the Blackfeet Went South and Other Stories.* London: The Boy's Own Paper Office, n.d.

PRIMARY SOURCES: UNPUBLISHED

Address from the Crees of Whitefish Native Lake, signed by Henry B. Steinhauer, 9 January 1871. Adams Archibald Collection. Provincial Archives of Manitoba, Winnipeg.

Archibald, Adams. Collection. Provincial Archives of Manitoba, Winnipeg.

Black, John. Collection. Provincial Archives of Manitoba, Winnipeg.

Board of Foreign Missions, General Board of the Women's Auxiliary to the Missionary Society of the Church of England in Canada. "Resolution Passed at the Annual Meeting," 1909. Presbyterian Church in Canada. Correspondence: Women's Foreign Mission Society 1909. United Church of Canada / Victoria University Archives, Toronto.

Bompas, Bishop William Carpenter. "Narrative of a Journey to Metlakatla: A Race with Winter." 1877. Anglican Church of Canada–General Synod Archives, Toronto.

———. Papers. Anglican Church of Canada–General Synod Archives, Toronto.

"Booklets and Manuscripts in the Indian Tongue Including a Nez Perce–English Dictionary." 1838–1840. Western Americana Collection. Beinecke Rare Book Library, Yale University.

Burman, Arthur. "Indian Work of the United Church of Canada." Stephenson Collection. United Church of Canada / Victoria University Archives, Toronto.

Cody, H. A. "Indians of the Yukon." Ca. 1900–1910. Anglican Church of Canada–General Synod Archives, Toronto.

———. Papers. Anglican Church of Canada–General Synod Archives, Toronto.

Cowley, Abraham. Diary, 1866–1867. Abraham Cowley Papers. British Columbia Archives, Victoria.

———. Original letters, journals, and papers. Incoming 1822–1880. Reel 86. Provincial Archives of Manitoba, Winnipeg.

Cowley, Arabella. Letterbook, 1858–1861. Abraham Cowley Papers. British Columbia Archives, Victoria.

Douse, John. Papers. Archives of Ontario, Toronto.

Duncan, William. Papers. Special Collections. University of British Columbia, Vancouver.

Eells, Edwin. "Eliza and the Nez Perce Indians: A Narrative of the Life and Work of Eliza Spalding Warren, the Second White Child Born in Oregon Territory (Original Narrative and a Transcript Thereof)." Tacoma, 1913. Western Americana Collection. Beinecke Rare Book Library, Yale University.

Eells, Myron. "The Hand of God in the History of the North Pacific Coast." Speech delivered at Whitman College, Washington, 1 June 1888. British Columbia Archives, Victoria.

———. "The Worship and Traditions of the Aborigines of America; or, Their Testimony to the Religion of the Bible." Paper read before the Victoria Institute, or Philosophical Society of Great Britain, 1885. British Columbia Archives.

Garrioch, Alfred Campbell, to John Murray, 1888. Alfred Garrioch Papers. Anglican Church of Canada–General Synod Archives, Toronto.

Good, John Booth. "Pioneer Pacific Pipings," n.d. British Columbia Archives, Victoria.

———. "The Utmost Bounds of the West," n.d. British Columbia Archives, Victoria.

Griffen, Desire, to Mary Walker, 15 February 1840. Western Americana Collection. Beinecke Rare Book Library, Yale University.

Hale, Horatio, to Elkanah Walker, 14 October 1841, Fort Colville. Western Americana Collection. Beinecke Rare Book Library, Yale University.

Horden, John. Correspondence. Moosonee Collection. National Archives of Canada, Ottawa.

———. Correspondence and letterbooks. Moosonee Collection. Anglican Church of Canada–General Synod Archives, Toronto.

Hudson's Bay Company. Clipping book, 1819–1833. Hudson's Bay Company Records. National Archives of Canada, Ottawa.

Journal of the Bella Bella Mission, 1880–1924. British Columbia Archives, Victoria.

Letter from the Methodist Missionary Society to the Superintendent-General of Indian Affairs Respecting British Columbia Troubles, [1889]. British Columbia Archives, Victoria.

"List of Indian Missionaries." File 165. Stephenson Collection. United Church of Canada/ Victoria University Archives, Toronto.

Maclean, John. Biographic file. United Church of Canada/Victoria University Archives, Toronto.

McDougall, George, and John McDougall. Papers. Glenbow-Alberta Institute, Calgary, Canada.

McFarlane, Roderick. Papers. National Archives of Canada, Ottawa.

Methodist Central Missionary Board. Minutes, 1872–1887. United Church of Canada/ Victoria University Archives, Toronto.

Morris, Alexander. Papers. Provincial Archives of Manitoba, Winnipeg.

Newnham, Bishop Jervois. Papers. National Archives of Canada, Ottawa.

Nisbet, James. Papers. United Church of Canada/Victoria University Archives, Toronto.

O'Meara, Frederick. "Report of the Committee on Indian Missions," n.d. Bishop Strachan Papers. Reel 9. Archives of Ontario, Toronto.

Reed, Hayter. Papers. National Archives of Canada, Ottawa.

Robson, Ebenezer. Collection. British Columbia Archives, Victoria.

Robson, John. Collection. British Columbia Archives, Victoria.

Roley, George Henry. Papers. British Columbia Archives, Victoria.

Rose, Samuel. Correspondence. Archives of Ontario, Toronto.

Scott, Robert Clyde. Papers. British Columbia Archives, Victoria.

Smith, Asa Bowen. Collection. Beinecke Rare Book Library, Yale University.

———. Letters. Western Americana Collection. Beinecke Rare Book Library, Yale University.

Smithurst, John. Collection. National Archives of Canada, Ottawa.

Spalding, Eliza Hart. Letters, 1840. Western Americana Collection. Beinecke Rare Book Library, Yale University.

Spalding, H. H., to Reverend David Greene, 7 June 1842. Western Americana Collection. Beinecke Rare Book Library, Yale University.

Spalding, H. H., to _____ McKinley, Fort Walla Walla. Western Americana Collection. Beinecke Rare Book Library, Yale University.

———. "Narrative of an Overland Journey to Fort Vancouver and Lapwai in 1836 together with an Account of the Beginning of the American Protestant Missions Beyond the Rockies." Typescript copy. Western Americana Collection. Beinecke Rare Book Library, Yale University.

Stringer, I. O. Papers. Anglican Church of Canada–General Synod Archives, Toronto.

Sutherland, Reverend A., to J. S. Corcoran, 24 August 1888. United Church of Canada/Victoria University Archives, Toronto.

Sutherland, Reverend A., to Honorable Superintendent General of Indian Affairs, 20 May 1889. United Church of Canada/Victoria University Archives, Toronto.

Tate, Caroline Sarah. C. M. Tate Family Collection and Papers. British Columbia Archives, Victoria.

Tims, Archdeacon John William. Collection. Glenbow-Alberta Institute, Calgary, Canada.

Walker, Elkanah. Letters. Western Americana Collection. Beinecke Rare Book Library, Yale University.

———. "Traditions, Superstitions, Manners and Customs of the Indians in the Northern Front of Oregon," 1847. Western Americana Collection. Beinecke Rare Book Library, Yale University.

West, John. "The British North American Indians with Free Thoughts on the Red River Settlement, 1820–1823." Provincial Archives of Manitoba, Winnipeg.

Whitman, Narcissa. Letters. Western Americana Collection. Beinecke Rare Book Library, Yale University.

Wilson, Edward Francis. "Autobiography of Edward Francis Wilson." Anglican Church of Canada–General Synod Archives, Toronto.

Young, Egerton Ryerson. Papers. Archives of Ontario, Toronto.

SECONDARY SOURCES

Albers, Patricia, and Beatrice Medicine. *The Hidden Half: Studies of Plains Indian Women.* New York: University Press of America, 1983.

Allen, Opal Sweasea. *Narcissa Whitman, an Historical Biography.* Portland, Ore.: Binfords and Mort, 1959.

Anderson, Gary Clayton. "Joseph Renville and the Ethos of Biculturism." In *Being and Becoming Indian: Biographical Studies of North American Frontiers,* edited by James Clifton. Prospect Heights, Ill.: Waveland Press, 1993.

Armitage, Susan, and Elizabeth Jameson. *The Women's West.* Norman: University of Oklahoma Press, 1987.

Axtell, James. *The European and the Indian: Essays in the Ethnohistory of Colonial North America.* New York: Oxford University Press, 1981.

Baird, W. David. "Cyrus Byington and the Presbyterian Choctaw Mission." In *Churchmen and the Western Indians, 1820–1920,* edited by Clyde A. Milner and Floyd O'Neil. Norman: University of Oklahoma Press, 1985.

Barman, Jean. *The West Beyond the West: A History of British Columbia.* Rev. ed. Toronto: University of Toronto Press, 1996.

Beaver, Robert Pierce. *American Protestant Women in World Mission: History of the First Feminist Movement in North America.* Grand Rapids, Mich.: W. B. Eerdmans, 1980.

————. *Church, State and the American Indians: Two and a Half Centuries of Partnership in Missions between Protestant Churches and the Government.* St. Louis: Concordia, 1966.

————. "Protestant Churches and the Indians." In *Handbook of North American Indians: Volume Four, History of Indian-White Relations,* edited by William C. Sturtevant. Washington, D.C.: Smithsonian Institution Press, 1988.

Berkhofer, Robert F., Jr. *Salvation and the Savage: An Analysis of Protestant Missions and American Indian Response, 1787–1862.* Lexington: University of Kentucky Press, 1965.

————. *The White Man's Indian: Images of the American Indian from Columbus to the Present.* New York: Vintage Books, 1978.

Bieder, Robert. *Science Encounters the Indian, 1820–1880: The Early Years of American Ethnology.* Tulsa: University of Oklahoma Press, 1986.

Bolt, Christine. *American Indian Policy and American Reform: Case Studies of the Campaign to Assimilate the American Indians.* London: Allen & Unwin, 1987.

Bolt, Clarence. "The Conversion of the Port Simpson Tsimshian: Indian Control or Missionary Manipulation." *BC Studies,* no. 57 (1983): 44–54.

Bowden, Henry Warner. *American Indians and Christian Missions: Studies in Cultural Conflict.* Chicago: University of Chicago Press, 1981.

Boyd, Lois A. *Presbyterian Women in America: Two Centuries of a Quest for Status.* Westport, Conn.: Greenwood Press, 1983.

Bronner, Simon. *American Folklore Studies.* Lawrence: University Press of Kansas, 1986.

Brown, Arthur Judson. *One Hundred Years: A History of the Foreign Missionary Work of the Presbyterian Church in the U.S.A., with Some Account of Countries, Peoples and the Policies and Problems of Modern Missions.* 2nd ed. New York: Fleming H. Revell, 1936.

Cannon, Miles. *Waiilatpu, Its Rise and Fall, 1836–1847: A Story of Pioneer Days in the Pacific Northwest Based Entirely upon Historical Research.* Boise, Idaho: Capital News Job Rooms, 1915.

Canse, John Martin. "Jason Lee: New Evidence on the Missionary and Colonizer." *The Washington Historical Quarterly* 6, no. 4 (1915): 252–260.

Carter, Sarah. *Lost Harvests: Prairie Indian Reserve Farmers and Government Policy.* Montreal: McGill-Queen's Press, 1990.

———. "Two Acres and a Cow." *Canadian Historical Review* 70, no. 1 (1989).

Chaudhuri, Nupur, and Margaret Strobel. *Western Women and Imperialism: Complicity and Resistance.* Bloomington: Indiana University Press, 1992.

Chester, Samuel Hall. *Behind the Scenes: An Administrative History of the Foreign Work of the Presbyterian Church in the United States.* Austin, Tex.: Press of Von Boeckmann-Jones, 1928.

Cloud, Henry. *Economic Background for Self-Support in Indian Missions.* New York: Board of National Missions, n.d.

Coates, Kenneth. "Anglican Clergy in the Yukon." *Journal of the Canadian Church Historical Society,* 1990.

Comaroff, John, and Jean Comaroff. *Of Revelation and Revolution.* Chicago: University of Chicago Press, 1991.

Cott, Nancy. *The Bonds of Womanhood: "Woman's Sphere" in New England, 1780–1835.* New Haven: Yale University Press, 1977.

Cro, Stelio. *The Noble Savage: Allegory of Freedom.* Waterloo, Canada: Wilfrid Laurier University Press, 1990.

Davis, E. A. *Commemorative Review of the Methodist, Presbyterian and Congregational Churches in British Columbia: A Retrospect of the Work and Personalities of the Churches in British Columbia, Up to the Time of Their Union into the United Church of Canada, together with a Prophetic Forecast for the Future.* Vancouver: Wrigley Printing, 1925.

Dickason, Olive. *Canada's First Nations: A History of Founding Peoples from Earliest Times.* Tulsa: University of Oklahoma Press, 1992.

Dippie, Brian. *The Vanishing American: White Attitudes and U.S. Indian Policy.* Middletown, Conn.: Wesleyan University Press, 1982.

Drury, Clifford. *Marcus and Narcissa Whitman, and the Opening of Old Oregon.* 2 vols. Glendale, Calif.: Clark, 1975.

———. *Presbyterian Panoram: One Hundred and Fifty Years of National Missions History.* Philadelphia: Board of Christian Education, Presbyterian Church of the U.S.A., 1952.

Dunlay, Thomas. *Wolves for the Blue Soldiers.* Lincoln: University of Nebraska Press, 1982.

Eddy, Daniel C. *Christian Heroines; or, Lives and Sufferings of Female Missionaries in Heathen Lands.* Boston: Estes and Lauriat, 1881.

Elsbree, Oliver W. *The Rise of the Missionary Spirit in America, 1790–1815.* Williamsport, Penn.: Williamsport Printing and Binding, 1928.

Evans, Karen, comp. *Masinahikan: Native Language Imprints in the Archives and Libraries of the Anglican Church of Canada.* Toronto: Anglican Book Centre, 1985.

Fagan, Brian. *The Great Journey: The Peopling of Ancient America.* London: Thames and Hudson, 1987.

Faris, John T. *Winning the Oregon Country.* Philadelphia: Westminster Press, 1922.

Farragher, John Mack. *Women and Men on the Overland Trail.* New Haven: Yale University Press, 1979.

Fisher, Robin. *Contact and Conflict.* Vancouver: University of British Columbia Press, 1977.

Flanagan, Thomas. *Louis 'David' Riel: Prophet of the New World.* Rev. ed. Buffalo, N.Y.: University of Toronto Press, c1996.

Garett, Richard. *The History of the London Missionary Society, 1795–1895.* 2 vols. London: Henry Frowde, 1899.

Getty, Ian, and Antoine Lussier, eds. *As Long as the Sun Shines and Water Flows: A Reader in Canadian Native Studies.* Vancouver: University of British Columbia Press, 1983.

Giraud, Marcel. *The Métis in the Canadian West.* Vols. 1–2. Translated by George Woodcock. Lincoln: University of Nebraska Press, 1986.

Gough, Barry M. "A Priest versus the Potlatch: the Reverend Alfred James Hall and the Fort Rupert Kwakiutl." *Journal of the Canadian Church Historical Society* 24, no. 2 (1982): 75–89.

Gould, S. *INASMUCH: Sketches of the Beginning of the Church of England in Canada in the Relation to the Indian and Eskimo Races.* Toronto: n.p., 1917.

Grant, John Webster. *Moon of Wintertime: Missionaries and the Indians of Canada in Encounter Since 1534.* Toronto: University of Toronto Press, 1989.

Gunson, Niel. *Messengers of Grace: Evangelical Missionaries in the South Seas, 1797–1860.* New York: Oxford University Press, 1978.

Handlin, Oscar. *Truth in History.* Cambridge: Belknap Press, 1979.

Hines, H. K. *Missionary History of the Pacific Northwest: Containing the Wonderful Story of Jason Lee: With Sketches of Many of His Co-Laborers: All Illustrating Life on the Plains and in the Mountains in Pioneer Days.* Portland, Ore.: H. K. Hines, 1899.

Hinsley, Curtis. *The Smithsonian and the American Indian: Making a Moral Anthropology in Victorian America.* Washington, D.C.: Smithsonian Institution Press, 1981.

Hitsman, J. Mackay. *Safeguarding Canada.* Toronto: University of Toronto Press, 1967.

Hoover, Dwight. *The Red and the Black.* Chicago: Rand McNally College Publishing, 1976.

Horsman, Reginald. *Race and Manifest Destiny: The Origins of American Racial Anglo-Saxonism.* Cambridge: Harvard University Press, 1981.

Hoxie, Frederick. *A Final Promise: The Campaign to Assimilate the Indians.* Lincoln: University of Nebraska Press, 1984.

Huddleston, Lee Eldridge. *Origins of the American Indians: European Concepts, 1492–1729.* Austin: University of Texas Press, 1967.

Hunter, Jane. *The Gospel of Gentility: American Women Missionaries in Turn-of-the-Century China.* New Haven: Yale University Press, 1984.

Jeffrey, Julie Roy. *Converting the West: A Biography of Narcissa Whitman.* Norman: University of Oklahoma Press, 1991.

Jennings, Francis. *The Invasion of America: Indians, Colonialism, and the Cant of Conquest.* New York: Norton, 1976.

Josephy, Alvin, Jr. *Now That the Buffalo's Gone: A Study of Today's American Indians.* New York: Alfred A. Knopf, 1982.

Judd, Neil. *The Bureau of American Ethnology: A Partial History.* Norman: University of Oklahoma Press, 1967.

Keller, Robert. *American Protestantism and United States Indian Policy, 1869–1882.* Lincoln: University of Nebraska Press, 1983.

Klein, Laura, and Lillian Ackerman. *Women and Power in Native North America.* Norman: University of Oklahoma Press, 1995.

Latourette, Kenneth S. *A History of the Expansion of Christianity.* Vol. 4 of *The Great Century in Europe and the United States of America, A.D. 1800–A.D. 1914.* New York: Harper, 1941.

Leckie, William. *The Military Conquest of the Southern Plains.* Tulsa: University of Oklahoma Press, 1963.

Limerick, Patricia. *Legacy of Conquest: The Unbroken Past of the American West.* New York: Norton, 1987.

Lipset, Seymour Martin. *Continental Divide: The Values and Institutions of the United States and Canada.* New York: Routledge, 1990.

Loetscher, Lefferts Augustine. *A Brief History of the Presbyterians.* Philadelphia: Westminster Press, 1978.

Long, John S. "Reverend Edwin Watkins: Missionary to the Cree, 1852–1857." In *Papers of the Sixteenth Algonquin Conference,* edited by William Cowan, 91–117. Ottawa: Carleton University, 1985.

Lovett, Richard. *The History of the London Missionary Society, 1795–1895.* 2 vols. London: Henry Frowde, 1899.

Lyman, W. D. "The Chief Features of the Life of Father Eells." *The Whitman College Quarterly* 1, no. 2 (1897).

Macleod, R. C. *The NWMP and Law Enforcement, 1873–1905.* Toronto: University of Toronto Press, 1976.

Maddox, Lucy. *Removals: Nineteenth-Century American Literature and the Politics of Indian Affairs.* New York: Oxford University Press, 1991.

Malchow, H. L. *Gothic Images of Race in Nineteenth-Century Britain.* Stanford: Stanford University Press, 1996.

Mandelbaum, David. *Society in India.* Berkeley: University of California Press, 1970.

Marty, Martin. *Righteous Empire: The Protestant Experience in America.* New York: Dial Press, 1970.

McGregor, Gaile. *The Noble Savage in the New World Garden: Notes toward a Syntactics of Place.* Toronto: University of Toronto Press, 1988.

McNab, John. *They Went Forth.* 2nd ed. Toronto: McClelland and Stewart, 1955.

Miller, Christopher. *Prophetic Worlds: Indians and Whites on the Columbia Plateau.* New Brunswick, N.J.: Rutgers University Press, 1985.

Miller, J. R. *Shingwauk's Vision: A History of Native Residential Schools.* Toronto: University of Toronto Press, 1997.

———. *Skyscrapers Hide the Heavens: A History of Indian-White Relations.* Toronto: University of Toronto Press, 1989.

Miller, Page Putnam. *The Evolving Role of Women in the Presbyterian Church in the Early Nineteenth Century.* N.p., 1979.

Milner, Clyde A., II, and Floyd A. O'Neil, eds. *Churchmen and the Western Indians, 1820–1920.* Norman: University of Oklahoma Press, 1985.

Mitchell, Lee Clark. *Witness to a Vanishing America: The Nineteenth-Century Response.* Princeton: Princeton University Press, 1981.

Miyakawa, Tetsuo. *Protestants and Pioneers: Individualism and Conformity on the American Frontier.* Chicago: University of Chicago Press, 1964.

Moir, John. *Enduring Witness: A History of the Presbyterian Church in Canada.* Toronto: Presbyterian Church in Canada, 1987.

Morrison, William Brown. *The Red Man's Trail.* Richmond, Va.: Presbyterian Committee of Publication, 1932.

Morton, Edmund. *A Short History of Canada.* Edmonton, Canada: Hurtig Publishers, 1983.

Murray, Peter. *The Devil and Mr. Duncan.* Victoria, Canada: Sono Nis Press, 1985.

Myres, Sandra. *Westering Women and the Frontier Experience, 1800–1915.* Albuquerque: University of New Mexico Press, 1982.

Nixon, Oliver Woodson. *How Marcus Whitman Saved Oregon, a True Romance of Patriotic Heroism, Christian Devotion and Final Martyrdom, with Sketches of Life on the Plains and Mountains in Pioneer Days.* Chicago: Starr Publishing, 1895.

Nock, David A. *A Victorian Missionary and Canadian Indian Policy: Cultural Synthesis vs. Cultural Replacement.* Waterloo, Canada: Published for the Canadian Corporation for Studies in Religion by Wilfrid Laurier University Press, 1988.

Ong, Walter. *Orality and Literacy: The Technologizing of the World.* London: Methuen, 1982.

Packer, Donald Dean. *Early Churches and Towns in South Dakota.* N.p.: South Dakota State University, 1964.

———. *Founding the Church in South Dakota.* Brookage: South Dakota State College, 1962.

Pascoe, Patricia. *Relations of Rescue: The Search for Female Authority in the American West.* New York: Oxford University Press, 1990.

Patterson, E. Palmer. *The Mission on the Nass: The Evangelization of the Nisga.* Waterloo, Canada: Eulachon, 1982.

Pearce, Roy Harvey. *The Savages of America: A Study of the Indian and the Idea of Civilization.* Baltimore: Johns Hopkins University Press, 1981; 1st ed. 1953.

Pecke, F. A. "John Booth Good in British Columbia: The Trials and Tribulations of the Church, 1861–1899." *Pacific Northwest Quarterly* 75, no. 2 (1984).

Peterson, Jacqueline, and Jennifer S. H. Brown, eds. *The New Peoples: Being and Becoming Métis in North America.* Lincoln: University of Nebraska Press, 1985.

Piggin, Stuart. *Making Evangelical Missionaries, 1789–1858: The Social Background, Motives and Training of the British Protestant Missionaries in India.* Abingdon, England: Sutton Courtenay Press, 1984.

Pilkington, James Penn. *The Methodist Publishing House.* Vol. 1. Nashville: Abingdon Press, 1968.

Posey, Walter. *Frontier Mission: A History of Religion West of the Southern Appalachians to 1861.* Lexington: University of Kentucky Press, 1966.

Prucha, Francis Paul. *American Indian Policy in Crisis: Christian Reformers and the Indian, 1865–1900.* Norman: University of Oklahoma Press, 1976.

———. *The Great Father: The United States Government and the American Indians.* Vol. 1. Lincoln: University of Nebraska Press, 1984.

Ray, A. J. *Indians in the Fur Trade: Their Role as Trappers, Hunters and Middlemen in the Lands Southwest of Hudson's Bay, 1660–1670.* Toronto: University of Toronto Press, 1974.

Riley, Glenda. *The Female Frontier: A Comparative View of Women of the Prairie and the Plains.* Lawrence: University of Kansas Press, 1988.

———. *Women and Indians on the Frontier.* Albuquerque: University of New Mexico Press, 1984.

Rohner, Ronald, ed. *The Ethnography of Franz Boas.* Chicago: University of Chicago Press, 1969.

Said, Edward. *Orientalism.* New York: Pantheon Books, 1978.

Schlissel, Lillian, Vicki Ruiz, and Janice Monk. *Western Women: Their Land, Their Lives.* Albuquerque: University of New Mexico Press, 1988.

Sharp, Paul. *Whoop-Up Country: The Canadian and American West, 1865–1885.* Minneapolis: University of Minnesota Press, 1955.

Sheehan, Bernard. *Savagism and Civility: Indians and Englishmen in Colonial Virginia.* London: Cambridge University Press, 1980.

Slotkin, Richard. *Regeneration Through Violence: The Mythology of the American Frontier, 1600–1860.* Middletown, Conn.: Wesleyan University Press, 1973.

Smith, S. F. *Missionary Sketches: A Concise History of the Work of the American Baptist Missionary Union.* Boston: W. G. Corthell, 1881.

Smith-Rosenberg, Carroll. *Disorderly Conduct: Visions of Gender in Victorian America.* New York: Alfred A. Knopf, 1985.

Speer, Robert C. *Servants of the King.* New York: Young People's Missionary Movement of the United States and Canada, 1909.

Sprague, D. N. *Canada and the Métis, 1869–1885.* Waterloo, Canada: Wilfred Laurier University Press, 1988.

Stanley, George F. *The Birth of Western Canada: A History of the Riel Rebellion.* Toronto: University of Toronto Press, 1963.

Stanton, William. *The Leopard's Spots: Scientific Attitudes Toward Race in America, 1815–1859.* Chicago: University of Chicago Press, 1960.

Stocking, George W., Jr. *Victorian Anthropology.* New York: Free Press, 1987.

———, ed. *Observers Observed: Essays in Ethnographic Fieldwork.* Madison: University of Wisconsin Press, 1983.

Sullivan, Zohreh. "Race, Gender, and Imperial Ideology; in the Nineteen [*sic*] Century." *Nineteenth Century Contexts* 13, no. 1 (1989): 19–32.

Surtees, Robert. "Canadian Indian Policies." Vol. 4 of *Handbook of North American Indians: History of Indian-White Relations.* Washington, D.C.: Smithsonian Institution Press, 1988.

Szasz, Margaret. *Indian Education in the American Colonies, 1607–1783.* Albuquerque: University of New Mexico Press, c1988.

Takaki, Ronald. *Iron Cages: Race and Culture in Nineteenth Century America.* New York: Alfred A. Knopf, 1979.

Tucker, L. Norman. *Western Canada.* London: A. R. Mowbray, 1908.

Usher, Jean. *William Duncan of Metlakatla: A Victorian Missionary in British Columbia.* Ottawa: National Museum of Canada, 1974.

Van Kirk, Sylvia. *Many Tender Ties: Women in Fur Trade Society, 1670–1870.* Norman: University of Oklahoma Press, 1983.

Whitehead, Margaret. *Now You Are My Brother: Missionaries in British Columbia.* Sound Heritage Series no. 34. Victoria: Provincial British Columbia Archives and Record Service, 1981.

Winks, Robin. *The Relevance of Canadian History: U.S. and Imperial Perspectives.* Toronto: Mcmillan of Canada, 1979.

Zumwalt, Rosemary. *American Folklore Scholarship: A Dialogue of Dissent.* Bloomington: Indiana University Press, 1988.

NAME INDEX

SUBJECT INDEX